S0-EFW-174

Céline and His Vision

Culture and the Ageing

Céline

AND HIS VISION

By Erika Ostrovsky

London • UNIVERSITY OF LONDON PRESS LIMITED
New York • NEW YORK UNIVERSITY PRESS

SBN 340 08930 x

First published by New York University Press 1967
Second impression 1968
Copyright © 1967 Erika Ostrovsky

University of London Press Ltd
St Paul's House, Warwick Lane, London EC4

Printed and bound in Great Britain by
Hazell Watson and Viney Ltd, Aylesbury, Bucks

LOUIS-FERDINAND Céline, one of the most controversial figures of contemporary French literature, has aroused vehement comment in literary and political circles, and violent reactions among the reading public. Exalted to the status of the foremost French writers of our century, denounced as boor, charlatan, and criminal, Céline's reputation is far from being settled. The recent Pléïade edition of his works does imply inclusion among the "classics," but laurels rest uneasily on a head such as his. Nothing about the man or his work suggests either truce or quietude. Both are complicated, unorthodox, paradoxical, highly individualistic in nature. Any study devoted to Céline must meet the demands of his multiform character and accept all the challenges his work presents.

The problems of analyzing Céline are augmented by his voluminous literary production, his agitated existence—complicated by wartime travel, exile, imprisonment, confiscation of property—as well as by the contentions over his literary estate, following his death a few years ago. Manuscripts have thus been lost, scattered, dismembered, sold piecemeal; accounts of his life are frequently colored by partisanship and personal bias, necessitating research and evaluation that sometimes resemble detective work rather than the calmer scholarly pursuits. In a sense, this adds to the excitement of the quest and also seems in keeping with the character of Céline and his art. The task is more arduous as a result, but lacks the fixity which the author himself so much despised. Considering himself in the ranks of those determined to unmask, to strip away all that is superficial, contingent, nonessential, the author merits treatment in like fashion.

The aim of this study, then, is to reveal the fundamental characteristics of Céline's work, to strip away the layers of contingency which envelop both his life and writing, to go beyond the various biases which tend to class him either among saints or demons, and to show what is most central to his literary vision. An undertaking of this kind demands many years of study and analysis, augmented and rendered more directly alive by firsthand knowledge of the milieu with which the author dealt. Preparatory research for this book, done mostly in Paris, began in 1960 and includes not only information contained in critical works but also material from valuable primary sources: manuscripts, correspondence, unpublished fragments, numerous interviews with the author's widow, his friends, critics, publishers, secretaries. While my own approach to Céline's work is essentially literary, the ideas of those interviewed—even in cases where they were colored by personal bias or emphasized mainly biographical factors—were of great interest, since they enlarged what might otherwise have been a purely academic evaluation of the man and the writer. By a fortunate coincidence, the publication of two important *cahiers* devoted to Céline occurred simultaneously with the formulation of my own ideas on the author and the writing of this book. It has provided a great deal of valuable information which might otherwise not have been at my disposal. Critical opinion and re-evaluation of Céline, aroused by these *cahiers*, as well as the publication of a work recently uncovered—*Pont de Londres* (Paris: Gallimard, 1964)—have provided important up-to-date material and created an atmosphere of renewed and passionate interest in "le cas Céline" about which it is exciting to write. It is even more rewarding, however, to have wanted to do so in past years when this was not so much the fashion.

Help in the research and preparation of this study has come from many sources, including the Penfield Fund, the Samuel S. Fels Foundation, New York University's Arts and Science Research Fund, the American Council of Learned Societies. I wish to express my gratitude for all these grants, as well as for the time and insights given me by the friends and critics of the author: Arletty, Marcel Aymé, Marie Canavaggia, Jeanne Carayon, J. Dellanoy, Bernard de Fallois, the late Roger Nimier, Robert Poulet, and Dominique de Roux. My thanks go also to the private owners of Céline manuscripts and correspondence for allowing me to consult these documents: Gwen-Aël Bolloré, Michel Bolloré, Marie Canavaggia, and Jean-Claude Descaves.

I am most grateful to Lucette Destouches, Céline's widow, for her warm welcome to the author's home in Meudon; for giving me access to the author's precious manuscripts and correspondence; for her willingness to discuss even the most controversial aspects of her husband's life with me; finally, for her friendship and the continued interest she has shown in my work.

In conclusion, I wish to express my appreciation for the help and encouragement I have received from my friends and former teachers: Germaine Brée, Elaine Marks, Thomas W. Bishop, Robert J. Clements, Bernard Garniez, Wilmarth H. Starr.

For Nina

CONTENTS

PREFACE   V

INTRODUCTION   1

PART I   NOX   27

1. *"Noircir et Se Noircir"*   29
    The Night Muses   29
    The Sullied Mirror   38
    "Noircir"   40
    "Se noircir"   56
    The Blackness Within   65

2. *Humanism À Rebours*   85
    Echoes of Semmelweiss   85
    Merciless Pity   91
    Céline and "Le Docteur Destouches"   97
    The Unheroic Hero   106
    "Coins de tendresse"   114
    The Cult of Perfect Forms   122

3. Totentanz   130
    The Muse of Death   130
    The Passing of Things   133
    The Quick, the Maimed, and the Dead   137
    From "La Comédie de la mort" to Tragedy   145

PART II   NOX IRAE   155

4. *The Horseman of the Apocalypse*   157
    The Sound of the First Trumpet   157
    Der Sündenbock   162
    The World of Goya, Bosch, and Brueghel   169
    Solvet Seclum in Favilla   177

5. *"L'Autre Côté de la Vie*   183
    Metamorphoses   183
    "L'Extra-voyant lucide"   188
    The Dancing God   194

BIBLIOGRAPHY   209

Céline, Louis-Ferdinand.

D'un Château l'autre. Paris: Gallimard, 1957. Referred to as *C.*

Entretiens avec le Professeur Y. Paris: Referred to as *Y.*

Féerie pour une autre fois, I. Paris: Gallimard, 1952. Referred to as *F., I.*

Féerie pour une autre fois, II. Normance. Paris: Gallimard, 1952. Referred to as *F., II.*

L'Eglise, comédie en cinq actes. Paris: Gallimard, 1952. Referred to as *E.*

L'Herne, Ed. Dominique de Roux, Paris, No. 3, 1963; No. 5, 1965, both devoted to Céline. Referred to as *L'Herne,* No. 3 and No. 5.

Mort à crédit (part of volume in the Bibliothèque de la Pléïade: *Voyage au bout de la nuit suivi de Mort à crédit*). Paris: Gallimard, 1962. Referred to as *M.C.*

Nord. Paris: Gallimard, 1960. Referred to as *N.*

Semmelweiss. Paris: Gallimard, 1952. Referred to as *S.*

Voyage au bout de la nuit (part of volume in the Bibliothèque de la Pléïade: *Voyage au bout de la nuit suivi de Mort à crédit*). Paris: Gallimard, 1962. Referred to as *V.*

Introduction

"IN THE HISTORY of contemporary letters, Louis-Ferdinand Céline is a true phenomenon. We must not explain him; we must simply note his existence as we would St. Elmo's fire or the Messina earthquake."[1] Undeniably, Céline can be considered one of the phenomena of twentieth-century French literature. Whether we should accept his advent as one would one of the cataclysms of nature is much more questionable. Since the critic or student of literature is engaged in a quest quite different from the act of faith implied in such a view, his task must be to explain, or at least to probe, analyze, dissect in order to reconstitute the work of art. In the case of Céline, both the artist and his creation merit this kind of attention.

The first step of the critic, then, should be an elucidation of those aspects of the writer's life which have direct bearing on the understanding of his work. For Céline, whose biography is obscured by many conflicting accounts—often influenced by ideological considerations and political factors—one finds oneself in the difficult position of having to separate fact from propaganda. I do not profess to have been completely successful in this attempt, for it would take years of study and searching through archives in order to corroborate the various sides of the story, which is still in the process of unfolding.[2] This is the task of a professional biographer or an intelligence agent. I shall content myself with presenting the principal and generally acknowledged facts which are relevant to the author's work. Céline's biography, even when reduced to these elements, reads like an adventure story:

1

Louis-Ferdinand Destouches, who was to become famous under the name of Céline, assumed in 1932, was born at Courbevoie (Seine), a Paris suburb, on May 27, 1894. His father, although holding advanced degrees, worked as a minor employee of an insurance firm. His mother, Louise-Céline Guillou, was a Parisian lacemaker. The paternal grandfather of the author, to whom the latter sometimes traced his interest in language and style, had been a professor of literature at the Lycée of Le Havre.

Louis-Ferdinand's childhood was spent entirely in Paris. During these years the family lived in the Passage Choiseuil, renamed le Passage des Bérésinas in Céline's novels and providing the setting for much of *Mort à crédit (Death on the Installment Plan)*. He attended public school on the Square Louvois and later on rue Argenteuil. In 1903, the boy was sent to Diepholz in lower Saxony in order to acquire a knowledge of German, which his family judged useful in preparing him for a commercial career. Upon his return, Louis-Ferdinand continued his schooling in Paris and accompanied his mother to the markets of the suburbs and Channel resorts where she sold the lace she manufactured. After obtaining his *certificat d'études* in 1905, the youth worked as an apprentice and messenger in several small business firms. His life during the adolescent years seems generally to have resembled that of the protagonist of *Mort à crédit*—with one important difference, indicating that the future author had a less defeatist outlook than his fictional namesake: he prepared, totally on his own, the work for the baccalaureate degree which he obtained in 1917, after completing military service.

In 1912, Destouches enlisted for three years in the 12th Cavalry Division, whose garrison was stationed at Rambouillet. In 1914, at Poelkapelle in Flanders, the young sergeant Destouches volunteered for a dangerous military mission during which he received severe head and arm wounds. He was awarded highest military honors for his heroism, trepanned for his head injury, given a 75 per cent disability rating, and withdrawn from active service. Material drawn from his cavalry experiences appears in the author's recently discovered "black notebook," [3] as well as in two novels, *Casse-pipe* and *Voyage au bout de la nuit (Journey to the End of Night).* References to his head injury and disability rating recur frequently in most of the works and are still in evidence in his last published novel, *Nord.*

A series of voyages followed Destouches' withdrawal from active service, which again furnished the groundwork for future literary productions: a trip to the Cameroons (Mikobimbo) in 1916 with the Occupation Services, resulting in malaria and amoebic dysentery from which the author was to suffer for the rest of his life; trips to London and work for the Armament Service which brought him into contact with the world of secret agents and international intrigue as well as with the centers of prostitution and underworld activities in Soho.[4] The London of those days would serve Céline as a setting for *Guignol's Band*, as well as for its newly discovered sequel, *Le Pont de Londres.*

The year 1918 marks the beginning of his medical career, which was of vital importance during his life and forms a part of the dual personality of Dr. Destouches and Louis-Ferdinand Céline. The young man undertook his studies at Rennes and during his first year made a lecture trip across Brittany for the Rockefeller Foundation, speaking on the prevention and cure of tuberculosis. In 1919, Destouches married Edith Follet, the daughter of the director of the medical school at Rennes; his only child, Colette, was born a year later. A short period of bourgeois existence followed. Upon completion of his medical studies in 1924 and the publication of his doctoral thesis, *La vie et l'oeuvre de Philippe Ignace Semmelweiss*, Destouches received his diploma from the Faculté de Médicine in Paris. The thesis, which dealt with the life, work, and scientific martyrdom of the Hungarian gynecologist Semmelweiss, already showed literary promise and far exceeded the concerns of the usual doctoral dissertation of this kind, by virtue of its preoccupation with style and treatment of the subject. The major themes introduced in this early and not specifically literary work form an important basis for the understanding of the evolution of Céline's writing; and *Semmelweiss* can be considered a point of departure from which, although it will greatly diverge later, Céline's work nevertheless springs. (More detailed discussion of this work will be found in the section of this book entitled "Echoes of Semmelweiss.")

Doctor Destouches, assured of a life of social and professional ease, being destined to become his father-in-law's successor, almost immediately abandoned such possibilities of terra firma and embarked on a series of missions for the Rockefeller Foundation which took him to Liverpool and Geneva. During one of the sea voyages of this period, he was informed that his wife had obtained a judgment of divorce. The years that followed (1925–1928) were filled with travels that took Destouches all over the globe: to Africa on an inspection tour of the European colonies there, to the Cameroons once more for research on yellow fever and sleeping sickness, finally to America, where he studied the problems of social medicine in the Ford factories and also visited Canada and Cuba. These extensive travel experiences were to be reflected in his works (most especially in *Voyage au bout de la nuit*), as was his subsequent return to Paris and the establishment of a medical practice there.

In 1928 we find Destouches in Clichy at 36 rue d'Alsace. The shingle—now gone—then informed one that he was not only a general practitioner but specialized in children's diseases. It was at this address also that the metamorphosis from Dr. Louis Destouches to Louis-Ferdinand Céline the writer took place. Leading a dual existence of work at a dispensary by day and at the writing table at night, he began the long labor which led to *Voyage au bout de la nuit*. It continued during the next four years and terminated in a manuscript which ran over a thousand pages at its completion. Two women played an important part in the life of the author at this time: one, a young proofreader named Jeanne Carayon, who was instrumental in bringing his first novel to publication; the other, his mistress, an American dancer named Elizabeth Craig, whom he fondly nicknamed "the Empress" and to whom his first great work is dedicated.

When the enormous manuscript was finished, the writer sent copies to Denoël and Steele as well as to Gallimard. The circumstances which led to his discovery by the publisher, Denoël, belong in the realm of literary anecdote: the manuscript, signed only with the pseudonym Céline (middle name of the author's mother, assumed for purposes of publication or, as he claimed, to shield him from suspicion from his patients or prejudice against a doctor who "scribbles") arrived at the publisher at the same time as the manuscript of a woman writer living at the same address—98 rue Lépic, where Céline had moved during 1931. Denoël, reputed to have read *Voyage* in one night without being able to put it down until dawn, was determined to publish it. There followed a hectic search for the author, during which Céline was identified as "that madman on the fourth floor" by his concierge, and finally located. The editors immediately contracted him; Gallimard offered publication a few days later, in vain. Preparations for publication, that is, reading of proofs, corrections of galleys, etc. were placed almost entirely in the hands of Jeanne Carayon, since the author himself refused to have anything to do with such "trivia" and would not even discuss the book once it was completed. This attitude remained characteristic of Céline during his entire literary career. While willing to labor in painstaking fashion on a work in progress and to make endless revisions, once he had finished, he considered it a product that was static, "figé," dead, almost. He would then no longer concern himself with it, preferring to go on immediately to the next creation.

Publication procedures were further complicated by the "corrections" made by overly enthusiastic typists who, disconcerted by the unorthodox punctuation, took it upon themselves to put the manuscript into "proper" form by adding commas and periods in the conventional manner. "They're trying to make me write like François Mauriac!" was Céline's curt and annoyed comment on this. Three or four revisions of the galleys were necessary before the novel, which revolutionized traditional prose form in France, could finally be rendered into typographical terms.

When *Voyage au bout de la nuit* appeared in November 1932, it created great furor in literary circles. Nominated almost immediately for the coveted Prix Goncourt, it failed to win by one vote. There was meager consolation in the fact that the book was awarded the Prix Théophraste Renaudot. Its author, however, was launched into literary fame. Translations into numerous languages were undertaken, discussions raged in the pages of magazines, literary journals, and newspapers of Europe. Voyage brought Céline adulation and even wealth, on the one hand, and violent attacks and enmity, on the other. There was no doubt in anyone's mind, however, that it was a major and revolutionary contribution to the world of French letters. The author himself, in the midst of this storm of varying reactions, immediately set to work on his second novel *Mort à crédit (Death on the Installment Plan).*

The year 1933 marked the publication of Céline's one and only play *L'Eglise,* written during the same period as Voyage and treating an essentially identical series of incidents, with additions of episodes dealing with the League of Nations and containing some antisemitic satire which foreshadows certain elements in the pamphlets which the author was to write a few years later. *L'Eglise* is, both in the opinion of critics and the author himself, inferior to his other writing, but holds a certain interest for comparison, or for the elucidation of the importance of form versus subject matter in Céline's work. The play, performed by a group of amateurs in Lyon in 1936, has recently been considered for a comeback.[5] While referred to as a "flop" by its author, it has been compared in quality and intent with some of Genet's works and thus may have a certain appeal for contemporary audiences.

In 1934, a lecture delivered by Céline, paying homage to Zola (published as *Hommage à Zola,* Paris: Denoël and Steele, 1936), is of interest since its backhanded praise of the nineteenth-century author serves to define more closely Céline's developing literary vision. The lecture indicates that Zola's naturalism was essentially an optimistic doctrine: motivated by a belief in science, progress, and social action, based on a scheme of values which enabled one to define virtue and vice and permitted the author to play the role of moralist who verbally chastised those guilty of vice. Providence was still functioning, Céline affirms, and man had not yet embarked on his vast suicidal and homicidal crusade. Since Zola's day, he adds, man's nightmarish conditions have been clarified, and even made "official." In summary, Céline tends to treat Zola as outmoded, and his concerns, although worthy of praise, untenable and even inapplicable in today's world.

Céline's second major work, *Mort à crédit* (*Death on the Installment Plan*), appeared in 1936, with Denoël and Steele as his publishers once again. In the preparation of the manuscript, the author had the help of a new secretary, Marie Canavaggia, whose skillful collaboration continued to facilitate his task and lasted until his death in 1961. *Mort à crédit*, although completed four years after *Voyage*, is the literary transposition of the period in the author's life just preceding *Voyage*. Together, they can be considered the first major stage of Céline's literary career. The second novel proved as successful as the first and many critics judge it to be even more interesting in terms of its stylistic explorations and innovations. It cemented the author's fame and firmly established him in the ranks of the foremost writers of the thirties.

In the same year, Céline undertook a trip to the U.S.S.R., financed by the royalties from the Russian translation of *Voyage* by Louis Aragon and Elsa Triolet. The Russian edition is the result of Céline's fame, which had spread to many countries and encouraged translations into numerous languages; it is probably also due to the fact that Leftists in France, judging the work to be in the populist tradition and its author an apologist for the proletariat, attempted to claim him as one of their spokesmen. Ironically, the writer for whom there had been high hopes in Communist circles [6] returned from the U.S.S.R. only to write *Mea culpa*, which was a scathing denunciation of the "proletariat paradise" he had failed to find there. It is noteworthy that Céline here refused, as he did during his entire career, to be associated with any particular group, political party, or "camp." This seems to be a fundamental trait of his personality, and needs to be remembered when considering his actions during the years that followed.

With the year 1937, a new stage in Céline's literary career began—one which critics favorable to the author sometimes tend to ignore. The works produced during this period, although called "pamphlets," are really novels of a sort. They contain no definite plot line whatever, but consist of a number of diverse passages, varying from violent diatribes on the dangers of war for France and attacks on Jewish factions, which the author accuses of bellicist agitation, to racist arguments of all

kinds, interspersed with fictional episodes, and even some
light-hearted fantasies entitled "ballets" (some of which would
later be published in a collection by Gallimard). The first of
the pamphlets, virulently racist and pacifist in nature, *Bagatelles
pour un massacre* (Denoël, 1937), was severely censured by the
Leftists. Céline immediately went on to write a second and
similar work, *L'Ecole des cadavres* (Denoël, 1938), which
caused the author and the work to be condemned for defama-
tion in 1939.

Paradoxically, having raged against all forms of bellicist
activity, when the Second World War broke out, Céline
attempted to enlist for its duration. Rejected because of ill
health, he embarked as a ship's doctor on the "Chella," which
traveled from Marseilles to Gibraltar. After the ship was
torpedoed and sunk by the Germans in the same year, Céline
returned to Paris to take the place of the physician, who had
been mobilized, at the dispensary of Sartrouville. During the
"Exodus," Céline left Paris in an ambulance with two new-
borns, an aged invalid, and Lucette Almanzor, the young
dancer from the Opéra Comique who was later to become his
wife. Although offered a post on a ship going to England,
Céline refused to abandon his ambulance service and went
on to serve in a medical capacity at a work camp. Upon his
return to Paris, he resumed practice at 4 rue Girardon, a
building which also housed a group of the Resistance movement. He apparently gave his medical services to patriots who
had been tortured by the Gestapo. At the same time, he wrote
the third of his pamphlets, *Les beaux draps* (Paris: Denoël,
Les Nouvelles Editions Françaises, 1941), which again affirmed
racist arguments and attacks on French policy.

The next period in Céline's life presents even more puzzling
and contradictory actions: the author visited Berlin in 1942 in
the company of several other French physicians. The visit,
ostensibly aimed at an inspection of hospitals there, really was
meant to serve for making arrangements for a trip to Copenhagen. Céline, who had apparently anticipated a holocaust even
during the thirties, had stored gold bullion in Denmark for
safekeeping at a time when his success as a writer had brought
him an excellent income. The exploratory trip to Berlin was

unsuccessful, however, and Céline returned to Paris. His marriage to Lucette Almanzor took place in the following year. In April 1944, Gallimard published *Guignol's Band*. In July, the couple decided to leave Paris, since Céline had been threatened with violence, probably because of accusations of collaboration based on ideas expressed in his pamphlets. Although offered a chance to join the maquis in Brittany by R. Champfleury, one of the leaders of the Resistance movement, or to go to England, Céline decided to try to reach Denmark. In 1944, the author, accompanied by his wife, an actor friend Le Vigan, and the cat Bébert, crossed the German frontier. On the way to Baden-Baden, their papers were confiscated and the group was forced to wait in that town until permission to continue to Denmark could be obtained. After long delays, Céline asked to be allowed to return to France or to go to Switzerland. He spent two weeks in Berlin striving to get visas, but to no avail. Having refused to make propaganda speeches for the Nazi radio, he was interned for three months at a camp for "freethinkers." There followed an unsuccessful attempt to cross into Denmark and a forced return to Kressling, Germany. Céline and his companions then decided to join their compatriots in voluntary exile at Siegmaringen. Céline performed his medical functions among his countrymen, reportedly sparing them neither efforts to save their lives, nor his caustic comments concerning their views.

In March of 1945, the author and his wife, accompanied by their cat Bébert, who never left his master's side, crossed Germany on foot, in the midst of bombardments and the turmoil of four armies in battle with each other. It took twenty-one days to get from Siegmaringen to the Danish border, where they were picked up by the Red Cross, almost dead of hunger and exhaustion. His experiences inside Germany during the last war years and the journey toward Denmark furnished the material for Céline's final works, *D'un château l'autre* and *Nord*.

After their arrival in Copenhagen a new period of difficulties began. Hidden in an apartment of the Ved Stranden, the author and his wife could emerge only after the Germans fled in June. At that time, Céline learned of the death of his mother, which had occurred in March of that year in Paris.

In December the attaché of the French Legation in Denmark, G. De Girard de Charbonnière, asked the minister of foreign affairs for the arrest and extradition of Céline on charges of collaboration. On December 25, 1945, both the author and his wife were imprisoned. While she was released after two months to undergo a serious surgical operation, Céline remained in a death cell for fourteen months, awaiting extradition and probable execution at any moment. Visits from his wife were restricted to ten minutes a week and conversations could take place only in the presence of two guards and in English, a language she was not well versed in. Céline fell ill, suffering from pellagra and serious loss of weight. In February 1947, he was allowed to leave prison to be interned at Copenhagen National Hospital on his written promise not to leave the premises without permission from the security police. The intervention of the French Legation, however, resulted in his being returned to prison a few more times. In June of that year, broken in health and spirit, the author was released, but only after signing a statement that he would not leave Denmark without permission from the authorities.

Céline and his wife lived in abject poverty in an attic of the Prinsessgade until autumn. When forced to leave this lodging, the author obtained permission to live near Körsor, under the supervision of his lawyer. Housed in a primitive hut on the latter's property, located at Klarskovgard on the edge of the Baltic sea, suffering material deprivation and all the rigors of exile, the couple existed in what was almost total isolation until the spring of 1951. The only solace came from a Danish pastor and a few loyal friends who attempted to help the author in clandestine fashion, but whose aid he frequently refused, being too proud to accept what he considered charity. Céline had begun to write again, however, slowly and painfully, ever since his release from prison. His literary activities continued throughout the rest of his Danish exile. He also undertook the preparation of his own defense against the charges of collaboration which had resulted in his condemnation by a Parisian court in February 1951 to a year in prison, a fine of 50,000 francs, and the confiscation of half his property. The point-by-point refutation by the author and the efforts of his

French friends (some of whom were Jewish) eventuated in his exoneration from all charges in a verdict pronounced by the military tribunal of Paris on April 26, 1951. In June of that year, the entire household, which included a variety of stray dogs and cats acquired during the years of exile, returned to France.

The last decade of Céline's life was spent in a house at Meudon, on the outskirts of Paris. Ill, exhausted, embittered, and often subject to hostile treatment, the author lived in almost total seclusion until his death in 1961. While continuing his functions as a doctor until the very last—but limiting his practice to a few patients of the vicinity—Céline continued to write, incessantly, feverishly, driven on by the need to finish saying what he had to express, before death overtook him. His life during the last years was one of great asceticism, isolation relieved only by visits from a few remaining friends, and seems to have been dominated by endless hours of work. His wife Lucette, caring for the aging author and the animals who were now the couple's only constant companions, showed the boundless devotion to which Céline pays homage in his books.

With Gallimard as his editor, the author published a large number of works during the years that lay between the return from exile and his death. None of these have yet been translated into English, which is unfortunate, since they constitute an impressive body of writing of great interest and importance for those concerned with the evolution of Céline's work. In order of publication, they include: *Féerie pour une autre fois.* (1952); *Normance. Féerie pour une autre fois. II* (1954): two consecutive novels dealing with the Paris of the war years and situated mainly in Montmartre. In them, one finds a mixture of transposed biographical material from the epoch during which Céline lived at rue Girardon (1940–1944), hallucinatory episodes during which reality merges into delirium—such as the fantastic bombardment of Montmartre—as well as humorously grotesque incidents such as those involving Jules, the legless satyr. The work which follows, *Entretiens avec le Professeur Y* (1956), is a series of imaginary conversations between the author and a literature professor suffering from a bladder condition. Here, Céline, with his characteristic talent for mingling humor and extremely serious concerns, reveals his aesthetic theories and techniques of stylistic innovation. *D'un château l'autre* (1957), followed by a second and related novel, *Nord* (1960), deals with the years in war-torn Germany. Both works depict the grotesque and macabre world of the Nazi *Götter-dämmerung* and show an entire civilization on the brink of annihilation. They present the nightmare vision of a whole continent about to crumble, with incidents of group and individual madness full of black humor. Transposed biographi-cal material and hallucinatory accounts merge once again, to create this account of a modern apocalypse in which Céline is both the chronicler and one of the victims. In the interim separating these two dread-filled works, the author's *Ballets sans musique, sans personne, sans rien* (1959) appeared, a delightful collection of wryly humorous sketches, which in-clude the scenario for an animated cartoon, "Scandale aux abysses," and a charming parody of Bernardin de Saint Pierre's famous *Paul et Virginie*, entitled "Voyou Paul. Brave Virginie" (Scoundrel Paul. Good Virginie). At the time of his death, the author had just completed another novel, "Rigodon," which Gallimard at this date is in the process of publishing. This last work apparently deals with the years of exile in Denmark and would thus provide the concluding portion of the author's final trilogy with *D'un château l'autre* and *Nord*.

When the author's death occurred on July 1, 1961, at his home at Meudon, the event was kept secret from the press and only a few friends attended the funeral in the small local cemetery at the edge of the railroad tracks. A simple gravestone marks the tomb of the author, tracing the double existence he led in the inscription: "Louis-Ferdinand Céline / le Docteur Destouches." Beneath it there is the carving of a ship, in memory of his lifelong love for the sea and its vessels.

The turmoil and hardship which characterized Céline did not cease with his death. They continued to be evident in the problematic nature of the settlement of his literary estate; in the fact that many manuscripts disappeared, emerged only in fragments, or in unexpected places. Some were salvaged or preserved, like the recently published *Pont de Londres* (Paris: Gallimard, 1964), dealing with the same London setting as

Guignol's Band and considered by the critic Robert Poulet to be a sequel to the latter. Other manuscripts, however, seem to have been broken up and are sold piecemeal by booksellers, auctioneers, or private individuals. "Rigodon" was for a long time stored away at a notary's for safekeeping. Libel suits raged over *Nord*, resulting in heavy fines imposed on the publisher and the author's estate and necessitating the publication of a revised edition of the novel (entitled "Edition définitive," Gallimard, September, 1964), in which the original names have been altered to avoid libel. Legal complications, connected with the charges of collaboration made against Céline, have stifled publication of certain of his works in this country. Many obituary notices and commemorative articles concluded on a note of violent attack. Even today, some critics still refer to the author as "Il Maledetto," "L'Impardonnable," reminding us that Céline, the heretic, is subject to the firebrand even posthumously. Recent critical works, the great variety of viewpoints presented in the two issues of *L'Herne*, the energetic response of the European press, the controversies which still rage about him, make the author seem as alive and disconcerting as when he first burst upon the literary scene in 1932. We can conclude that Céline will remain for a long time among the unquiet dead, which is probably the best testimony to his immortality.

Essentially, it is Céline the writer who is our main concern in this study, and biographical data—no matter how intriguing —simply serve as a backdrop against which his works can be placed for greater scope and insight. While it seems wrong to view an author's writings in a vacuum, like a series of disembodied creations that have no link with his life, it is just as erroneous to tie them too closely to his everyday existence. It is true that in Céline's case one is easily tempted to draw parallels between his life and his art, but I prefer to emphasize only one fundamental resemblance: that of nonfixity, upheaval, uncertainty, contradiction. That this is true for his life the short biography presented above has shown. It is even more characteristic of the internal workings of his novels, and for the author's entire *situation* on the literary scene of the twentieth century.

Céline's position in French literature, both in regard to importance and to membership in a particular *famille d'esprit*, has been subject to quite varied interpretation. While there is general agreement concerning Céline's place among the major writers of modern Europe, its exact nature and the extent of its import are amorphous. On the one hand he is ranked among such giants as Kafka, Proust, and Joyce, or considered—at least by one major French critic—a figure of such stature that the contemporary literature of that country could be divided into two periods: before and after Céline; on the other, he has been dismissed by a number of equally important critics or simply classed with a number of lesser writers who expressed pessimistic or nihilistic feelings in the 1930s. The fact remains that it is not easy to fix or pin down Céline's *situation* in contemporary literature.

One might of course say the same of any writer of one's own age. Being forced to view contemporary works from within the century rather than from a safe vantage point in time which permits one to render judgments imbued with retrospective wisdom makes evaluation much more difficult. In Céline's case, detached consideration is further complicated by what appears to be a strong, emotional, almost personal reaction in both reader and critic. While such involvement is one of Céline's major aims in writing, it tends to produce either a defensive or aggressive attitude and makes establishment of the author's place or stature in contemporary letters that much more problematic.

The dearth of major studies on Céline may be a reaction to this dilemma. On the other hand, the recent appearance of three book-length works on the author in France [7] certainly would indicate a growing or renewed interest in the critics concerning his writing. The studies in question, all published in the years immediately following Céline's death, together with the recent *cahiers* devoted to him, constitute the only major contributions to an elucidation of his writing. Of a somewhat different nature, although providing some insights into the author's ideas and major concerns, are Poulet's interviews [8] and Hindus' study, which is a combination of personal observations and critical remarks, [9] severely criticized by Céline himself.

While the present state of Céline studies is not characterized by an overabundance of critical works, it is ameliorated by the pages devoted to the author in various survey studies of contemporary literature, as well as by the numerous and sometimes excellent articles to be found in literary magazines.

My own contribution to Céline studies will differ from that of the three French critical works that have appeared to date and which, although competent and valuable for introductory purposes, tend sometimes to diverge from the central concern of literary criticism and substitute appreciation for exploration by means of textual analysis and examination. The need for the latter approach, although met in part by the studies mentioned above, is evident and suggests treatment on a more extensive scale. It is my hope that this book will contribute to the understanding of Céline by applying to him the only truly meaningful criterion, that of his own writing. The technique used will be an explicative one, based both on analysis in depth and synthesis of major themes. The principal aim of such a procedure is to determine the inner structure of the writing, the consistency of themes, the architecture of the works when seen as a whole, the development and durability of the literary vision, and its applicability to our world. These seem to me the measuring stick of the greatness of a writer, not only when examined as an isolated figure, but also in relation to his contribution to the literary scene of his time.

My study will deal with what are considered Céline's greatest books and these will be treated in detailed fashion and with a view to synthesis of central themes. They are: *Voyage au bout de la nuit* and *Mort à crédit*, written at the start of his literary career; *D'un château l'autre* and *Nord*, produced during the last decade of Céline's life. Everything characteristic of the writer is contained in these four works: all the main themes and stylistic innovations, every stage of the evolution his writing underwent. In themselves, they constitute a whole, a statement as complete as anything designed to define an author's vision of man's position in the universe. At the same time, they can also be seen as a cycle, for it has been noted that Céline's last great work, *Nord*, meets and in many respects parallels his first, *Voyage au bout de la nuit*.[10] In choosing this quartet of long and complex novels and exploring each in depth, I believe that the clearest and the most meaningful insight into Céline's literary vision can be gained.[11]

The method of study on which this book is based is a combination of cataloguing and synthesizing: of culling detailed examples that illustrate the complex network of phrases and incidents which underlies each of Céline's major themes; of combining these themes into the structure which upholds the author's central vision, and to examine the shape of this structure during the course of his literary career with an eye for both consistency and change. Since Céline can be included among those authors whose work proceeds in a vertical rather than in a horizontal direction because they develop their particular literary vision in an ever-deepening fashion, no radical metamorphoses could be expected. It was more a question of noting how the concepts, hinted at or stated partially in the early works, were further clarified or accentuated as his writing progressed. Just as Céline proceeded, in the many successive versions of each phrase and paragraph of his novels, to build, to amplify, to add volume and complexity, so does his work as a whole grow in scope and amplitude. Both the micro- and the macrostructure of his writing follows this pattern. The architecture of one repeats and reflects the other.

Thus, one must examine Céline's work both as with a magnifying glass and through a telescope: dissect and synthesize, note the minute detail and the enormous edifice. Moreover, this examination must take place in the very center of the author's disquieting universe, where the critic is assailed by shifting, moving, terrifying words and thoughts. The setting in which he works is as precarious as that of a voyager about to be shipwrecked or of a passenger on one of the barges, galleys, phantom ships that lurch and plow their way through Céline's novels. Neither microscope nor telescope finds stable footing, and exploration cannot proceed in the peaceful and removed domain of the laboratory or observatory.

In training the telescope on Céline in an effort to place him within the context of past and future, or to relate him to major currents in Western literature, one becomes immediately aware of further difficulties. Disclaiming almost all the predecessors which perspicacious critics have assigned him, and leaving behind but few true disciples, Céline, the arch-individualist among modern French novelists, refuses to be labeled or categorized. He goes so far as to delight in mystifying his critics, to lead them astray, to poke fun at their attempts to impale and classify the writer like a specimen. If we wish to do so at all, we must provide only the largest and broadest sort of lineage for Céline. We might then point to his relatedness with the ancient tradition of irrationalist, mystical, obscurantist literature which, in French writing, would link him most closely to the Middle Ages and the sixteenth century and to a tradition which preceded that of the Classical Age with its emphasis on reason, formal beauty, elimination of excess. We might also ally him to this current as it comes to the surface again in the nineteenth century and manifests itself in the rejection of the dictates of classicism.

Linking Céline to particular writers, such as Aristophanes or Rabelais,[12] Rousseau, Voltaire,[13] Swift, and Cervantes, has its attractions. However, while such comparisons emphasize his capacity to produce laughter of a robust or satirical sort, it seems even more important to dwell on Céline's adherence to another, blacker current in literature. It is one filled with militant pessimism and violent derision, denoting a vision that spares nothing of man's existence, and a humor that is no less somber than its poetic strength. This stream flows from Villon to Beckett and comes to the surface at various points during the centuries. One of its tributaries—attaining particular fame in the postwar years—is that of existentialism. In the group of thinkers and writers considered the precursors of its present-day doctrines are those familiar figures among whom Céline would not have felt out of place: Pascal, Nietzsche, Kierkegaard, Dostoevsky, Flaubert, and others.

Céline's link with existentialist thought is much more crucial than the obvious influence he has exercised on the best-known exponent of the doctrine, Jean-Paul Sartre. It is based not only on his ability to figure in the ranks of those who are its precursors—for, like them, he has seen and voiced all the pain, hideousness, meaninglessness, and despair of the human condition—but also on the fact, and this is one of his major contributions, that he has translated his vision into a particularly modern idiom. His work can thus be considered as a juncture of existentialist thought and contemporary style, that is, the eruption of the spoken word into literature. The importance of this particular combination is great. For it establishes the problem of existence *not* in abstract philosophical terms or couched in traditional literary language, both of which might serve to remove it from the sphere of direct experience. It is the confrontation of the reader with an overpowering vision of his desperate situation, presented in terms of his actual, living speech, which makes the existential dilemma so real, so palpable, that it becomes almost unbearable.

Céline's contribution is vital not only because it is a journey to the end of past statements on the nature of human existence, but also because it points the way to an expression of these ideas through stylistic means that force the reader into direct contact with basic emotions and spoken language. Thus, the stripping away of protective layers of consolation, illusion, contingency which may serve as palliatives, occurs on two planes at once: the sweeping demand for a *tabula rasa* is met both by thought and expression. In this resides Céline's unusual power as a writer, as well as the anger or terror of the reader, who is subject to such ruthless and exacting action.

There can be no doubt that Céline belongs in the ranks of the great destroyers. Uprooting secure concepts of existence and literature at the same time, he commits what for many is an unpardonable sin—that of leaving us no refuge of any kind, no exit from the trap he has shown our world to be. The first attack is leveled at beliefs we generally cling to in order to maintain a safe view of our universe: thus, religion is dismissed or rejected; moral codes are proven a sham, an empty shell; human brotherhood reveals itself as a hollow dream. The second uprooting is no less thorough, for traditional literary style is scrupulously dismembered, exploded, destroyed. Céline's entire work—both in theme and style—is an illustration of the view that existence is an endgame played out on a cannibal isle or in a cosmic jungle, in an irrational and vicious setting with a multiple décor of slaughterhouse, asylum, and dunghill. Moreover, this vision is hammered into us in a

language as brutal, direct and visceral as raw human emotion
—the apparent directness being due to Céline's consummate
skill as a writer which allows him to produce this effect of style,
while hiding the meticulous craftsmanship that lurks behind it.

Allusion to Céline's cohorts in the sphere of existentialist
thought and the overthrow of safe concepts of existence has
already been made. For his precursors in the second domain—
the destruction of safe literary tradition—we must look among
the poets. (This is in keeping with Céline's own affirmations,
since he considered poets and not prose writers his mentors in
the realm of style.) We might then point to some of those
nineteenth-century poets who were determined to "break the
neck of eloquence" and cut the flow of lyrical effusion, so
much in vogue in their day. The best known among them,
Baudelaire, Laforgue, and Corbière, providing striking illustrations of this concept in their works. Other efforts along similar
lines include the revolutionary treatment of syntax in the hands
of such poets as Mallarmé, Rimbaud, and later Apollinaire.

Prose, however, had been much slower to change. The
novel in France, at the time of Céline's appearance, had not
really undergone an equally radical evolution. It is of course
true that severe quakes had been produced on the French
literary scene by surrealist experimentation, and that the concepts of Proust and Gide were upsetting the accepted notions
of the novel. Style, however—at least insofar as the important
breakdown of the barrier between the written and spoken
language [14] was concerned—remained within its safe and traditional boundaries. It is in this realm that Cèline created a major
revolution from which the novel in France has not recovered
since. The status quo of the genre can truly be said to have been
destroyed with the advent of *Voyage au bout de la nuit*.

The new stylistic trend, as well as the vision of existence
it served to present in such forceful terms, has had an enduring
impact on French literature which is both great and diffuse.
Strengthened by the influence of certain American writers, such
as Hemingway, Dos Passos, Faulkner, and others, reflected and
carried on in the work of the young Sartre,[15] it grew and continued to exercise its influence during the late 30s and 40s.

Céline's contribution, at its source, is both profound and difficult to pinpoint. While some critics draw up long lists of writers both in France and abroad who have felt the impact of the latter's work,[16] one has to admit that it is impossible to speak of Céline as the founder of a school of literature or to depict him surrounded by a coterie of disciples. The reasons for this are manifold: the unique combination of factors which constitute his particular literary genius; the highly individualistic or even nonconformist nature of his personality; his hatred for any state of fixity or adherence to group action, including that of a school of writing; his refusal to accept discipleship or following of any kind; his claim to the total freedom and lone pursuits of the arch-destroyer.

Although the impact of Céline is not specific, it runs in a deeper—if often hidden—current. Essentially, it consists of the creation of a new tone, a literary ambiance which pervades an entire sector of modern letters and exceeds the limits of national boundaries or personal orientation and background. It has made possible the indebtedness to Céline felt by French authors of such diverse persuasion as Aymé, Queneau, and Bernanos, as well as the kinship expressed by foreign writers like the Slovakian Géjra Vanoš, or the Americans Henry Miller, William Burroughs, Allen Ginsberg, and Jack Kerouac, among others. The homage paid by non-French writers is often based mainly on an appreciation of Céline's vision rather than of his style—since the latter demands an extremely thorough knowledge and familiarity, even intimacy with the French language, down to its subtlest innuendos and spoken or *argotique* terms. Translations, while giving a general idea of Céline's work, have until now been fairly inadequate,[17] rendering little if any of the vital aspects of what the author considers his major contribution, his "music." Even with this severe limitation, however, Céline's writing seems to have had a great enough impact to cross language barriers and affect the work of authors with quite different national backgrounds.

In American literature alone, Céline's work has had a strong appeal for two generations of writers and manifests itself both in prose and poetry. The effect on poetry is less

frequently noticed than that on prose, but if we give credence
to the opinions of Allen Ginsberg, the best known poet of the
San Francisco Renaissance, Céline and William Carlos Williams
have related aims in regard to incorporating "the diction and
rhythms of actual speech," [18] a concept which is certainly a
fundamental one in the stylistic realm. Ginsberg voices his own
indebtedness to the French writer and points out that his
important collection *Kaddish* contains not only his impressions
of Céline (in "Ignu") but that the main poem is based on
syntax inspired by the methods characteristic of the latter. In
an appraisal of which qualities of Céline's stylistic innovation
most appeal to American writers today, Ginsberg states that
"the rapidity of transitions and shiftings made possible by the
3-dot syntax [Céline's] . . . that's what impresses us in US
who are interested in the use of aural speech patterns transferred to written language." The last part of Ginsberg's statement can thus be applied to a group of writers which includes
both poets and prose writers interested in the vitality and
immediacy that can be gained by means of stylistic devices
related to those developed by Céline and grafted or transformed to suit the American speech medium.

Among prose writers in this country who best exemplify
the meaningfulness of certain aspects of Céline's writings for
American authors, one must certainly include Henry Miller,
William Burroughs, and Jack Kerouac. Burroughs' interest in
the French writer very likely dates back to the 1940s, since
Ginsberg states that the author of *Naked Lunch* introduced
Céline's *Voyage au bout de la nuit* to him and Kerouac in
1945, and that both of them have always been "entertained and
'influenced'" by it. Miller's link with Céline goes back further
in time and appears more deeply rooted. One might add that
for all the writers cited, however, the appeal of Céline resides
in what Ginsberg lists as his "Spenglerian melancholy," the
long "tirades on social corruption and bêtiserie appropriate to
USA obviously," as well as Céline's "surreal vision which
touches us directly [so that we can] see our landscape through
his eyes." In a sweeping final statement, the American spokesman for the poets of the San Francisco Renaissance points

out that the French author is "a nut, a freak, an eccentric—
like our tradition of Poe, Emily Dickinson, Thoreau, Pound—
all our geniuses verily."

Kerouac, closely related to the group of Burroughs, Ginsberg, Corso, Ferlinghetti, summarizes Céline's contribution to
contemporary letters as "that flamboyant tone, that shrug of
the shoulders, that laugh which is like a deliverance," [19] and
goes on to pay homage to the French writer in terms which
reveal many of his own preoccupations. Thus, Kerouac emphasizes Céline's great compassion, his sensitivity to suffering, his
being falsely accused of vitriolic viciousness. In looking at
Kerouac's own work, it becomes evident that while he appre-
ciates "the clarity of personal modern grief in Céline," [20] and
strives to elucidate the same problem in his writings, these
lack the strength and originality of the French author. While
Kerouac's momentary confrontations with such grief provide
us with some pages of fine writing—as in the striking passages
on the corpse of Waldo Meister [21]—they are unfortunately
often marred by sentimentality or cliché of concept and image.
Some of the other similarities in the work of Céline and
Kerouac, such as the attempts to achieve the impression of
spontaneous prose or the use of hallucinatory visions,[22] tend
to underscore the discrepancy in the art of the two writers and
point up Céline's superiority. The clearest comparison presents
itself if one places Kerouac's fellow travelers in *On the Road*
—Dean Moriarty and Sal Paradise—next to their counterparts
in *Voyage au bout de la nuit*—Robinson and Bardamu; while
a superficial resemblance seems apparent, the stature of the
latter overshadows the former in every way.

William Burroughs' best work, *Naked Lunch*, certainly de-
serves some comparison with Céline on the basis of an expression of personal suffering, black or grotesque humor, the
torrential flow of verbal abuse, the hallucinatory nature of
many episodes, the obsessive repetition of certain erotico-
sadistic sequences, the use of special terminology characteristic
of a particular group of society—argot in Céline, "junkie" talk
in Burroughs—the concern with spoken language and its
literary notation. For Burroughs and other similar writers, the
most obvious relationship with Céline lies in the creation or

portrayal of a protagonist who is a neo-romantic version of the outsider: the wanderer, the outcast, the deviate, the junkie, the subterranean. In all cases, we note the emergence of a central figure on the verge of dissolution and of a universe which echoes his state. It is significant of an orientation that is similar in the group of American writers discussed so far and a certain sector of French literature in the 1930s whose vision found its culmination in the works of Céline.

It is perhaps significant that Miller comes closest to being Céline's contemporary and that he thus partook of the same literary ambiance in which the French writer created his works, for among American authors at least, Miller has sensed and incorporated Céline most completely. This becomes evident, less in the admittedly numerous references and evaluations of Céline found in Miller's writings [23] than in the very quality of these allusions: one is under the impression that Miller treats Céline's works as a kind of reference point or as memories which spring forth in his mind as naturally as some of his own life experiences.[24] A similar feeling transpires, even in the character of Miller's homage to the French author, for he states simply: "Céline lives within me. He always will." [25] This affirmation is upheld by the relationships in the works of the two writers which go far beyond surface manifestations or a few similarities of theme. The links are more fundamental, diffuse, sometimes not obvious, and manifest themselves mainly in the realm of style: in the word accumulations, the thickly textured and often rapid outpourings, in the devices used to build up an idea, a feeling or a description which include the use of a flood of related images or utterings, of a method by which the subject is surrounded from all possible sides, represented by means of the cumulative effect of its various component facets. In more general terms, we note that both authors use language to obtain an impression of immediacy, personal involvement or direct participation, and are concerned with the creation of a style in which spoken language (or, more precisely, the literary rendering of the spoken word) figures prominently.

Their closeness is not based only on stylistic links, however, and resides also in their penchant and ability for creating scenes of a hallucinatory nature and sometimes with strong erotic content (transmuted into an aesthetic, or mystical concept in Céline while remaining mainly physical in Miller), as well as in their tendency to mingle the crudest aspects of reality with poetic elements in almost inextricable fashion. The nature of their outcry also shows similarities: both express themselves in a harsh, defiant, angry, often cruel tone, but this gives way to sudden—if infrequent—bursts of great warmth or tenderness. The point at which the two authors diverge is in their conclusions about the nature of human existence. Here, Miller shows a more affirmative view, since he considers evil, pain, and viciousness a possible source or matrix for joy and beauty. Céline's vision is in sharp contrast, centering darkly on death, evil, and pain, offering no consolation by metamorphosis but insisting on the inevitability of final dissolution and decay.

While it might be too simplistic to reduce the parting of the ways of the two writers to the inevitable differences in the viewpoint of the Old World and the New, it must be admitted that Céline's true *famille d'esprit* must trace its genealogy on European soil and probably even locate its main branch within the boundaries of the country of his birth. The writer's closest relations are to be found among those men of letters of the nineteenth and twentieth century whose central preoccupation has been with the sordid, absurd, desperate aspects of existence on the one hand, and with concentration on style on the other. Added to this, they share a basic need to mercilessly destroy all illusions which could serve to spread a veil of false security, order, or reason across the dreadful workings of our universe. Among them, we find such authors as Flaubert, Jarry, Lautréamont, Gide (in some measure), Artaud, the young Sartre, Ionesco, Genet, Michaux, Beckett, Robbe-Grillet, Du Bouchet. For all of these men, the first aim in shaking the foundations of accepted and often smug beliefs is the forced confrontation with the precarious, hostile, or frankly hopeless nature of human existence. In some instances, once this revelation is made, there follows a leap toward affirmation, a promise of new meaning once all former meaning has been destroyed. The case of Pascal and religion is too well known to reiterate. But it is no less true for Flaubert and aesthetic perfection; for Gide and self-fulfillment, authenticity, and multiform reality; for Sartre and existential involvement.

In Céline, the arch-destroyer, this kind of affirmative leap does not occur, however. The path he follows is the pursuit of a black vision to its very end, the compulsion to embark on voyage after voyage of discovery into the various realms of despair which existence can offer. The only fellow travelers one might indicate are Michaux and Beckett, whose central vision is closely linked to his. Finally affirming nothing but the power of the word—just as Michaux and Beckett were to do after him—Céline subjects himself to the demanding tasks of the word-maker's craft. Literature then becomes an exorcism rather than a salvation, a sign that everything is lost except the word.

It is evident why only a few men were truly able to follow in Céline's path. In the wake of scorched-earth policies, the harvest must be meager. Once monuments have been razed to the ground and foundations shattered, one can hardly explore or survey the same terrain. The greatness of Céline resides not only in his stylistic revolt, but also in his having ventured to the very end of an already desperate line of thought and feeling. It is true that the totality of his pursuit might be qualified as "monstrous," [26] being admittedly excessive, totally unrelenting, determined to break the tether of reason which counsels a balance of opposites and the wise middle course. Contemporary literature has known other such "monsters," now revered: Kafka, Joyce, Proust. It is not unlikely that Céline will one day join their ranks.

Notes

1 Robert Poulet, *La Lanterne magique* (Paris: Nouvelles Editions Debresses, 1956), p. 23.

2 *L'Herne*, Nos. 3 and 5 provide a great deal of interesting information concerning Céline's life.

3 "Carnet du cuirassier Destouches," *L'Herne*, No. 5, 9–11.

4 Georges Geoffroy, "Céline en Angleterre," *L'Herne*, No. 3, 11.

5 Jean Paget, "Hermantier retrouve une pièce de Céline," *Arts et spectacles* (December 16–22, 1964), 4.

6 The recently discovered introduction to the Russian edition by the Soviet critic Ivan Anissimov (*L'Herne*, No. 5, 165–72), however, mingles praise of Céline's attacks on capitalism with criticism for his not having

sufficiently affirmed social revolution and rejected capitalistic decadence, as well as for having fallen into the trap of despair and nihilism.

7 Nicole Debrie-Panel, *Louis-Ferdinand Céline* (Lyon: E. Vitte, 1961); Marc Hanrez, *Céline* (Paris: Gallimard, 1961); Pol Vandromme, *Louis-Ferdinand Céline* (Paris: Editions Universitaires, 1963).

8 Robert Poulet, *Entretiens familiers avec L.-F. Céline* (Paris: Plon, 1958).

9 Milton Hindus, *The Crippled Giant* (New York: Boar's Head Books, 1950).

10 Milton Hindus, "Dire, redire et se contredire," *L'Herne*, No. 3, 246.

11 Needless to say, all of Céline's work served as a frame of reference for the analyses presented and will be referred to whenever pertinent. Greatest emphasis, however, will be placed on the four works mentioned above.

12 Claude Jamet, *Images de la litterature* (Paris, F. Sorlot, 1943), p. 16.

13 Debrie-Panel, op. cit., pp. 82–85.

14 A barrier appreciably greater in French than in American literature.

15 Sartre's first novel, *La Nausée*, shows that he has felt the impact of Céline in terms of both vision and style.

16 Such critics as Boisdeffre, Nimier, or Jamet mention the following as Céline's disciples: Bernanos, Blondin, Boudart, Calaferte, Clébert, Guérin, Huguénin, Kerouac, Miller, Mouloudji, Nimier, Paraz, Queneau, Sartre, Vian, Vanoš, etc.

17 Fortunately, what appears to me an unusually fine translation of *Mort à crédit* by Ralph Manheim (for New American Library) is to appear in November 1966. Hopefully, it will point the way to further translations of Céline's works in the near future.

18 Letter from Allen Ginsberg to the author of this book, September 24, 1965. All direct quotes from Ginsberg are contained in this letter.

19 Homage to Céline. Letter by Jack Kerouac, *L'Herne*, No. 3, 205.

20 *The Subterraneans* (New York: Grove Press, 1958), p. 46.

21 *The Town and the City* (New York: Grosset & Dunlap, 1950), pp. 432–37.

22 For example: *On the Road* (New York: Compass Books, 1963), p. 295.

23 For example, Miller lists *Journey to the End of Night* as one of the hundred books which influenced him most ("Books in My Life"); *Voyage au bout de la nuit, Mort à crédit, Mea Culpa, Semmelweiss, Hommage à Zola* are in the list of books which Miller states he remembers having read (French edition only of "Books in My Life"). Other references occur in *The Air-conditioned Nightmare* (pp. 37, 156), *The Intimate Henry Miller* (pp. 152, 166), *The Red Notebook* (last page), *A Devil in Paradise* (p. 103), etc.

24 *The Air-conditioned Nightmare* (New York: Avon Books, 1945), pp. 35, 156.

25 *L'Herne*, No. 3, 202.

26 The term seems to be a favorite with critics when referring to Céline. We find it, among other places, in Roger Ikor's "Au feu de l'enfer," *L'Herne*, No. 3, 251; and in Geoffrey Brereton's *A Short History of French Literature* (London: Penguin Books, 1961), p. 246. M. Hindus' study on Céline also was originally entitled "The Monstrous Giant" (see *L'Herne*, No. 5, 68).

Part I   Nox

1 · "Noircir et Se Noircir"

THE NIGHT MUSES

Céline's literary universe lies *sub luce maligna*. Heretical, full of dread, giving off a dark gleam, his works conjure up a host of night terrors. Grotesque underground creatures, incubi, monsters, imbeciles and grinning gargoyles, scapegoats and tormentors, beasts and mockeries of men wander about in the shadowy zones of endless and repetitive nightmares. The world of day, of sun and light, is foreign to Céline. "I don't like the sun, as you might well guess," [1] he states with characteristic wryness. True, an almost total eclipse reigns in his writing so that only the dark side of existence can reveal itself. "Everything interesting happens in the shadows," [2] he assures us and, having voiced this conviction early in his literary career, Céline holds to it with unrelenting consistency. During the course of the years his vision does not change but, on the contrary, grows in scope and substance. If *Semmelweiss* already depicted a night world, *Nord* only projects it on a larger canvas, but the basic image remains unaltered.

One can, in fact, see all of Céline's work as a long contemplation of the same major theme. If his writings constitute " a continual deepening of the truth he has in his possession," [3] or pursues, it is because this "truth" is central to his vision. In attempting to define it, we might summarize it as a universe created through a "noircissement" (blackening) [4] of existence, reality. This night world forms a constant theme whose all-pervasive quality proves that it is more than a simple motif, a

mere device, or an intriguing décor. Appearing at first only to
be a shadowy, amorphous mass, this blackness—when probed
and analyzed—can be shown to have a clear and definable
shape.

What then is this night? How does it function in the
works of Céline? What are its origins, its boundaries? Critics
are at variance concerning the roots and interpretation of
Céline's terrifying literary vision which has upset, intrigued,
captivated, or frankly outraged readers for two generations. It
is hard to agree with those scholars who consider Céline's preoccupation with ugliness, viciousness, pain, corruption, and dissolution primarily an attempt to shock the reader or terrorize
him; [5] or with those who accuse the author of exhibitionism or
of taking pleasure in obscenity for its own sake.[6] Such evaluations tend to dismiss Céline's predilection for describing the
hideous or dark side of existence too lightly. It is obvious to
many critics that Céline has indeed chosen strange muses—
those of death and ugliness [7]—and is determined to show us
an image of man that exhibits his congenital ignominies, illuminates his very vitals in order to reveal that soft, shapeless, dreadful core of being which most of us generally prefer to hide
from view to protect our emotional equilibrium.[8]

One might be led to attribute Céline's orientation to the
aim of a moralist or social reformer, and see him mainly in the
guise of an indefatigable pamphleteer, unrelenting in his denunciation of man's present condition, his accusation of our
age and its abysmal stupidity, a railing and incurable idealist.
Such a view could arise if one concentrates on the author's
statements concerning the ill-effects of poverty, or interprets his
cry of "Everything needs redoing!" [9] in the light of social com-
mentary. However, the idea that Céline is interested in achieving changes in a particular social system is fallacious. Not only
does he refuse to attribute to literature the ability to reform
existence, but he also firmly believes that the present social
system is as rotten as any other, past or future. His horror and
disgust go much further; the attacks are directed against life
itself.[10] His goal is *not* to reconstruct society, nor even to suggest palliatives. "He offers no remedy for the suffering which
he denounces . . . yet is obsessed by this suffering." [11] It is

evident that Céline's greatest power lies in denunciation and in the ability to rule out easy remedies or utopian illusions. In order to do this, he cannot allow himself to be limited by the framework set up by any social system and, of necessity, "divests himself of all canons, transgresses all conventions." [12]

It is probably as a result of such action that the idea of Céline as a nihilist, an anarchist, a kind of *homme révolté*, has arisen. Critics tend to emphasize the tendency toward negation and accuse the author of "not giving a damn," [13] or moving continually toward an absolute refusal of the status quo. The rather one-sided perception of his work as containing primarily attacks and derision, the arch-pessimism of the author which is often read as true nihilism, have earned him such titles as "negation personified," [14] or "apocalyptic pessimist." [15] The matter is much more complex, however, since we find in his works pure negation countered by fierce involvement and a furious kind of compassion which would seem to be the very opposite of true nihilism. The same kind of paradox can be found in what has been termed Céline's "anarchism." While it is quite true that the author himself has stated, "I am, always have been, always will be an anarchist, and I don't give a damn for anyone's opinion" (N., 111), he has considerably clarified this pronouncement by other remarks. Thus, he states for example: "[In literature] one needs a great deal of anarchy. Not for the principle of the thing, but because our lives are so completely askew and upside down." [16] From this it becomes clear that Céline advocates a semblance of anarchy in literature mainly in order to reflect the state of the world in which we live, and rejects any doctrinaire approach. He is clearly too much of a skeptic to believe in the methodical application of anarchy or any other theory. Actually, he is "merely an anarchist out to destroy all anarchies. Surely if anarchy reigned somewhere, he would be opposed to it, just as he is opposed to everything else. . . ." [17] We might once again connect this attitude with the opposition or even abhorrence the author feels toward any strictly delimited action, category, or school of thought, that is, anything that resembles a state of fixity.

This is true not only for the designation of anarchist but for any other label applied to Céline, for he himself refuses to be fixed or confined to any category, no matter how provocative. Instead, he "breaks all boundaries, just as he ruptures all eardrums," [18] and remains alien to anything one attributes to him, complex, disturbing, difficult to capture. This is due in part to his insistence upon remaining uninvolved and truly individualistic, in part to his ability to disentangle himself from most conventional bonds and disregard the petty, the contingent. "He never had to renounce any party, since he belonged to none, nor any master, having none . . . he is the picture of a totally free man." [19]

Being free, Céline is also elusive. It is not only difficult to affix any tag to him, but also to analyze him in any one particular light. Some may admit that the writer is "outside of any classification, beyond competition, beyond the law." [20] This does not eliminate attempts to determine the framework and internal laws of his work. To probe and clarify its author's dominant vision is not to delimit his writing in any manner but simply to unify its complicated and paradoxical structure into a central statement. This might be condensed into the expression of a desire to depict "a world blackened but true." [21]

If Céline's reasons for dwelling on such a vision of the world are not those of the moralist, the anarchist, or the nihilist, what does his preoccupation stem from? Some critics suggest that the author has an obsessional penchant for the cloaca of life or an almost pathological liking for themes of stupidity, suffering, and cruelty.[22] A cursory examination of his work might well result in such an impression: the long monologues seem to pour out of the farthest recesses of a mind laid bare, the hallucinatory tales that resemble fever dreams, the frenetic accounts at which Céline excels—all may give an impression of delirium or of mania. Is it this quality in his work which has led some scholars to conclude that the author himself is nothing short of a madman? [23] We cannot seriously consider such an interpretation or accept it as an explanation of Céline's central vision. This would be to show no greater insight than the author's concierge and would force us, by the same token, to dismiss the works of great writers like Nerval, Nietzsche, Baudelaire, or Kafka as being the ravings—albeit talented—of mental patients.

Just as unacceptable as ascribing Céline's tendency to blacken reality to dementia is his portrayal as a leering, satanic monster—a cross between Nero and the Marquis de Sade—who delights in human abjection and misery. Unfortunately, this is often the case and even appears in the preface of the Pléiade edition of his works where Henri Mondor assures us that Céline "too often delights in evil . . . and that his gourmandise for debility and physical decrepitude seems to equal his predilection for blindness and terror. . . ." [24] Some venture the guess that the author shows pleasure both in seeing and inflicting pain, and enjoys self-abasement.[25] Others add that Céline wishes to take all the hatred and evil of the world upon himself and thus rid humanity of them.[26] Such views tend to portray the author either as a satanic or a Christlike figure. Both are equally untrue or at least exaggerated. While the first tends to present him as a sado-masochistic case study or as the demonic enemy of mankind, the second makes him into a sacred scapegoat, a view which is just as hard to accept. Certainly, Céline is no docile Lamb of God willing to suffer in silent acquiescence. How far from the "So be it!" necessary for that role are his furious railings, his violent streams of invectives alone! If one wishes to resort to biblical comparisons at all, the "modern Jeremiah" of Poulet,[27] or the "Ezekiel of the faubourg" used by Vandromme,[28] are certainly more fitting. But, although such picturesque epithets are interesting, they do not lead us much closer to the truth. Nor does the explanation we seek lie in any portrait of the author, drawn either in psychological or mythical terms.

Actually, this answer is a fairly obvious one, neither unique nor overly complex, although only a very few critics seem to have arrived at it. Céline's constant involvement with a dark and wrathful universe arises from a literary choice. Simple as it is, this insight forms the basis for an understanding of the author's entire work. It is surprising that it is not emphasized more frequently, since it clarifies so much and does away with the majority of the conjectures enumerated above, which prove to be rather unfruitful. Once this becomes clear, we see why some critics have suggested that all of Céline's books are composed in the same manner, that the spirit of anger gives them a remarkable structure,[29] and—we might add—a particular ambiance and unusual unity. The procedure used by the author, as described by Michel Beaujour in a lecture delivered at the Institut Français of New York in March 1963, is to choose out of reality the evil, ugliness, and despair and to make them his themes. He will not release his hold on this segment of reality throughout the course of his literary career.

Beaujour goes further when he states that Céline "chooses himself" and the malediction which lies over his life, thus making both an existential and an aesthetic choice. The second of these is quite clear: it is the same one as is contained or implied in Céline's phrase, "noircir et se noircir," a key concept, since it seems to serve as the springboard for his literary production as a whole. The first notion, that it is also an existential choice, might somewhat obscure issues. While it is certainly linked to the literary one, it might foster the erroneous idea that Céline and his protagonists are one, that there is little difference between his life and its literary rendition. In Céline's case, one can fall into this trap more easily than with many other writers. Various factors contribute to this: his works are written in the first person, so that the author and the narrator seem at times to fuse into one; several of Celine's protagonists (Ferdinand, Bardamu, Robinson of the early novels, and Ferdine of the last two) have many of their author's own characteristics;[30] Céline's style, because of its directness, immediacy, and resemblance to spoken language, creates the illusion that one is participating in the author's own experiences. The appearance of fusion between Céline and his work is purposeful, but has sometimes resulted in misplaced emphasis on the part of even the best critics. On occasion, it has fostered an attitude which treats Céline as though he were speaking, not through a literary medium, but in purely realistic, experiential terms. It would certainly be more accurate to be aware of the author's artistic theory of transposition[31] than to consider his writings as a "journal intime." In that case, we must say that Céline did not choose the malediction which pursues the figures in his literary universe to weigh upon his own destiny as well.[32]

The concept of an "existential choice" might then best be used in the largest sense of the word, as an orientation in which both the man and the writer partake. One of the major aspects

of this orientation, and one which indeed becomes a corner-
stone of Céline's writing, is what Beaujour terms the firm belief in "the sublime nature of ugliness." What interests us most,
however, is the method for achieving this sublime ugliness, the
"trick" by which the author proceeds. It is revealed as early
as *Voyage* (pp. 331–32) and analyzed by Beaujour as an effort
to "corrode the world, undermine it." To carry this project out,
the writer needs a corrosive agent, an effective means of sabo-
tage. *Hate* would seem to be the most useful tool for performing both these functions. It has even been suggested that
Céline's pen is effectual only when spurred on by fury or
hostility, or that hate almost amounts to a faith for him.[33]
Whether, however, hate is a tool, an incentive, a basic theme,
or a faith, what is central is that it is the agent of metamorphosis, the golden bough that opens the gates of the underworld, the precipice from which "le docteur Destouches" flings
himself to land in the stormy element of literature, to be transformed into Céline.

Once one accepts this conception, many ideas of Céline
and his critics become quite revealing. The author makes it
clear that the nightmare visions he shows us have a literary
foundation. Thus he points to *Voyage au bout de la nuit* saying: "There you have the lyricism of baseness." [34] Couldn't
this very phrase be applied to all of his writings? One critic has
referred to Céline's "vulgar, one might even say filthy, lyricism,
which magnifies human vileness and paints everything larger
than life, emphasizing above all its sick and harmful aspects." [35]
Doesn't such an observation bring us back to Céline's prescription of "noircir et se noircir," to which he might have
added—defining the tone a writer with his aims must use—
"crier et décrier" (to cry out and decry)? Céline would probably have agreed that among the numberless voices and noises
of our time, only a loud and ugly cry would succeed in being
heard,[36] but it is even more likely that Céline's "cry" is not so
much the result of a reasoning attitude, or a rational comment,
as the expression of deeply felt anger and disgust. It is an authentic outburst of emotion, better described as "the outcry of
a real human being, appearing in the midst of an assembly of
dummies and automatons."[37]

On the other hand, the strident note of his utterance is

also based on the knowledge that this tone of voice is best
suited to his talent, that the anger it contains most fully releases the brilliant verbal flood of which he is capable. But
hatred, wrath, and the black invectives they liberate, are not
only an art form: they are an essential part of the author's
personality and seem to spring from early experiences deeply
rooted in his mind. (M.C., 631) At the same time, they are a
weapon, a spice that keeps thought active and alive,[38] and a
vital spur to that remorseless lucidity which gives justification
and meaning to life.[39] Most important of all is the fact that
this torrent of black bile is his authentic literary voice. While
for Destouches, the doctor, it might have been natural to speak
softly and to alleviate pain, for Céline, the writer, true expression is possible only in the form of a cry full of hate and fury
that offers no palliative, no soothing tranquilizer. The author
makes it quite clear that to arrive at artistic authenticity and
individuality, disgust and brutality are valuable means.[40] Reality
is altered by a lyrical, black, and muddy reconstruction of its
components, a task for which anger, hatred, or wrath provide
the energy as well as the tools.

Only a few critics have seen the specific function of hatred
in Céline's writing, that is, its use as a literary springboard.
While some have sensed that it is a necessary condition for
his creative function, others have defined Céline's wrath as its
basic component, a kind of fuse which fired his verbal ava-
lanches and set off the explosions of his style: "He needed
enemies; his technique and creative spirit demanded it. He
needed them just as a poet needs rhyme." [41] Céline, whose
horrendous outpourings reeking of sulphur and brimstone seem
to rise from some gigantic infernal maw, had to resort to the
primitive flint of rage to unleash them. He himself gives us a
wonderfully apt description of the combustion agent, in Voyage
(211–12), in which the concierge quite fittingly becomes the
keeper of the spark, the repository of the corrosive fumes:

> Our *concierges* furnish those who know how to take it and
> keep it warm next to their hearts, enough all-purpose hatred,
> free of charge, to make a whole world explode . . . [hatred]
> that vital, hot spice, so mean and alive, so irrefutable, without
> which the mind is stifled and reduced to slandering and

maligning in a vague fashion only, or stammering pale insults. There is nothing which can bite, wound, cut, annoy, obsess, without the concierge, nor anything which could add to universal hatred the inflammatory power of a thousand undeniable details.

Is not Céline himself a more grandiose version of this concierge, a kind of Cerberus whose furious snarls establish him as the undisputed guardian of all the shameful secrets of man?

Undoubtedly, Céline's tinderbox of hate is a dangerous tool, one that threatens to scorch the hands of its user. He runs the risk of all those who have snatched at forbidden fire: that of being himself consumed. Although no Prometheus who sought after the divine flame of the gods, but rather one who has striven after that of infernal regions, his punishment is not too dissimilar from that of the rebellious Titan. Or possibly he is closer to the figure of another rebel against the established order. It seems to have been his lot to live condemned to hatred, shouldering the burden of his curses or, as he himself notes, to wander about in the bitterly humorous guise of a "Sisyphus with a paper rock!" [42]

It is certainly true that, from the start of his literary career, Céline ran great risks and "was a dangerous burden to himself." [43] But he was well aware of his choices, knew that attacks would inevitably result from his writing and, in a sense, accepted them. "I know what I'm doing and what risks I run," he states, "it's all very well like this. . . ." [44] In the same manner, the protagonist of *Mort à crédit* informs us: "I'll tell such stories that they'll come back from the four corners of the globe, expressly to kill me. Then it'll be all over and I'll be damned glad." (502) A similar idea is expressed in Céline's preface to *Voyage au bout de la nuit* (Pléiàde edition) where the author attributes all persecution and hatred he has experienced to the writing of that book. And although these statements, on the simplest level, could be interpreted merely as a desire for self-destruction, they indicate something quite different. In larger, less literal terms, they remind us of Céline's recognition of the dangers of lucidity, the risks of the prophet or the seer, of the artist who dares go to the end of that night which is his own poetic vision.

THE SULLIED MIRROR

One critic remarks that Céline "was the first to force us to look at man in a defiled looking glass." [45] Many others have concurred. From the start of his literary career, with *Voyage au bout de la nuit*, the prototype of the Célinian novel is established: "a black epic, charred and tainted, in which modern man is magnificently insulted." [46] Were we to analyze this work alone, we should have a good indication of the author's themes throughout his literary career, although we would have to allow for some changes due to the evolution his writing underwent. Most often, this evolution takes the form of an enlargement, a further *noircissement*. *Voyage*, however, is already an exhaustive catalogue of human failings or vices—found under all climes and in most circumstances—a kind of Baedeker for every sort of night journey. We are led from continent to continent to learn what endless variety of "rottenness" man is capable of, to what horrid and constantly new lengths he can go. Each time we feel we have come to the end of degradation and pain, a new vista opens before us, another pit of despair, a further abyss which must be explored. We cannot plead exhaustion, for Céline is there before us, dragging us relentlessly along, screaming into our ears, forcing our eyes open. The book is truly a "travelogue through the gutter of the twentieth century . . . a journey through a hellish terrain in which everything is at war with everything else." [47] And, we might add, in which the author is also at war with most of his readers. In the simplest terms, *Voyage* can be called an epic of all that's foul in man, in which nothing is spared of the human animal except his earliest beginnings: childhood remains relatively unsullied, and the child himself is an innocent victim who, momentarily at least, is free from the stain of man's vileness.

In his second book, Céline goes further: he shows us that childhood itself is repulsive, imbecilic, miserable, "sullied" to the point of being "merdeux." Céline has taken the final step: he grasps life by the nape of the neck and "drowns it in filth and ignominy," [48] without exempting even its earliest manifestations which we so fondly think of as full of delights and free from taint. The child Ferdinand, the protagonist of *Mort à crédit*, appears in all his abject misery, truly as though seen in a defiled mirror. The book depicts his wanderings through a grotesque labyrinth typical of Céline's universe, his total failure in every corner of an implacably sordid world, which is both absurd and futile. There is no moment of easy compassion, no relenting in the harsh outline of the image thrown back by Céline's mirror, no relief from the nightmare vision. It is true that, practically without exception, "Céline's books besmirch rather than pity the sufferings of mankind." [49] The almost unbearable quality which they have, the bitter view of existence they present, is based on a feeling of degradation without any hope of redemption. It is this double confrontation which many have found so disturbing. It must be admitted that one does not read Céline with impunity,[50] even in his early novels, and that portrayals grow increasingly harsher and more devastating as his work progresses. The tendency to thrust before us "new 'letters from the underground,' a new 'ship of fools,' " [51] becomes continually more pronounced. And the glimmers of even the most furtive beauty or warmth, the small "recesses of tenderness," [52] which could still be uncovered here and there in *Voyage* and in *Mort à crédit*, are totally eliminated in the last major works.

D'un château l'autre* and *Nord*, those gigantic and terrifying frescoes of destruction, madness, and unrelieved grotesqueness which conjure up visions similar to Michelangelo's *Last Judgment* or Picasso's *Guernica*, portray a universe so tainted as to be about to fall to rot. Nothing and no one escapes the hatred, disgust and brutality of Céline's gaze.[53] Acting as the "inspired grave-digger of a decaying world," [54] he holds a black funeral mass for Western man. "[The author] buries the corpse of an entire civilization . . . and tells us quite brutally . . . that this corpse was an unclean one," [55] a hideous mass swarming with maggots and giving off the unbearable stench of its putrefaction. It is Céline's great and dangerous task to force us to stand facing that cadaver without averting our eyes; the awful responsibility both of the doctor and the writer to inspect even the most dreaded of sights; and to hold the mirror unflinchingly before the face of the corpse, even at the risk of being destroyed by contamination or the wrath of the onlookers.

"NOIRCIR"

Let us look, then, at the images in the mirror which Céline holds up for us and scrutinize them in greater detail. They can be grouped, some being self-images, some depicting others, some describing the reaction to what the mirror shows. While they form a sort of triptych, fitting together like the panels of a many-sided glass, they can also be considered separately for greater clarity. The themes which each contains will shift somewhat, grow sharper or dimmer, as Céline's work progresses, change from a slight glimmer to an almost shattering sight, but always remain part of a unified vision: one that is characterized by the will to attack, corrode, soil.

The first and most violent manifestation of this tendency to "blacken" is contained in the picture of mankind in general. Céline has called men by all the vile names imaginable. He refers to them as "les salauds" (V., 219) long before his famous fellow writer Jean-Paul Sartre, with the important difference that for Céline, hell is to be found not only in "the others," but in himself as well.[56] Man then, is shown to be almost totally malevolent, stupid, absurd, grotesque, squalid, and *sale* (dirty) in the true sense of the word. This brutal indictment does not change from *Voyage* to *Nord*, written almost thirty years later. If anything, it only deepens. For even the most cursory glance reveals that while the first diptych of *Voyage au bout de la nuit* and *Mort à crédit* depicts the "vileness," absurdity, and futility of individuals, the second, comprising *D'un château l'autre* and *Nord*, performs the same function for entire civilizations. While Bardamu, man and child, had wandered without aim or hope from Africa to Passy, from Detroit to Courbevoie, from Toulouse to Blême-le-Petit, in the early novels, entire peoples migrate in similar fashion and to the same end in the final works. The only difference is that the circles of their hell become more and more circumscribed as the catastrophe grows larger. They turn about in a continually tighter yet more gigantic trap. But the outcome is the same. The "No Exit" sign has not changed, only the lettering has become more grotesque. The vehicles which carry off the dead or dying, those who have succumbed within the trap, have also grown more nightmarish. The tugboat that draws away everything in its path so that silence may reign at the end of *Voyage au bout de la nuit* (492) becomes "Charon's boat" with its hideous captain and mutilated passengers of *D'un château l'autre* (83–95), or the cow-drawn chariot of *Nord* which carts off its load of drugged victims to a limbo even more shadowy than that of the tugboat of old (455, 458).

Man himself, however, is the most terrifying creature in Céline's terrifying universe. Bardamu had already concluded: "It is of man, and of man alone, that one must always be afraid . . ." (V., 19). In addition to being feared, man was also to be hated and finally rejected. These steps in the reaction toward man—hate and fear, followed both by disgust and a total exploration of all the disgusting aspects, resulting finally in flight, avoidance, renunciation, and indifference—are repeated in every individual novel and again in the larger structure of the four works we are considering, if they are examined as a unit. Thus man is blackened and his night side explored to the fullest. In each case, however, when the end of that voyage is reached, there occurs a drawing back as though in horror, a weary dismissal, renunciation, silence. In this impassioned and painful journey, Céline becomes the Virgil of a Dantesque exploration which never emerges toward Purgatory or Paradise, but leaves the traveler stranded on the shores of day, in the cold and indifferent light of morning.

In this hellish domain, it is not Satan but man who is gigantically evil. What Céline terms "vacherie" (vileness) in *argotique* and deceptively off-handed fashion is really Evil of epic proportions. The cataloguing of all its possible manifestations, the dwelling upon its endless forms, is a vast undertaking. Céline devotes himself to this task with something resembling cold passion. Not a single aspect of man's hideousness is neglected, no corner of his black recesses is left unilluminated. Nothing and no one is spared. Ignominy covers the unborn child and the dying man, the woman in the throes of childbirth and the aged cancer patient. Neither poverty nor wealth, learning nor ignorance, health nor disease, voluptuousness nor abstinence, cowardice nor bravery, victory nor submission, life nor death, confer any dignity or worth upon man. All that he can evoke is horror and sometimes pity. But, just as one could not accuse Dante of revelling in the horrors of Hell, only of feeling compelled to depict them, so would it be absurd to consider Céline's trip to a lay underworld as a leering descent into the sewer (as some of the critics mentioned earlier have done). There is no gladness in his task, no Beatrice to give the hero spiritual succor—only a few prostitutes here and there to bring him a little earthly warmth—no hope of redemption. Both have an equally urgent mission, however: there is the task of the seer to be performed, the revelation of a world order to be set down. If Céline's work is no divine comedy but more like a *tragi-comédie humaine*, it is an undertaking of similar scope and involvement: a total rendering, not of a theological, but of a godforsaken universe.

One can follow Céline on every lap of this relentless journey which stretches across his four greatest novels and lasts for nearly three decades. If we consider these works as a unity, we find that the "blackening" of man from womb to coffin proceeds with great clarity and almost absolute consistency.[57] It begins from the moment of conception, with the horrors of pregnancy, abortion, stillbirth, and culminates in childbirth *with* fear and pain. In *Voyage au bout de la nuit* alone, there are descriptions of all such incidents. Bardamu's medical route in Rancy includes a visit to a young woman slowly bleeding to death of an abortion, whose family refuses to save her by sending her to a hospital, fearing the shame involved (359–62); a woman who will probably die of a stillbirth and whose husband, unable to decide whether she should be cared for in a hospital or not, resolves the dilemma by adjourning to a bistro (296–300). In *D'un château l'autre*, "the motherhood of the world" is depicted in the image of numberless women who "produce, bleed, confess, scream!" (218) The result of all these horrors, the newborn child, is a bundle of abominable cries, doomed to lifelong misery, revolting and pitiful at the same time (V., 271).

In *Mort à crédit*, childhood is utterly and systematically "blackened." Not only is *man* shown to be a creature dying on the installment plan, but even the child experiences death, degradation, and misery in repeated and unrelenting doses. In *Voyage au bout de la nuit*, children had still managed to retain a certain measure of human dignity. They were victims to be pitied and depicted in a compassionate light: Bébert, the sickly nephew of the concierge who dies of typhoid despite Bardamu's efforts to save him; Alcide's orphaned niece; the imbecile daughter of Baryton, the director of the asylum; the unnamed young girl, beaten to stimulate her parents' erotic appetites.[58] Children are favorably compared to adults because they are not as "rotten" (at least for the time being) and therefore less to be feared. It is still possible to feel affection for them, and "as long as one has to love something, one runs less of a risk with children than with grown men." (V., 242) They are still only a potential danger, for it is "when mankind is no longer a child that it becomes deadly" (N., 127). In general, the state of childhood has not been besmirched in *Voyage au bout de la nuit*. There is, however, one place in the novel where it already appears in a bad light: Robinson, when reminiscing over his youth, "found nothing there which didn't make him despair to the point of wanting to vomit in all the corners, as one would in a house where there are only disgusting things that give off a stench!" (326)

Mort à crédit will go on to describe this enormous house of childhood in which there are only repugnant things that give off a vile odor and provoke such violent disgust and despair that one can only react by endless vomiting. They also elicit other excretory manifestations, as we might expect, since Céline's explorations of man's internal cloaca leave nothing unsaid. Thus, Ferdinand, the youthful protagonist of *Mort à crédit* simply sums up the state of his life as "Youth! . . . Shit! . . ." (973). This equation has been applied by one critic to Ferdinand himself, stating that the latter is "both physically and mentally *le merdeux*, haunted by his inability to keep himself clean." [59] Not only clean, one might add, but also to keep himself innocent, that is, not guilty of all the crimes he is constantly accused of: ingratitude, laziness, lechery, stupidity, viciousness, depravity, failure, and finally the greatest crime of all—that of having been born (M.C., 541).

Similar crimes had already been attributed to some of the children in *Voyage au bout de la nuit*, as evidenced by the fact that Bébert's aunt asks Bardamu to prescribe "an anti-vice

syrup for the kid," which would "keep him from touching himself all the time" (244). As much later as *D'un château l'autre*,
the description of a Sunday excursion on one of the *bateaux-
mouches* arouses comments of a similar nature. Children are
still referred to as "Shit-house critters! always picking their
noses and fooling around with their flies." And their treatment
is similar to the one they undergo in all the novels: "Those
slaps in the face! the beatings . . . screams . . . tears!" For
the adults seem to believe in the innately evil nature of children, in the fact that "the kid who isn't beaten inevitably turns
into a criminal . . ." (*C.*, 79). Thus they justify their sadistic
treatment of children by self-righteous remarks—when they
bother to do so at all—and go on to torment their helpless
victims.

Of course, in *Mort à crédit* we find a picture of childhood
with these general characteristics, only drawn in much greater
detail and with nightmarish repetition. Its hero, that "idiot
child," is accused of all the types of "uncleanness" described
above. It grows increasingly clear that the child is seen not
only as *le merdeux* but also as *le vicieux* (the depraved one)
and finally, as *le maudit* (the accursed one). His existence is
wretched from the very start. Life begins in that dreadful,
half-lit, airless place that is the Passage des Bérésinas:

> made for croaking slowly but surely, what with the piss of
> little dogs, the shit, the globs of spit, the leaking gas pipes.
> More foul than the inside of a jail. Under the glass roof,
> way down, the sun filters through so weakly that one could
> eclipse it with a candle. (*M.C.*, 557)

Ferdinand's childhood consists of being fed on endless plates
of "waterlogged noodles," of beatings, reproaches, failures that
grow increasingly more upsetting, a feeling of guilt for every
action undertaken, the realization that even one's initial motion
had been an irrevocable error, that above all, "one shouldn't
have been born!" (*M.C.*, 541) And if, in general, "life is a
misery from one end to the other," (*N.*, 418) this particular
end—or beginning—of existence is characterized by the most
degrading of all miseries, those of the victimized child. The
catalogue of his sufferings is truly exhaustive; nothing is left
out. Ferdinand has to endure the rages of his father, as con-

tinual and horrible to witness as to bear (M.C., 539, 553, 593);
the admonitions of a mother who drags her crippled body
through a labyrinth of poverty and turns into a hideous martyr,
a creature both pitiful and revolting at the same time (539–40);
food prepared in a filthy recess where soiled laundry and moldy
merchandise are kept, served on cracked plates, so nauseating
it induces repeated vomiting (543); the endless search for work,
for even the most meager niche to hide in; the continual defeat. But worst of all, viciousness everywhere, and directed especially against children. Thus, Céline sees man as revolting,
persecuted, and miserable from birth on. Like a hunted animal,
the child cringes, fawns, crawls, and only at rare intervals turns
to snarl briefly. In general, his state makes him both disgusted
and disgusting.

Ferdinand alone embodies all these traits. He is miserable,
persecuted, revolting: guilty of "uncleanness" on several counts.
It has been pointed out that his "immediate response . . .
to almost any beauty anywhere . . . is masturbation," an activity which "returns like a leitmotif, as a symbol of frustration." [60] One might add that this motif is not only a symbol
of frustration, but also one of escape. In general, however, it
is quite true that masturbation, among other forbidden and
punishable offenses of childhood, plays an important role in
Mort à crédit. It contributes to the total picture of unwhole-
someness, unsavoriness, and unpleasantness which are an important part of the "blackening" to which Céline subjects this
portion of man's life. Nor is it the only "crime" of which
Ferdinand is accused. Besides his penchant for autoeroticism,
"he's as filthy as 36 pigs! He has no self-respect at all! He'll
never earn his living! . . . He smells bad! . . . We'll end up
by having to support him!" (555) his outraged parents add.
And the list of accusations goes on, for he is also "the ungrate-
ful bum! . . . the little bastard who takes advantage of others
in his sneaky way . . . the little rotter crammed full of our
sacrifices" (556).[61] The only escape from this hideousness without relief, is into fever dreams, eroticism, flight, silence (583,
etc.), and the world of the imagination. The last of these,
which takes shape in the creation of a legend, that of *le Roi
Krogold,* is not without dangers. It proves to be so disastrous

(636) that this activity is hereafter scrupulously repressed, thus closing another one of the doors that seemed to lead to a world less hideous than that of the everyday.

Ferdinand is not alone in this dark fresco of childhood. His is only the main portrait in an entire gallery of sickly, fearful, squalid children who appear in *Mort à crédit*. They include those pale "kids" in the Passage des Bérésinas who die of the shock of being allowed to breathe the country air (556); the little cripple, André, whom Ferdinand is accused of having debauched by his legend (637) and who, like the latter, is one of those "untouchable children . . . [who] smell so bad . . . that sour smell, the smell of the totally impoverished" (629); the nearsighted imbecile of Meanwell College, Jonkind, who constantly repeats the pathetic phrase "No trouble, Jonkind!" (709); finally, the wild horde of children on Courtial des Pereires' farm, where the latter planned to cultivate "the new Race, Flower of the Fields," (993) and succeeded only in raising a crop of youngsters as disastrous as his agricultural products which spread corruption throughout the countryside!

The squalor, sickness, and corruption of childhood are depicted at great length in the early two novels.[62] Almost all the children who appear there are either physically or mentally ill, and quite a few die in the course of the novel. In *Voyage au bout de la nuit* alone, we find stories of the small boy who has died a violent death in the war (41), Bébert, who succumbs to typhoid, Aymée, who is mentally ill, plus a number of other such children who are more briefly alluded to (95, 308). In *Mort à crédit*, their number grows: le petit André; endless series or uncared-for infants of the poverty-stricken tenants of Ferdinand's grandmother (583); Paulo, who suffers from alcoholism and is already well versed in perversion (592), Jonkind, the idiot child; and finally Ferdinand. It is he, of course, who embodies all miseries of body and spirit: the constant torment and failure; the various trials of the body, the hunger, thirst, aching feet, sweating back, uncleanness, disease, unsatisfied desire; the emotional anguish of misunderstanding, ill treatment, guilt; the morbidity of his surroundings; the utter hopelessness of his existence.

Moreover, the relationship of the child to the adult is very frequently that of victim and tormenter. This had already been true in the most sadistic incident of *Voyage au bout de la nuit*, (pp. 265–67) and is almost always the case in *Mort à crédit*. And of all the child-adult relationships described, that of the family proves to be the most vicious. The protagonist, after having suffered from its cruelty, makes a severe indictment of the institution, exclaiming "Families! . . . they're rotten, all of them, and crawling with pollution." (699) The parents meant to care for the child in his most difficult moments, to offer affection and support when needed, become the enemies, the torturers of the helpless creature. The helplessness of the child, probably the most terrible of his attributes, is depicted by Céline with implacable accuracy and pitiless compassion, as is the plight of all victims: animals, the sick, the wretched, and the vulnerable of every kind. It is a quality which manifests itself in Ferdinand in two important ways: in the inability to be anything but a total failure, and in the inability to fight back.

Thus the hero of *Mort à crédit* is "a miserable adult telling the story of a miserable child fumbling with life. Everything young Ferdinand touches . . . crumbles as soon as he approaches it." [63] Not only does everything crumble which he touches, but he himself falls apart as an individual and is left without recourse to anything but penitence, self-recrimination, the cunning of the beaten animal, silence, withdrawal, despair. There is only one instance of active rebellion in the book which takes a violent, almost deadly form: Ferdinand's maddened attack upon his father (806). But it has disastrous consequences, almost ending in the boy's death and bringing on serious illness (807–809). The end of childhood, according to *Mort à crédit*, is defeat. The repeated cry of: "I want to leave!" (1078) uttered at the close of the book, the tired "Non!" which echoes through the final pages, are all that is left to say.

Having unmasked childhood as an inferno rather than a lost paradise, Céline proceeds to do so for all the states of being which men like to think of generally as endowed with some beauty, meaning, dignity, or splendor. Among these, some people might include patriotism, or heroism in wartime, as well as the gentler virtues of harmonious coexistence in time of peace. Céline, however, negates them and insists that—especially for the impoverished of this world—either of the two paths can only lead to destruction. "There are," he assures us, "two main ways of dying, either through the total indifference of one's fellow-men in peacetime, or their homicidal passion when war breaks out." (V., 82) One of the tasks of his books will be to provide us with numberless accounts of both these "ways of dying."

His pages on war, especially those at the beginning of *Voyage au bout de la nuit* (pointed out by most critics), as well as the lesser known but even more complete accounts contained in *D'un château l'autre* and *Nord*, are among the most devastating ever written. Céline's reaction to war is not only immense fury and violent denunciation by means of a portrayal of all its vilest aspects, but also contains the startling revelation of the "rottenness" of men which is one of his blackest discoveries. The often quoted remark from *Voyage*, "one is as virgin to Horror as one is to sensuality," (17) is indicative of this fact. Even more revealing, however, are the statements that follow, for the author goes on to say: "Who could have foreseen, before really going into war, all that the filthy, heroic, good-for-nothing heart of man contains?" (17) And almost thirty years later, Céline again explains: "It's war which created the feeling of revolt in me. It's *there* that I first understood." [64] Man is revealed in his essential viciousness, absurdity, and helplessness in war as nowhere else. There are, of course, several varieties of war or near-war, all of which have this in common, that they liberate man's lowest instincts and reveal him in his true and hideous form. These situations include life in the tropics, in prison, in all the cannibal isles where the human being drops his civilized mask and shows his real nature. The incident of the "Amiral Bragueton" is one which describes a private war, that of the lynch mob, in the course of which occurs "the biological confession" of man. In the tropics the nature of existence is revealed as not dissimilar from the revelations of war: "the truth: stagnant pools full of a heavy stench, crabs, carrion, and turds" (112–23). Prison is considered another one of the places where one learns "real lessons" about human nature. Céline states, just as he had about war, that "those who haven't been [in prison] are nothing

more than filthy virgins, gabby, futile ham-actors" (*C.,* 67). In
L'Eglise, moreover, Céline had stated that "Life is a jail" (253),
thus enlarging the prison image to apply to all of existence

In the pages on war in *Voyage,* what becomes clearest is
Céline's realization of the imbecilities, madnesses, and utter
horrors human beings are capable of. Thus, he speaks of war
as that "enormous, universal mockery" (16), "that diabolical
imbecility" (17). Heroism itself becomes nothing more than
buffoonery (39); the warrior's actions are meaningless but are
nevertheless continued, as though existence would go on and
the absurdity of the entire situation were not apparent (38).
Men, so habitually blind that, even when faced with death
they cannot imagine it, persist in their shortsighted, menial
ways "just as the sheep, in the fields, lying on its side in its
death-agony, continues to graze" (39). What is more unfor-
givable though than any of these feelings, is man's utter viciousness. Thus the fighting men are "a hundred times madder
than a thousand dogs and so much more depraved" (17). It
is quite natural that one can never be virgin to horror again,
once one has contemplated the unforgettable image of the
warrior, "a man built like you or I but much more of a monster
than the crocodiles or the sharks who hang around in the . . .
waters, their jaws snapping, circling the ships full of garbage
and rotten meat" (27).

From such revelations arises the conviction that it is man
and man alone who must always be feared. This develops into
a belief that "to trust men is already to allow oneself to be
killed a little." (176) A similar theory is also expressed by
Bardamu's strange and larger-than-life *Doppelgänger* Robinson,
when he states that "men, when they're healthy . . . scare one
. . . especially since the war . . . whereas if they're sick, there's
no denying it, they're much less frightening." It is quite clear
that the terror of man, for those who have once seen him at
his vilest, remains alive always. It can only be lessened or
momentarily allayed, either by facing an incapacitated and therefore harmless opponent, or by resorting to the ruses, the cowardice of the frightened animal. For Céline states quite clearly:
"As soon as life gets a little easier, one starts to think only of
the dirty tricks one can play . . ." (*M.C.,* 928).

The last idea throws light on two important themes in

the work of Céline: that of the victim—the child, the animal, the prisoner, the sick person, or the madman—and that of the coward. The first becomes sympathetic because not frightening. This explains the fact that when Céline shows compassion in his writing, it is always for a member of this victim class, since it is impossible to feel pity or compassion for those who terrorize one even if they are essentially miserable. The second theme is of great interest also, because it clarifies the only other position Céline leaves open to his heroes in the face of fear. Both are facets of the same vision, reactions to the same predicament. For fear is one of the predominant modes of all the novels. One might even say that Céline's vision depicts "the night of fear . . . a fear that bellows and creaks, a sinister fear which never releases its prey . . . cosmic fear." [65]

More specifically, it can be shown that fear is closely related to the sudden vision of *man's* terrible face, rather than that of superhuman forces. God is contemptuously dismissed, for he is "undergoing repairs" (Epigraph, *Ecole des cadavres*, Paris: Denoël, 1938) and Nature, although "a terrifying thing" (V., 57), "a bitch" (299), cannot match man for horror. In *Voyage au bout de la nuit*, this head of the Gorgon reveals itself in war and results in Bardamu's becoming "sick, feverish, insane . . . with fear" (61). His comrades also, having committed one kind of folly by believing in "an ideal of absurdity"—that of patriotism—then become "stupefied by war . . . driven mad in another fashion: crazed by fear. The two sides of the coin of war." (65) Dread resulting in madness is also the outcome of another kind of war, that of adult against child, of father against son, depicted in *Mort à crédit*. Brutality so great, absurd, and grotesque that it brings about an attack of madness, followed by physical and mental collapse (806–809), is the fate of both Bardamu and Ferdinand. The lesson becomes clear: both in war and peace, human vileness is to be feared. The victim's choice is either attack—which is generally squelched by the overwhelming odds against him—or cowardice.

Céline has elevated "cowardice" almost to a cult. From Bardamu's question at the beginning of *Voyage au bout de la nuit*, "Can it be that I'm the only coward on this earth?" we proceed to his conclusion that "one is never fearful enough," (113) and to the affirmation that cowardice is a boon and can provide "a marvelous ray of hope for one who becomes expert in it" (119). Of course, the almost ironic glorification of cowardice is voiced after Bardamu's "trial by humiliation," by means of which he has narrowly escaped massacre by the passengers of the "Amiral Bragueton" (118–20). It is then that he decides that "it's probably fear one needs most often to get out of scrapes in this life" (121). Thus, cowardice becomes really the only way to escape being destroyed by men, "[those] most vicious and aggressive organisms which exist in the world . . ." (123). Fear then turns into a weapon, almost a virtue or at least a protective device, a shell to cover man's vulnerable parts, a valuable armor no matter how ugly or lowly its form. The uses of this device are widespread, explaining many of man's actions, aims, aspirations, and contaminating even some of his highest activities. Thus Céline assures us that, basically, "to philosophize is just another way of being frightened and leads to nothing but cowardly simulations . . ." (205).

The author goes even further. His analysis of terror and its results for human existence have truly caused him to pronounce one of the blackest utterances ever made about man and which expresses the apotheosis of fear and cowardice: [66] "To soil one's pants is the beginning of genius" (E., 85). In a sense, this statement is only a more extreme version of those which preach the usefulness of fear, and indicates an adherence to a policy of self-preservation. It is possible, as has been suggested, that the "cowardice" of Céline's protagonists constitutes "whatever stability they have, whatever makes them men and gives them an identity." [67] It could, however, also be argued that this is their only solidarity: the communion in fear of all those night creatures who live in a world where there exists "no longer any road or light" (V., 335); the others, "the day people," never enter here for "one is separated from them, by fear" (idem).

The apotheosis of fear can have two outcomes: either one of catharsis, in which "to accept being afraid, is to be no longer afraid"; [68] or one of abandon, a dissociation of the will which manifests itself in "an ecstasy of dispersion . . . a gradual abdication of consciousness." [69] Of the two possible choices, Céline seems to reserve one for himself and assign the other to his protagonists. While Bardamu, Robinson, Ferdinand, and even Ferdine of the last works, come to the second conclusion (that of abdication or dissolution), Céline himself definitely takes the first path and makes it one of the cornerstones of his literary vision. Thus, he not only indicates that he believes that to accept being afraid is to no longer be afraid, but also that to go to the very end of night is to be no longer wrapped in darkness. Lucidity takes the place of the abdication of consciousness; "the ecstasy of dispersion" is replaced by the act of gathering together, of forming, of creating.

However, even the protagonists of the novels do not always react only by abandon, cowardice, or fearful withdrawal. Sometimes they resort to other weapons: those of silence, deception, suspiciousness, indirect attack. Bardamu, for example, discovers that by inspiring the fear of death, of the void in Lola, he is able to overpower her and "those other bastards" (219) who find lucidity completely unbearable. The armor of silence is also quite effective. Ferdinand of Mort à crédit excels in its use. During his three months' stay at Meanwell College he states: "I didn't protest" (721), "the isolation there suited me better and better" (723). Silence also includes an obstinate, bitter refusal of tenderness or intimacy. He states: "I've had my fill of feelings, confessions" (699), or "it was repeating on me, mounting from my spleen, making my balls ache just to think about it . . . all that treachery! . . . the moment one lets oneself be enveloped . . ." (702). Thus, having suffered as a result of trusting in men, one does not easily fall into the same trap, no matter how powerful the temptation—even when it is in the form of an exquisitely beautiful woman—because one has learned that "to confess attracts misfortune" (583). Nora Merrywin's beauty, kindness, and sensitivity create a feeling of such enchantment and desire in Ferdinand that he almost succumbs to the temptation of intimacy. The danger becomes especially great when the woman's charm is coupled with that of imagination, or literature, and it takes an immense effort for Ferdinand to resist involvement, confidence (710–15, 727, 729, and especially, 736).

One of the other ways of not becoming involved, enveloped, and possibly betrayed by tenderness, is to run. This explains the instinct to flee people, places, life itself, the compulsive fidgeting, characteristic of almost all of Céline's protagonists. His works portray the endless migrations of a long line of aimless globetrotters. Their continual departures are motivated either by danger, refusal of involvement, persecution, failure, or the threat of stagnation or dissolution. In many different ways they express the idea that "as one remains in a place, things and people become messy, they rot and begin to stink expressly for you." (V., 272)

Man's "rottenness" is not only apparent in times of stress or during childhood, when helpless victims abound, but it also erupts in an area of human experience which we generally think of as pleasurable and devoid of horror: eroticism and sexual gratification. Céline tends to blacken most descriptions of such acts. Sometimes, this is done in a spirit of mockery, because the author "finds this business of 'I lo-o-ve you' vulgar, heavy-handed," [70] and cheaply sentimental. More often, however, the indictment is more severe. In tracing the theme throughout his four great novels, we find that eroticism is quite frequently linked to violence.[71] It becomes part of a pattern which shows that "the human bent is toward the carnivorous," [72] as well as the carnal. In *Voyage au bout de la nuit*, we meet the concierge of the hospital at Issy-les-Moulineux, "a depraved female," "a bitch," who spies on the sick war veterans and often is instrumental in bringing about their execution. Nevertheless, "in bed . . . she was a splendid piece," precisely because of her "bitchiness," which, we are told, is "like pepper in a fine sauce . . . it's indispensable and gives it body" (63). At other times, however, viciousness linked to eroticism can be quite unpleasant or even dangerous. Bardamu discovers this during his adventure on the "Amiral Bragueton" where, to stimulate the bored and tired female passengers, he is chosen to be the subject of a "scene of super-carnage which foreshadowed an awakening of their wrinkled ovaries. It was as good as being raped by a gorilla" (117). Later in the same novel, the description of the fair at the *Tir des Nations*, where one can enjoy "violence mixed with fun and games! the whole accordion

of pleasures" (468) echoes the concept of violence and sexual
gratification mingled. In *Mort à crédit*, there are quite a few
scenes written under the sign of "the divine Sade" as the
author will refer to him later (*C.*, 113). Among these, there is
a hallucinatory account of violence and sexual perversion (*M.C.*,
524–25), and the "spectacle" of brutal and grotesque eroticism
which Ferdinand and his friend watch secretly, but which turns
out to be so frightening a "corrida" that they flee in haste
(663–65). The theme is continued in the last novels, in the
orgies of *D'un château l'autre* which are inspired by war and
the "attraction of fresh meat," valuable aphrodisiacs, for "it
takes hunger and gunpowder to make people surrender themselves and fornicate without looking" (168). The holocaust of
war provides the necessary setting and inspiration for all the
frenzied and calloused coupling. This is especially true for
women, Céline assures us: "the more cities burn, the more one
massacres, hangs, draws and quarters, the more they are crazy
about sex" (*N.*, 205). Perfect specimens of "the bitch" can be
found in the last works: Hilda, the sixteen-year-old "master-
piece of depravity," who waits for troop trains, like all her
sisters excited into paroxysms of desire by the dangers of war
and the closeness of death (*C.*, 172–74); or Frau Frucht—whose
name is a beautiful play on words, containing allusions to
Furcht (fear) and also the term for fruit (*Frucht*)—a lady
long addicted to various sexual aberrations who, now that war
has exacerbated desire, "takes it all in," including Ferdine's wife
Lili, if she can procure such entertainment for the price of a
plate of ravioli! (267–71)

Women reach the height of their "carnivorous bent" in
those Maenadlike creatures, the former prostitutes of Munich
who have gone berserk, beating two men nearly to death and
killing a horse to devour enormous chunks of its bloody flesh
(*N.*, 352–58). However, an equally black tale of violence,
eroticism, and victimization had already been told by Céline
in *Voyage au bout de la nuit*, where a child is beaten mercilessly
by her mother in order to awaken the father's sexual appetites
(265–66). Céline seems to feel that hideousness can have no
further bounds, that one has reached the "very end." But since
the author's world, admittedly, "is a trap," [73] he demands not

only that his characters contemplate "the abyss within them, around them," [74] but he also forces the reader to do the same. He asks of the latter the kind of lucidity and courage which Bardamu exhibits when, caught in the trap of the courtyard, that world of "hideousness without relief," he does not avert his eyes or stuff his ears:

> I stayed there, listening only, as always, everywhere. However, I think I got strength from listening to those things, to go further, a funny kind of strength—and the next time I could go down even further, the next time, and listen to other laments I hadn't yet heard, or which I had trouble understanding before, because it seems that always, at the end, there are still other laments, which one has not yet heard or understood. (V., 266)

Céline forces the reader to accompany him on this dreadful night journey, to listen to all the wailing, to descend ever lower into the depths of terror and pain, to understand.

From the courtyard in *Voyage*, unrelievedly hideous, to the airless Passage des Bérésinas of *Mort à crédit*, on to the terrible castles of *D'un château l'autre* and the entrance to the underworld which is "the room no. 36" in that novel (162), Céline guides the reader in a constant downward journey, an ever-widening exploration of the recesses of terrestrial hell in which man is still and always the most fearful creature. And the blackness of the night which enveloped the first novel, has so thickened and spread that it finally covers an entire continent. From one war to the other, nothing has changed. Man, more terrible than the vilest of beasts, remains the same or has become more efficiently murderous: "Man has been identically the same for 500 million years . . . he doesn't change one iota . . . in a cave or skyscraper! . . . a motorized gibbon then? . . . airported? . . . all the quicker to rob and kill!" (C., 174–75) And the awful round of life goes on, for "our species is never out of commission; it fornicates, procreates, butchers, quarters, never stops." (264)

Absolutely nothing is left untouched. Céline's black vision does not stop at man's activities and at the evolution of his life. It attacks his very substance, his definition of human being. Repeatedly, the author reduces man to the level of a hideous

creature, one of the lowest forms of life on earth, and reveals
him in "his true form of an enormous and greedy maggot" (V.,
332). At other times, man is the container of these vile animals,
a kind of walking corpse, carrion swarming with corruption,
"[a] bag of worms . . . stuffed with maggots . . ." (V., 116).
Similarly, he is seen only in terms of his lowest functions, his
most insignificant components. Thus Céline informs us that
"we're only enclosures of luke-warm and unhealthy, rotting
guts" (V., 332); our bodies are merely "a travesty of agitated
and banal molecules . . ." (333), or simply "meat" (21).

Man's entire existence is summed up in this series of
statements: "We're all putrid from birth on . . . the earth is
dead . . . we're nothing but worms on its disgusting, fat corpse,
always busy feeding on its entrails and its poisons . . ." (V.,
370). Thus, man is not only futile, absurd, meaningless—he is
also corrupt, revolting as any carrion, and more vicious than the
fiercest beast. Existence itself loses all meaning, for "life in
the company of that malevolent animal is no more significant
than a nightmare." [75] The blackness has so successfully enveloped every aspect of living that one might conclude that
the author's statement is now complete. He has however only
begun his journey.

"SE NOIRCIR"

"It seems almost as if the moralist who is so ruthless to
himself had been repelled by his own image in the mirror, and
smashed the glass, cutting his hands." [76] Is it that Céline,
having held up a sullied mirror to human existence, has also
perceived himself in the glass? Or simply that, knowing himself
human, would assume his own reflection to be no less hideous
than that of the others? In any case, Céline does *not* smash the
glass, but continues to hold it as relentlessly in front of his
face as before that of the world. It is an interesting phenomenon
and not one frequently found in literature. For it goes beyond
the *confessions* of other writers, the display of one's inner
wares on the marketplace to be appraised by all passersby. Once
again, we might conclude that it is the phenomenon at work
of which we have already spoken, a "blackening" for purposes
of literary transposition.

Somehow, though, the matter becomes more complicated.
We find that, partly because his black vision is so hard to face;
partly because he presents himself in as sullied a fashion as his
characters, and does it so successfully that the picture is frequently taken as literal truth, partly because he plays an
enigmatic role in his own works, partly as a result of a reticence,
almost a shyness to display any tender or delicate feelings,
Céline has become a monstrous figure in the eyes of many—a
kind of filthy antichrist who is the sum of all his own black
literary creations.

Sometimes the author has encouraged such a view. In referring to his "habitual sacrificial mania," [77] he tends to indicate
that he is quite willing to accept the burden of such a role.
But the concept itself is a fairly complicated one; it encompasses many things: a literary theory; a close identification of
the author with his work; a sense of reticence, prudence, or
modesty (*pudeur*) which prevents one from revealing one's
deeper feelings, for fear that they might be misunderstood or
betrayed; a belief that the authentic artist will inevitably be
persecuted; (Y., 9, 10, 29); an image imposed from the outside
by those who have taken Céline's statements about himself
literally and which he has refused to contradict; finally, a
possible belief that it is necessary to suffer, to be hated as well
as to hate. Any facile explanation of the phenomenon is bound
to be partial or false. We must also be careful not to fall into
any of the nets which Céline the *mystificateur* [78] has laid for
us, not to be caught in the lime of his ironic traps.

It is not easy to determine how Céline really sees himself.
Many of his remarks about the "je" are contradictory. In his
Entretiens avec le Professeur Y—where we must make allow-
ances for a lot of spoofing—he makes several statements which
are as revealing as they are mutually exclusive, or at least
paradoxical: on the one hand, he states that his "I" is carefully disguised when shown; on the other, that he reveals himself more than naked, almost flayed before us. In the first case
he insists: "My 'I' isn't audacious at all! I only present it with
such great care! a thousand prudent gestures, discretions! I
always cover it over entirely, most cautiously, with excrement!"
(66–67) and he goes on to give us this formula: "The 'I'

always soiled and 'detached' " (67). Only two pages later, however, he states, in speaking about what he feels is a central
aspect of his writing—"comic lyricism"—that in order to achieve
this quality "you've got to plunge, to show yourself with your
nerves raw . . . your nerves raw! . . . *yours!* . . . not someone else's nerves! . . . and more than naked . . . raw!" (69)

Both these views, when analyzed, have an identical aim:
"*se noircir*." The first is an obvious case of doing so, by fairly
drastic means, as well as a way of masking the true personality.
The second is basically the same action, since Céline's view of
man is so black that any presentation of the latter, in all his
nakedness, is more like presenting an open cadaver with his
rotting entrails exposed than a display of inner grandeur. In
both instances, it is a defiant picture of the self, as well as a
cry of *mea culpa*.

It also seems true, however, that the author's "self-castiga-
tion . . . suggests a dialectical reservation. Céline is *eager*
to condemn himself and mankind—so eager that his work takes
on the nature of a *long confession*. It is not the confession of a
penitent. The admission of sin and crime is made in the
manner of a provocative challenge. He confesses with a snarl." [79]
And of course this snarl or "cry" is Céline's literary voice.
Another interesting phenomenon occurs, however: the snarl
of the author is also directed at his self. For "Céline *wraps
himself up* in his object as he snaps at it," [80] and that object
is frequently his own person. If Céline is "an atheist in
spiritual agony" concerning man's condition, and if "his arraign-
ment is self-flagellation," [81] then such punishment is inflicted
because he himself is a part of mankind. There is a certain
honesty in including oneself in this negative scheme of things,
in not flinching before one's own fallibility, humanity, and therefore criminality. Thus it is rather difficult to agree with Sartre
that Céline, in his writing, "reacts out of fear of the human
condition." [82] It would be to ignore the relentlessness with
which he depicts all its blackest aspects, not sparing even his
own existence.

Part of the author's reasons for the *noircissement* is also
a desire to be completely truthful, authentic, sincere, and to
probe the dark corners of one's own inner world: "to hide

nothing of oneself, to slander oneself methodically and give voice only to the furor of one's revulsions and vulgarities." [83] Sometimes, though, the calumny of the self goes too far, and scrupulous honesty demands the rectification of a picture which is too one-sided to have any meaning. Thus Céline will sometimes dispute the portrait which his self-accusation has etched in the minds of others, and defend himself as though on trial. "I'm not really as rotten as they think. I'm ashamed of not being any richer in feeling and all that . . . It's that tenderness makes a lump in one's throat that isn't easy to swallow." [84] We detect in these words the echo of Bardamu's confession when confronted with the dying Robinson:

> At such moments, it's a little embarrassing to have become so poor and so hardened. . . . One has hardly anything left inside except what's useful for an everyday existence, the life of comfort, plain existence, lousiness. One has lost one's confidence on the way. One has harassed and chased away pity, pushed it to the very end of one's entrails, with the excrement. (V., 486)

It seems as though Céline and his protagonist almost apologize, muse in a sad and regretful tone, over the ruthlessness of their actions and the loss incurred as a result. It is an admission of failure, of reticence or repression, of poverty in the realm of feeling. One wonders whether the author, having chosen a pitiless view of man and of himself as his literary vision, does not sometimes feel that he must justify or even expiate this choice.

Certainly, it is only a question of justification or of expiation, for Céline never once refutes his vision. He either accepts, refuses to negate, or almost encourages the charges made against him. Thus, "the more one considered him guilty, the more he worked at assuming the air of culpability." [85] It is equally true that the greater the danger became, the more he bristled, showing sharp quills, a black shell: actions which would also tend to deepen the impression of his viciousness or guilt. Since the act of "bristling" is only an illusory sort of defense, creating more severe attacks and greater danger, one sometimes wonders whether Céline did not truly suffer from that sacrificial mania to which he himself refers. Especially during the last part of his life autodestruction becomes an important motif in the work. This is evident in the various references to suicide; [86] in the endless ruminations on his sordid, wretched state, which seem almost masochistic in nature; the renunciation of human contact, the ascetic existence in which only work, that "torture," remains. Finally, a feeling prevails, not unlike that expressed in the monologue at the start of *Mort à crédit*, where the narrator states: "soon I'll be old. And it'll finally all be over . . . . I would like the storm to make even more of a racket, the roofs to fall in, the spring never to return, our house to cave in." (501) All of Céline's wishes have indeed been granted: he grew old, the tempests of an entire continent broke before his eyes, the roofs fell in, his house disappeared, the spring no longer returned. All "was finally over."

The fact that one can go back and forth between Céline's work and his life, as we have just done, is worth exploring. It shows *not* that the two are synonymous, but simply that the author has so successfully presented a literary transposition of himself among the other characters of his books that it is often difficult to determine whether one is confronted by a character wearing the author's mask or vice versa. This is more than mere play-acting or delight in mystification. It is a union of the artist and his work, so deep that Céline, in his usual fashion, is compelled to mock or blacken it,[87] just as he feels it necessary to disparage medicine, that other art which is central to his life.[88] Yet he is both a fine and devoted doctor and a great writer. Seldom has anyone denounced his own person and chosen craft with such vehemence. However, and here Céline's paradoxical nature affirms itself once more, there are also times when he defiantly affirms his own ability. Then he insists that he is the only genius of the century (*Y.*, 83, 85), a writer with almost Orphic powers who, if he chooses, can "make alligators dance to Pan's flute," [89] no mean feat for a man who elsewhere claims he only writes to pay his rent! (*C.*, 55)

We can see a somewhat puzzling, or at least contradictory pattern emerging in which *noircissement* alternates with self-glorification, defiance, or the arrogance of genius. This kind of vacillation is also characteristic of the works—and we are once again aware of the close relation between the man and his literary creation. Thus, "there are, in his works, two contrasting views, a hard and a soft pole, the freedom and lightheartedness of the thoroughbred . . . and the humility of the hunted animal." [90] There seems to be a similar movement in Céline's fluctuating self-image: at times he portrays himself as "the thoroughbred," proud, powerful, skillful and defiant; at other moments, it is the cowering, weak, cornered "hunted animal" which he depicts. The second image is much more current, however; the mirror is only infrequently unsullied, the glints of light are extremely rare.

During the last years, the picture grows increasingly dark and embittered. The theme of *le maudit* (the accursed)— already announced in the early works (*Semmelweiss, Mort à crédit*)—predominates in the author's references to himself. He considers himself foremost among the persecuted, the insulted, and the injured. His self-image has become that of "the scapegoat," the victim of a human corrida. Both *D'un château l'autre* and *Nord* depict him in this manner. And while it may not be right to take this image of an aged Céline—bitter, hurt, humiliated—and superimpose it on the man who has been likened to a defiant, laughing wrestler in his prime,[91] it seems almost inevitable that his evolution proceeded in such a direction. If one believes the author's poetic vision (rather than his personal reactions) to be the expression of his most profound convictions, then it becomes evident that his view of existence was equally black at the beginning of his career. The fate of his early protagonists alone bears witness to this fact. If one feels that they are reflections or literary doubles of Céline—as he himself has stated—then there is some logic in the fact that his earliest literary creations foreshadow his own final image. We might compare Céline's heroes and their author to Robinson and Bardamu, the first moving always one step ahead of his double, throwing his shadow before them as they proceed on their voyage. So do Céline's protagonists precede him in his life's journey.

Already in *Semmelweiss*, with the figure of this *médecin maudit* whose "terrible story" (Preface, *S.*) he has chosen to tell, we can find many parallels with Céline's future life: both make revolutionary discoveries—one in medicine, the other in literature—which are unacceptable, unprofitable, uncomfortable to many; frenzied, fanatical, and too violent insistence [92] on the truth of these discoveries results in their exile, persecution, illness, and death. The story of Semmelweiss, "which seems to exhaust all possible images of misfortune," (54) is both the kernel of all Céline's literary production and a kind of prophecy of his own fate.

As we go on to Voyage au bout de la nuit, the theme of the persecuted hero who suffers from a malediction continues, only in a somewhat different vein. Less sad, more brutal and grotesque, and certainly not so heroic, Bardamu-Robinson emerges from Semmelweiss and surpasses him in blackness (noirceur).[93] His life, like that of Semmelweiss and all future protagonists of Céline, ends in a stalemate, in failure. In almost every case, death, madness, apathy, and misery triumph.

In Mort à crédit, the pattern of the hero becomes even grimmer. From le maudit, who had had a certain grandeur, he becomes an unclean, unloved creature, hounded by guilt and shame, who spreads unhappiness and destruction wherever he goes. He is "a real curse," or "a living catastrophe," (680) "a selfish monster" (763)—descriptions not unlike those often given of the author himself. At the end of the book, Ferdinand seems to have internalized the black image of himself. He repeats the insults of others like a fatigued and discouraged parrot: "I had a rotten, depraved nature . . . I leaked pus all over the place . . . repulsive pervert that I was! I had neither feelings nor a future . . . . A bird of evil omen . . . . I was affliction personified" (M.C., 766).[94] At the end, the malediction which pursues Ferdinand becomes so extreme that he cries out: "What can it be that I'm guilty of?" (793) It is a question quite similar to the one which will echo obsessively throughout Céline's last works like a droning, endless refrain.

In a sense, the numerous plaintes and complaintes of the last novels—which sometimes have the unpleasant ring of self-pity—are really an enlarged version of Ferdinand's reiterations of all the accusations which have been heaped upon him. If we find them decidedly less palatable in D'un château l'autre and

Nord, it is because the author enters too obviously into his work and does not transpose as much during certain passages as we might like him to.[95] At other times, however, there is both consistency and literary value in those laments on his condition of miserable and hunted animal of prey. They reveal his ability to "wail, clearer, more loudly and more continuously than any of the wild cats which he harbored" [96] in a hut on the Baltic during the long years of exile. The quality of his "wailing" can truly be likened to that of the wildcat, both plaintive and fierce, pitiful and dangerous, usually shut out by more civilized and less upsetting noises. But it is Céline's true literary voice that once again resounds, and we are forced to heed it.

In general, Céline's blackened self-image is much less successful in those instances where there is little or no literary transposition. This is more frequently the case in the last works than in the first.[97] When the author himself appears almost undisguised in his work, his tales of woe sound too much like the plaintive or angry whine of an embittered man and descend from the literary to the personal level. Their scope is narrowed and they decrease in artistic value. In this connection, though, we note another phenomenon: the evolution of the narrator— who is also Céline's "double" and the protagonist of the novel —and that of the other participants in his dramas. As the literary transposition of the author's self becomes less pronounced and the narrator is more of an individual,[98] not as amorphous a figure, the general scope of the novel grows larger, more universal: the other actors in the drama are whole nations, the tragedies are those of continents, the holocausts involve entire civilizations. It is as though, as the self-image grows clearer, narrower, and more personalized in its *noirceur,* the setting becomes vaster, vaguer, and more overwhelming.

Céline's voice has also changed. The tone is sadder, less jubilantly defiant. While the early "cry" was one of both hurt and anger, that of the last works is one of pain and wailing. The black humor of former days, grotesque and deeply rebellious, has become exclusively that of the gravedigger or the condemned man.[99] While the younger Céline delighted in the kind of game which Bardamu plays and "which consists . . .

of creating oneself enemies, being overjoyed at their hatred, and then suddenly sneaking out from under their hold by means of an apparent submission," [100] the author of the last novels *actually* created these enemies for himself, rejoiced and triumphed in their hatred (during the first years of his fame), only to find that he could not escape their clutches by apparent submission (as the severe punishment of Céline during his years in Denmark has shown). For reality does not match the possibilities of literary adventures, and truth is blacker than fiction. Another game which the author delighted in, early in his career, "that comedy which is a take-off from real life . . . and allows [Céline] to recount, to invent out of himself another self (or a hundred other selves)," [101] has turned into a contest in deadly earnest. It is no longer a comedy but a tragedy, based upon reality and real-life experience. The blackened mask, which Céline has created and chosen to wear more frequently than most others, has become fixed to his features, fastened so inextricably to his face that he can no longer discard it at will. It is as though, in a play between art and reality as subtle and enigmatic as any work of Pirandello, the author, who had at first chosen to be a character, side by side with the other characters of his works, is finally constrained to wear the costume, which he had donned for literary purposes, as his everyday garb.

The same kind of strange turnabout of art and life occurs in other areas also: Céline, whose work suggests preoccupation with lonely pursuits—both in its frequent treatment of solitude and in the concern with innovation and uniqueness in terms of style—will have to suffer the fate of the solitary. While in his youth he appeared to some in the romantic guise of a "lone rider," [102] his last years were spent in almost hermetic and often forced isolation: the solitary confinement of a Danish prison; the lonely hut on the Baltic coast, miles away from other human beings; the old house in Meudon where life ends in almost total reclusion. The writer who has depicted so many types of flight, of persecution by men and by fate, and has announced that the pariah (who is the central character of his works) inevitably must suffer the wrath of society, becomes himself the living proof of his theories. Finally, he who has described childhood as an endless succession of insults, hard labor, disease, and deprivation in *Mort à crédit*, spends his old age in almost identical circumstances.[103]

There is no moral to this strange tale, no warning to young writers on the dangers of wearing a mask too well. There is only the story of an artist whose portrait of himself, drawn larger than life, became life itself, who, in the attempt to "noircir et se noircir," became enveloped by the blackness, whose night vision turned into a forced march to the end of that night.

THE BLACKNESS WITHIN

Much has been said about nausea in the works of Céline. But they also contain a movement which goes beyond nausea, and is essentially a kind of visceral revolt. It is a phenomenon similar to the desire to "noircir et se noircir" which is its parallel and at the same time its outgrowth. We might call it, risking an *argotique* pun, the theme of "gueuler et dégueuler" (to yell and to vomit). It is an outcry from the most central portion of man: his viscera. Once again, Céline's use of this measure is in the nature of a literary device, not the tool of the moralist or the reformer, as has sometimes been suggested. While it is possible that Céline "thought that he was performing a salutory task by putting everyone's nose in his own excrement," [104] it is much more likely that his concerns were more specifically literary ones. To the statement that the author has the "courage to vomit the collective poison, to spit the bitter taste of the world into the faces of all those who want to turn away from it," [105] we must add that this again is not his central or only concern. Nor is it a mere obsession with the cloaca of life—which we have already alluded to and ruled out—or a case of "emotional diarrhea," from which Céline suffers, as one critic has suggested.[106]

It has been submitted that the sewer is Céline's favorite metaphor, and that themes of this kind tend to "communicate his 'evacuative' scheme of values. They are cathartic, ejaculatory, scatological; they are a series of discharges; they spit and eject. They are the idiom of his universal purge. The sole remedy for our sewer world. . . ." [107] But one must emphasize the

fact that Céline is neither a devotee of the sewer, nor a reformer who wishes to clean up that subterranean realm. He
simply wishes to disclose this black labyrinth which lies, like a
filthy copy of our daylight streets, far below their surface. It is
by the strength of his vision that "he bares the roots. From
underneath the veils of decorum he exposes the mud and
blood," [108] and, we might add, the mucus, the vomit, the
excrement. A gigantic flow of images, almost oceanic in scope,
attacks all our senses; "we are subjected to [a] flood of words,
ejected, vomited, in a series of painful cramps. . . ." [109] And,
as if holding up a sullied mirror had not been enough, Céline
now adds the smells, the sounds, the tactile horrors which
complete the vision.

It is no wonder that such a venture has outraged readers
and provoked outcries from critics. Some feel that "the views
of Louis-Ferdinand Céline . . . are manifestly the product of
a man who speaks in terms of what is most visceral, most
animal-like in human beings," [110] or that "this basically pessimistic view of the world and of man can only appear unbearable . . . the 'no' he utters is an organic one." [111] More
than the outraged protest against Céline's "unbearable" visions,
certain aspects of the opinions of these critics have value for
our subject. The emphasis on the visceral and the organic "no"
pronounced by the author is central. For it leads to an understanding of the "inner" revolt depicted, that reaction which
goes beyond la nausée expressed by other writers, and is the
response of the entire human being, on the physical as well as
mental level, to the horror of existence. It is a violent protest,
one that involves man's very entrails, rather than the stagnant,
and essentially passive state of nausea. And for Céline himself,
such protest is closely linked to hate since "it was not nausea
which pervaded Céline's thinking . . . it was a robust and
powerful hatred," [112] and this "hatred was organic with him,
hate in its pure state." [113] Thus, the spewing forth, the visceral
revolt and the fury which it both depicts and embodies, is a
valuable literary device and one which gives Céline's work
much of its distinctive quality.

As was the case for Céline's "noircissement," it is indeed
clear that the use of visceral reactions—which are the discharges

of the inner blackness in man—is part of an aesthetic choice. For although it is possible to trace the theme of nausea in the *work* of Céline, to show as J.-P. Richard has done that the author depicts the internal rot and "liquefication" of the individual, it is equally important to point out that Céline, the *man*, despised such a state. One of his close friends reports: "His greatest fury was always aroused by anything he considered an abasement of man, a surrender of the self." [114] This statement is actually a substantiation of two ideas: first, that the sullied image is a literary one, and second, that such an image provoked rage and hatred in Céline. We might conclude that the author felt compelled to show us this hated picture in all its loathsome detail, surrounded by all the possible expressions of disgust which it elicits. The result is a purge of both writer and reader.

The theme of visceral reactions in the work of Céline falls into several categories, although when taken together, these form a unified whole. All are reactions by which the human animal ejects substances from within his body: bleeding, vomiting, defecation, urination, ejaculation. In Céline's work, the first three are especially pronounced. The key to the importance of these activities is already found in *Voyage au bout de la nuit* (in the episode of the Abbé Protiste) where man is reduced to his lowest and most revolting common denominator: a packet of lukewarm and rotting entrails (V., 332), and thus capable only of producing offal and ejecting the rot within. It is of course impossible to then see man in a grandiose fashion, although he is the creature "which they beseech us to transpose into an ideal." (332) The constant refusal to see the human being in this idealized fashion, as well as the insistence upon dwelling on his "biological ignominy," (333) leads Céline to concentrate on those activities which bring the rotting contents of man's inner core into view. For not only does each living man harbor death within him, but he also contains lesser products of waste and putrefaction in his entrails.

The contents of man's body are not only revolting, malodorous, in a state of decay, but his innards are also the seat of devouring death. Thus he is portrayed as a rotting, walking corpse, "already filled with maggots" (V., 116) during his lifetime, or as one of those revolting creatures who is himself "an enormous . . . . greedy maggot" (332). It is a world of worm eat worm, and Céline leaves no stone unturned, if under it there lurks some hideous thing to which he can liken man. But mainly, he is concerned with the revelation to man of his own mortality, the brutal and sickening awakening to the fact "that the flesh is nothing more than meat . . . meat destined for sacrifice, and that this meat, is first of all a bunch of innards, basically soft and full of cowardice." [115]

This realization is thrust at us in that awful vision at the beginning of *Voyage au bout de la nuit* consisting of two descriptions: one dealing with the death of two men in warfare, the other with the slaughtering of animals. If we put the two accounts side by side and note the protagonist's reactions to the incidents, many things become apparent. The first concerns the bloody death of the colonel and the messenger of Bardamu's regiment:

> The cavalryman no longer had his head, nothing but an opening above the neck, with blood in it, simmering and bubbling like jam in a pot. The colonel's belly was ripped open. . . . All this meat was bleeding, enormously. . . . (21)

Only a few pages later, we find this description of an open-air slaughterhouse:

> On bags and pieces of canvas, spread all over, even on the grass, there were pounds and pounds of entrails, scattered fat in yellow and pale flakes, disemboweled sheep with their insides in a mess. . . . And blood, and more blood everywhere, all over the grass, in soft and flowing puddles. . . . (24)

Bardamu's reaction to the slaughter of men and beasts is overwhelming: "I had to yield to an enormous desire to vomit, and not just a little, but to the point of fainting." (24)

The juxtaposition of the two incidents, one describing the death of men and the other animal carnage, is obviously meaningful. It permits Céline to indicate that, first of all, all living beings are basically subject to the same laws, the same dangers. Men as well as beasts are mortal and thus threatened by constantly imminent death. The act of dying reduces them to the level of object, in which they become only a bleeding mass of entrails, an unrecognizable heap of useless organs, in short, just "meat." Secondly, to show that in war, especially, men are on the level of beasts. As a result, the death of the first is no more tragic than the slaughter of the second. The only possible difference between them is that men are sometimes aware of the fate which awaits them, while animals are not. And finally, that once death has occurred, once the inner core of man is revealed, he is seen to be as revolting, meaningless, unhallowed as the carcass of the sheep, or the side of beef hanging on a tree. The disemboweled colonel and the sheep "with his insides in a mess" are of equal stature, the swarming flies make no distinction between them, the same stench of blood and excrement rises from both.

Bardamu's confrontation with this vision results in vomiting so intense that it blots out consciousness. It is both a mental and physical gesture of total revulsion. Moreover, it is an action that can only be described in a play on words: for it is both *lâche* (cowardly) and designed to *tout lâcher* (to let everything go). Essentially, it is a complex form of abandonment and occurs on three planes: the conscious one which results in flight; the physical one which brings about reactions common in revulsion or fear (vomiting or diarrhea); the need to wipe out consciousness (fainting). Such a reaction, either in part or in total, will recur in many other incidents of a similar nature in Céline's works. This is especially true because the author considers fear to be one of man's fundamental conditions—as we have already noted—and revulsion a necessary reaction to the vision of this condition. Thus, both fear and revulsion become almost constants, and their outward manifestation will be portrayed in a fairly consistent manner.

The various visceral outpourings of man are portrayed in several other places in *Voyage au bout de la nuit*. In the tropics, where man is, according to Céline, just as clearly revealed as in time of war, we see him almost rot before our eyes. We witness the "immense and basic flowing apart" of the individual, his "internal dispersion." [116] Thus, the colonialists have come to "make their boss a present of their meat . . . their blood, their lives . . . down to the very last red corpuscle coveted by the ten millionth mosquito" (V., 132–33); their wives, on the other hand, suffer from an endless menstrual flow, a series of "slow hemorrhages which bleed [them] white . . ." (142) and empty them of their life's substance; even the children, "an unpleasant species of fat European maggot . . . were dissolving from the heat and permanent diarrhea" (144). Some die, and their "bloodless remains" (145) are buried quickly in the jungle, while others lie in the hospital, wasting away from dysentery and skin diseases midst the heat and flies, alternating masturbation with fever dreams caused by malaria (144).

Further in the depths of the tropical jungle, where even the water has turned "yellowish," "nauseating," "slimy and muddy," (163) the horror increases. It seems concretized in the hordes of those "heavy caterpillars with shells, who constantly attacked our forest hut anew, trembling and dribbling," whose insides seem to contain the rot of the ages. For, "if you crush them, clumsy one, Heaven help you! You'll be punished by eight consecutive days of intense stench which rises slowly from their unforgettable, gruel-like mass." Are these creatures, "these weighty horrors which constitute the most ancient creatures in the world," (167) so far removed from that "enormous, greedy maggot," (332) that is man?

Various incidents in Voyage au bout de la nuit provide examples of all the visceral themes which appear in the work of Céline: the bleeding of various victims: the soldiers, animals, colonialists, women living in the tropics or dying of abortions and stillbirths; the vomiting of Bardamu when confronted with the horrors of war, and that of Robinson's memories of childhood; the internal putrefaction of man, as discussed in the episode of l'Abbé Protiste; the tropics where man is prone to autoeroticism, dissolution by heat, disease, madness, bleeding, and where even the children suffer from a permanent case of diarrhea, a condition which has been described as "the most striking and most sickening physiological image of the break-up which the world is undergoing." [117]

Certainly the "break-up" of the universe continues to concern Céline in Mort à crédit, for its physiological counterpart is constantly present in the book. As a matter of fact, seen in a certain light, the entire work can be regarded as an endless series of three major physiological reactions in the face of existence: vomiting, defecation, and masturbation. If we concede that they are the symbols of mental states, they represent, respectively, disgust, fear, and frustration (or possible *évasion*). And indeed, these are the prevailing feeling states in *Mort à crédit* which, when taken together, create the picture of failure, misery, shame, guilt, and torment which characterizes Céline's vision of childhood.

While all such reactions tend to indicate a state of despair, of all-engulfing nausea, of letting go and of giving up, they also point to a quite opposite impulsion. Just as we had found—in reference to another matter—a contrasting movement in Céline's thought and style which results in a cringing as well as a defiant action, we note that here too, a characteristic process takes place in which "softness is allied . . . with aggressiveness." [118] For Ferdinand not only succumbs to repeated expressions of his nausea, his defeat in the face of life, but he also revolts. And while the vomiting and diarrhea he is so prone to, express a breaking down of will and hope, they are also an action of defiance, a violent protest of the viscera (the central organs of the human being) against the misery and despair of existence. We might already interpret Bardamu's reaction to the human and animal carnage of the war and Robinson's comments on his youth in such a light, but the facts become even clearer in the next novel (*Mort à crédit*).

If we analyze the major incidents in the book that deal with this matter, we find that they support the view of protest. The first of these occurs early in the novel and concerns the exchange of stories between La Vitruve and Ferdinand's mother in which both women exalt parental sacrifice and decry the ingratitude of children. Ferdinand is so sickened by this display, that he announces: "I have to go and vomit in the toilet." (M.C., 529) Shortly afterwards, we see his physical revolt turn into a verbal outburst, a violent objection to all lies, which ends in an actual battle (532). Another incident describes vomiting as a reaction to death and callousness in a manner similar to the one in *Voyage au bout de la nuit* of which we have spoken. In this instance, the family of Ferdinand visits the grave of his grandmother Caroline. In the cemetery, the child becomes aware of the fact that, from the burial ground:

> a peculiar little odor was rising . . . a peppery, subtle, sour little odor . . . quite suggestive . . . once you've smelled it . . . you'll smell it everywhere . . . in spite of the flowers . . . in their very scent . . . in one's own smell . . . it makes your stomach turn . . . it comes from the grave. . . . (M.C., 597–98)

The odor of death is inescapable and it will linger on in all of Céline's works. In the present case, however, it is combined with that of food, for one of the neighbors whose appetite is sharpened by the excursion to the graveyard, insists that they "have a snack" upon leaving the grounds. Ferdinand reacts to this with extreme revulsion:

> Suddenly I got the idea to vomit it all out right then and there. . . . I couldn't think about anything except vomiting. . . . I thought of the cake . . . of what her face must look like by now, down there, Caroline's . . . of all the worms . . . the fat ones . . . the big ones with legs . . . who must be gnawing . . . swarming . . . in there. . . . All that rot . . . millions of them in all that swollen pus, the wind which stinks. . . . (Ibid., 598)

One of the most incredible descriptions of general nausea, so immense as to assume epic proportions, occurs in the pages describing the Channel crossing in Mort à crédit (610–13). Céline begins the account with the simple mention of the passengers' seasickness, but goes on to transform the entire ship into an enormous mass of open, spewing mouths, a group effort of "turning their entrails inside out and spilling them on the deck" (611). Men, women, children, even dogs empty their stomachs of everything they have eaten for days. The detailed description of the contents of their gullets is as amusing as it is revolting. With Ferdinand's mother in the lead, the passengers join in a gigantic display of what is hidden in their innards, down to the last raspberry and fishtail. The episode is one of fantastic and truly superrealistic proportions, a gigantic cinerama of revulsion. Grotesquely humorous, a tour de force of nausea, it must be read in its entirety in order to be really appreciated. It is, however, less important than other passages for purposes of illustrating the fact that visceral action, in Céline's work, is frequently a symbol of revolt in the face of fear, misery, or despair.

This concept becomes much clearer in the incident concerning the *Ecole Communale* (574–75), and reaches its highpoint in the visceral paroxysm which follows Ferdinand's frenzied attack upon his father (806–807). Extreme vomiting and diarrhea occur, as well as violent inner upheaval. "It's a real stampede of the insides. . . . One might think that everything is coming apart, or going to pieces . . . it trembles like during a storm, it shakes up one's whole carcass . . ." (808). Ferdinand is upset and amazed that he can "contain such a tempest within his body," (808) such uncontrollable terror, such cramps of his entire being, such a serious "break-down." At the same time, he is shaken and horrified by his father's vulnerability and weakness, in other words, his mortality. "I would never have believed that he was so weak, so soft . . . what a surprise!" (808) Essentially, it is the discovery, once again, that the human being is only "a bunch of entrails," or "just meat," easily shaken, hurt, destroyed. Ferdinand's reaction to this realization is so strong that it almost resembles total disintegration: "I fell down again in a heap and let go of everything on the tile floor." (*M.C.*, 809) It is literally a falling apart of the individual, a reduction to a completely helpless, revolting, and almost untouchable state; but it is also an active expression of despair, one which goes beyond nausea. This profound pessimism or anguish, when linked to anger or true fury, results in that "tempest" inside the person which is akin to revolt or "riot." It should not be underestimated as evidence of an important *"élan* and even a sort of *élan vital."* [119] Although Céline sometimes speaks to us in a "nauseating voice, shaken by terrible heaves," (*M.C.*, 30) the very fact that he gives voice to despair, that he spews it out before us and thus "relieves himself of the bitterness which soils him," (30, 58) is a positive action. If this visceral revolt is seen only in its physical reality, it might seem a childlike mechanism, not unlike a tantrum. But it can also be interpreted as the reaction of a living organism wishing to survive, and which must expel *détritus* or rid itself of objectionable material. In slightly more complex terms, or on a symbolic level, it is the same opposition of the two principal aspects of existence, the "soft" and the "hard," which we have already noted. In this sense, fear or terror resulting in a "softening" or disintegration of the individual is contrasted with revolt, "hardening," or "bristling." When the objectionable material has been expelled, the poison ejected, the organism that is purged of inward putrefaction can function once again. This is catharsis in its most literal and vivid sense, a paroxysm of the entire being which removes the festering rot. The cure, however, is not long in duration; the "offal" of life piles up again, both outside and inside the individual. Man is condemned to wander in that circle of hell where excrement forever rises to drown him.

Thus, Ferdinand lives in that *Passage des Bérésinas* which is "a kind of sewer," (*M.C.*, 561) or "a piss-house without an exit" (603) abounding in evil smells. He himself is covered with filth from his feet (609) to his head, continually and hopelessly unclean (622). Not only is he physically unsavory, but we have seen that all moral degradation is heaped upon him as well. Any of his activities in both of these areas are disparaged. We have already mentioned the frequent occurrence of onanism in *Mort à crédit*—that forbidden activity of childhood which can be considered the symbol of frustration, but also that of loneliness, of a turning inward upon the self, or of *évasion*, a flight into that equally forbidden realm, the imagination.[120] Other leading themes indicate, however, that almost all bodily activities of the human being are treated as suspect and can easily become obnoxious or nauseating. It is as though the fundamental concept of man as a "container of lukewarm and rotting entrails" (*V.*, 332) makes everything that has to do with the life of the viscera, the "mucous membranes," the "unmentionable activities of the interior epidermes which are so limp, so damp," [121] necessarily revolting. And if we consider the bodily functions which are shown in this unpleasant light—eating, regurgitation, defecation, urination, menstrual and other bleeding, masturbation, copulation—we find that all of them originate in the central, inner reservoir of man.

Not only the activities themselves, but also the places where they occur, are subject to hideous descriptions in the work of Céline. Thus, we find the disgusting kitchen of Ferdinand's mother in *Mort à crédit* which resembles "a filthy museum" (543); the toilets of America that are likened to a "disgusting swimming pool," "a fecal cavern," (V., 195–96) where men indulge in a "sudden debauchery of digestion and vulgarity" (196), and those of Siegmaringen, upon which all the five thousand ill-fed inhabitants of the town converge and almost succeed in burying the entire building in offal (C., 148–49); the various "bed recesses" where the sexual act takes place, most often in a repugnant fashion, combining "sinking and frenetic feelings," eroticism and horror (for example: M.C., 663–65; 668–70).

All these awful places converge upon a central courtyard, that "*cour*" of *Voyage au bout de la nuit*, the enclosure which offers only "hideousness without relief." There, darkness reigns, for "the sun never got to the bottom of it" (266) and an all-pervasive, suffocating stench: "Everything stank. There was no longer any air . . . there were only smells" (267). This is the kingdom of the concierge, that divinity of offal. She sits enthroned in her *loge* where all the putrefaction of life ends up and collects: "Oh! savory scrapings! Rubbish, drippings which ooze down from the bed chambers, the kitchens, the attics, and run in cascades into the home of the concierge, full force into life, what a savory hell!" (211) And we remember that it is also the concierge who is the keeper, not only of the filthy secrets of life, but of hate as well.

Céline, that "witness to universal putrefaction," [122] reveals the sewer world and, in reaction to it, speaks in that voice which is so fitting to the vision he portrays, "a voice that vomits." [123] He continues to spew out what he has already known in *Voyage au bout de la nuit*, to spit at the passerby from a great height, like a vindictive gargoyle at the summit of a great cathedral, the truth which he had already put in the mouth of his protagonist of former years. For it is in the bitter words of Robinson, shouted at Madelon in an attempt to awaken her to a truth as revolting as the "grub" contained in the chestnut she is eating and which she attempts to spit

out (V., 473). After having experienced all of life and gone
to the end of night, Robinson defiantly abdicates, choosing his
death and Madelon as his executioner. He rejects everything as
being putrid, disgusting; his speech is like an enormous bout
of mental vomiting, a rebellion against life, a repugnance beyond nausea, so vast that he can only be stilled by death, by
a total void:

> Well then, *everything* revolts and disgusts me now! not only
> you! . . . Everything! . . . Especially love! . . . Yours as
> well as that of the others. . . . That business of feeling you're
> after, do you want me to tell you what it reminds me of? It's
> like making love in an outhouse! . . . You want to eat rotten
> meat? With your love-sauce on it? . . . You can manage to
> get it down? . . . Not me! . . . If you don't smell anything,
> it's your luck! It's only because your nose is stuffed! One has
> to be a halfwit like you not to be disgusted. . . . You want to
> know what there is between you and me? . . . Well, between
> you and me, there's the whole of life. (V., 483)

Thus Robinson, on the way to annihilation, on the path to
becoming himself a "bag of worms" in his final state, still feels
his gorge rise at the sight of life and the endless intertwining of
"rotten meat" which occurs there. The cry of "No!" rings most
defiantly through this part of the novel. For Robinson, that
demon and hero of despair, rejects the nauseating spectacle and
steps outside of the cesspool preferring grave to sewer, and
death to death-in-life. (We might contrast him with Schertz,
the double amputee of *Nord* who dies by being drowned in a
cesspool [395].)

In some ways, Courtial des Pereires of *Mort à crédit* is not
so different from Robinson. Adventurer par excellence, *inventeur
maudit*, he moves from one grandiose failure to the next, until
he comes to his final and most grotesque experiment which
results in the creation of an "agricultural plague" (*M.C.*,
1009). The crops, which he raises by the mock-scientific method
named "téllurgie," are catastrophic, nauseating, threatening:
potatoes that are "gnawed, gnarled, monstrously rotten . . .
and what's more, full of maggots!" They are also "just swarming
with bugs, grubs with a thousand legs . . . and besides, what
an awful odor! infinitely nauseating!" (1008) The results remind
one of those worms that devoured the corpse of Ferdinand's

grandmother and the odor of death that rose from human
cadavers. The perpetrator of this "awful scourge" is accused of
creating "a new and completely special race of depraved,
hideously corrosive bugs" which threaten to turn the countryside into "an enormous field of putrefaction . . . a dreadful
turf . . . A vast cloaca of maggots! . . . an earthquake of
swarming worms," and convert the entire continent into "a
desert of decomposition." (1009) Once the earth is turned
into a rotting wasteland, only death remains as a way out,
and Courtial des Pereires—just as Robinson had done—takes
this path.

Having explored the air, the sea, and finally the land, and
failed, des Pereires commits suicide. His death is as bloody as
that of the colonel in *Voyage au bout de la nuit* and there are
many parallels in the description. The corpse is mangled:

> the head was a complete mess . . . a jelly . . . the flesh all
> chopped up! . . . His face is nothing but a hole . . . with
> the edges all sticky . . . and then, a kind of lump of blood
> which blocked . . . the middle . . . coagulated . . . a big
> blob. . . .(*M.C.*, 1020)

Once again man is reduced to an unrecognizable, shapeless
mass. The inventor's old wife, maddened by the sight of this
horror, cries out continually: "It's a placenta! . . . His head!
. . . His poor head! . . . It's a placenta! . . ." (1030). And
so end those who are accused of having "corrupted the
earth" (1009), to return to their hideous original state of
placental darkness, or their final corruption. The horror of
engendering meets the horror of decomposition, until the two
grow into an overwhelming vision to which herculean retching
is the only possible response.

To a world in a state of siege, a world that is a trap, a disgrace, an outrage, there can be only two basic reactions: abject
acceptance or defiant negation. The first results in the final
apathy, the downfall of the individual, which is the fate of
many of Céline's protagonists. It is, as Richard states, a kind
of "last stop: the state of refuse," a sort of limbo which is
actually the union of being and nonbeing, where all is reduced
to the condition of *détritus* (that which flowers on the edge of
nothingness). This is characteristic of the outcasts, of the outer

borders of the city—that vague and hideous *banlieue* which is
so often the setting of his novels—and of the "marginal zones
of being," which Céline tends to describe. However, while this
is one path taken by the characters in his works, it is not the
only one. For we cannot agree that "everything there announces
the fall into the amorphous," [124] since the author also indicates
another way, that of furious negation, manifested in a desire to
"gueuler et dégueuler," and finally, in a need to destroy oneself by violent means. Once more, we find the opposition between "soft" and "hard," stagnation versus destruction.

It is true that neither road can be called an acceptance of
life and that both lead to the ultimate decomposition of the
individual. There is, however, an important difference between
the weary request of Bardamu to "speak no more about it" and
the furious invectives of Robinson which provoke his death, the
sick and defeated "I want to go away" of Ferdinand, and the
violent departure of Courtial des Pereires. The first is that of
the terrified and worn out animal which lies still in the trap
that has closed upon it; the other is the desperate struggle to
shatter this trap even at the price of one's life. While Céline,
on the one hand, describes "a certain type of modern man who
is falling apart and losing his very entrails," [125] he is equally
concerned with depicting one who will rebel against his condition, even at the risk of retching out his entrails or spilling
them on the ground.

We note, however, that the theme of nausea and of
visceral reactions in general does not occur as frequently in
the last novels. While it is true that there are references to
these matters now and then, they do not predominate but
merely reflect the fact that they are a commonplace in human
existence. It is as though Céline has gone far beyond nausea or
any other specific reaction to the traplike nature of life. He is
now concerned with much vaster struggles than those of
individuals, so that the retching of Ferdinand has become the
gigantic spewing of cannons and aircraft shells, and the suicide
of Robinson or Courtial des Pereires the mass immolation of
entire nations. The possibility of taking the road of apathy is
gone; there remains only desperate, aimless flight, or *évasion*
by madness. It is no longer significant to decide that "one will

speak no more" or that one wishes to "go away." For there is nothing left to say, and nowhere to go. All that remains is either blind self-preservation or equally blind destruction.

It is no longer the individual alone who is the "bag of worms," but the entire continent. And the author's concerns go beyond one particular "bunch of innards" to show us the entrails of a gigantic, disemboweled corpse which is all of Europe. The sewer, the courtyard, the Passage des Bérésinas, the concierge's *loge*, have grown to such dimensions that they are now the vast stretches of a sulphurous hell, an endless "desert of putrefaction" (which exceeds the wildest imaginings of des Pereires' accusers). The pestilence, the "scourge" are no longer mock-apocalyptic threats, as in *Mort à crédit*, but have attained the terrible scope of a true apocalypse. Death is no longer on the installment plan, but wholesale and ever present. The sewers are now running blood. And the cloaca of life have turned into the charnel houses of death.

Notes

1 Letter to Eveline Pollet, September 1933, *L'Herne*, No. 3, 101.

2 *Voyage au bout de la nuit suivi de Mort à crédit*, "Bibliothèque de la Pléiade," Vol. CLVII (Paris: Gallimard, 1962), 64. All references to *Voyage au bout de la nuit* or *Mort à crédit* will be to this edition.

3 Nicole Debrie-Panel, *Louis-Ferdinand Céline* (Lyon: E. Vitte, 1961), p. 65.

4 Céline's prescription for literature: "Il faut noircir et se noircir" (one must blacken and blacken oneself). Quoted by J. Carayon, "Le docteur écrit un roman," *L'Herne*, No. 3, 22.

5 See for example: A. Suarès, "A propos de Céline," *La Nouvelle Revue Française*, IX, No. 104, 327; Claude Jamet, *Images de la littérature* (Paris: F. Sorlot, 1915), p. 166.

6 See for example: Manès Sperber, "Louis-Ferdinand Céline," *Preuves*, CXXVII, 20; Maurice Nadeau, *Littérature présente* (Paris: Corréa, 1952), p. 157.

7 Debrie-Panel, *op. cit.*, p. 16; H. Clouard, *Histoire de la littérature française du Symbolisme à nos jours, 1915–1960* (Paris: Albin Michel, 1962), II, 336.

8 Debrie-Panel, *op. cit.*, p. 16; Robert Stromberg, "La source qui ne rafraîchit pas," *L'Herne*, No. 3, 209.

9 These can be found especially in *Voyage . . .* (for example, pp. 82, 95, 206). They also recur, however, in all of Céline's work and appear as late as *Nord* (p. 135, etc.). "Everything needs redoing!" is still heard in *D'un château l'autre*, p. 76.

10 Suarès, *op. cit.*, pp. 326–27.

11 Marcel Arland, *Essais et nouveaux essais critiques* (Paris: Gallimard, 1952), p. 232.

12 Leon Trotsky, "Céline—Novelist and Politician," *Atlantic Monthly*, CLVI, No. 4, 419.

13 Walter Orlando, "Grandeurs et misères de Bardamu," *La Table Ronde*, No. 57, 172.

14 Suarès, *op. cit.*, p. 329.

15 Pierre Brodin, *Présences contemporaines* (Paris: Debresse, 1957), III, 152.

16 Letter to E. Pollet, *L'Herne*, No. 3, 100.

17 Suarès, *op. cit.*, p. 329.

18 Poulet, *La Lanterne* . . . , p. 23.

19 Paul Morand, "Céline et Bernanos," *L'Herne*, No. 3, 257.

20 Orlando, *op. cit.*, p. 174.

21 Remark cited by J. Carayon, Céline's first secretary, during a personal interview with the author of this study (September 1962).

22 Nadeau, *Littérature* . . . , p. 158; Simon, "Céline le forcéné," *Le Monde* (June 6, 1961), p. 1; Brasillach, *op. cit.*, p. 230; H. E. Kaminski, *Céline en chemise brune ou le Mal du présent* (Paris: Les Nouvelles Editions Excelsior, 1938), p. 27.

23 Kaminski, *op. cit.*, pp. 31, 114; Milton Hindus, *The Crippled Giant*, p. 45; Simon, *op. cit.*, p. 1; P. Etiemble, *Hygiène des lettres. II. Littérature dégagée. 1942–1953* (Paris: Gallimard, 1955), pp. 167, 177; Sperber, *op. cit.*, p. 20; etc.

24 "Avant-propos," p. xi.

25 Kaminski, *op. cit.*, p. 27; Nadeau, *Littérature* . . . , p. 158; Poulet, *Entretiens* . . . , p. 66.

26 Nadeau, *Littérature* . . . , p. 158.

27 *Entretiens* . . . , p. 33.

28 *Céline*, p. 13.

29 Dominique Rolin, "Ni avant, ni après, ni ailleurs," *L'Herne*, No. 3, 290.

30 Bardamu is a doctor, suffers head injuries in the war (just as Céline did) and follows the course of his author's journeys. Céline himself states: "Bardamu?—he isn't me. He's my double. But Robinson too!" (Jeanne C. . . ; "Le docteur écrit un roman," *L'Herne*, No. 3, 22.) We find a small, but interesting detail in *Voyage* to substantiate this: Robinson is also trepanned, just as Bardamu and Céline himself (p. 446). Ferdine of the last two novels bears such close resemblance to Céline and his life during this period, that he could also pass for the author's double.

31 Céline considers this to be an extremely important aspect of his writing. These are some of his statements concerning it: "A writer must, above all . . . transpose." Letter to Ernst Bendz, 1948. *L'Herne*, No. 3, 119. Or again: "I only write to transpose" (Letter to Milton Hindus, March 1947, *Texas Quarterly*, V, No. 4, 25). "I turn around and strangle a kind of present actuality. Transpose it . . ." (*idem.*, 28).

32 We must admit however that Céline, in his novels, appears to have prophesied the course of his own life with appalling accuracy. Rather than subscribing to a mysterious origin of such predictions, one might venture the comment Céline made about "La Vitruve" in *Mort à crédit*: "She judged low, she judged correctly" (p. 516).

33 Beaujour lecture; William Waller, "Journey into Nihilism," *The South Atlantic Monthly*, Vol. XLIII, No. 3, 290; Jean-Paul Sartre, "Portrait de l'antisémite," *Les Temps Modernes*, Ière année, No. 3, 449.

34 Jeanne C. . . , "Le docteur . . . ," p. 23.

35 Mondor, *op. cit.*, p. XIV.

36 Karl Epting, *Frankreich im Widerspruch* (Hamburg: Hanseatische Verlagsanstalt, 1934), p. 55.

37 Poulet, *Entretiens* . . . , p. 3.

38 In *D'un château l'autre* we find this remark: "I subsist even more frequently on hate than noodles!" In one of Céline's letters we find the following: "An immense hatred keeps me alive." (Letter to Albert Paraz, cited in *Le Gala des vaches; journal*, Paris: Editions de l'Elan, 1948, p. 86.)

39 A letter from Céline states: "I want to see, to believe the abject nature of man. I have seen. I shall thus not have lived for nothing." (Pierre Monnier, "Résidence surveillée," *L'Herne*, No. 3, 79.) Compare the above with a passage from *Voyage* which expresses a similar idea:

> The biggest defeat of all is to forget, especially what it is that makes you croak, and to croak without ever having understood just how rotten men really are. One has to tell everything one has seen of what is most depraved in man. . . . That's enough of a job to keep one going for a whole lifetime (pp. 27–28).

40 Letter to E. Pollet (June 1933), *L'Herne*, No. 3, 99.

41 Jacques Laurent, "Céline," *Le Nouveau Candide*, X, 13.

42 Letters to Hindus, *Texas Quarterly*, V, No. 4 (1962), 35.

43 Vinding, *L'Herne*, No. 3, 69.

44 Letter to Eveline Pollet, January 31, 1938, *L'Herne*, No. 3, 105.

45 Pierre de Boisdeffre, *Histoire vivante de la littérature d'aujour-d'hui* (Paris: Le Livre Contemporain) p. 257.

46 Robert Brasillach, "Céline prophète," *Les quatre jeudis. Image d'avant guerre* (Paris: Ed Balzac, 1944), p. 229.

47 Harry Slochower, *No Voice is Wholly Lost. Writers and Thinkers in War and Peace* (London: Dennis Dobson, 1946), p. 90.

48 Suarès, *op. cit.*, p. 327.

49 *Ibid.*

50 Jean-Louis Bory, "Du Braoum dans la littérature," *L'Herne*, No. 3, 224.

51 Epting, *op. cit.*, p. 54.

52 Expression used by Robert Poulet in a personal interview on August 27, 1962, to refer to the delicate or compassionate passages in Céline's work.

53 Except animals, an aged patient, and Lili or Lucette (Céline's wife in real life)—all innocent victims.

54 Jacques Darribehaude, "Souvenirs," *L'Herne*, No. 3, 184.

55 Vandromme, *op. cit.*, p. 47.

56 During an interview with the author of this study (September 1962), Bernard de Fallois suggested that for Sartre "les salauds ce sont les autres," while for Céline, "le salaud c'est d'abord lui-même."

57 Only a very few exceptions to this pattern can be found in all the novels: Alcide and Molly of *Voyage*, L'Oncle Edouard and Nora of *Mort*

à crédit, Mme. Bonnard of *D'un château l'autre*, and Lili of the last two works. More detailed discussion of these will follow in the chapter entitled "Humanism A Rebours."

58 Her story is prefaced by these words: "There is an end to everything. It isn't always death, but often something different and much worse, especially with children" (V., p. 265).

59 W. M. Frohock, "Céline's quest for love," *Accent*, Vol. II, No. 2 (Winter 1942), 79. One must also note here, however, that in French argot "les merdeux" means children in general (see *Dictionnaire de l'Argot Moderne*, Aux Quais de Paris, Ed. du Dauphin, 1953, p. 130).

60 Frohock, *op. cit.*, p. 81.

61 *Note:* One should call attention to the concept of "the scapegoat" which is an important theme and will be treated in greater detail in Chapter IV.

62 It is interesting to note that Céline, the author of this black picture, could also say: "I hate sickness, penitence, anything morbid. . . . I admire the wholesomeness of childhood." (Letter to Milton Hindus, *Texas Quarterly*, p. 34.) The opposition of these two concepts is not really as paradoxical as it might at first appear. If we concede that Céline's system of "noircissement" is a literary one, this case becomes an excellent example of that very phenomenon.

63 Frohock, *op. cit.*, p. 81.

64 Claude Bonnefoy, "Dernier adieu à sa jeunesse" (Interview with Céline), *Arts*, No. 833 (August 3–9, 1961), 5.

65 Vandromme, *op. cit.*, p. 33.

66 Suarès, *op. cit.*, p. 328. One might add that, aside from indicating terror and cowardice, the action described by Celine is also a gesture of defiance; the author might be implying that such anger or defiance is the beginning of genius, his own included.

67 Arland, *op. cit.*, p. 230.

68 Jean-Pierre Richard, "La Nausée de Céline," *La Nouvelle Revue Française*, No. 116, 245.

69 *Ibid.*, X, No. 115, 45.

70 Hanrez, *Céline*, p. 275.

71 Although there is another current, the "erotico-mystical," to be found in Céline's works which is equally important and diametrically opposed. This will be treated in detail in the chapter entitled "L'Autre Côté de la vie."

72 Céline, *Entretiens avec le professeur Y* (Paris: Gallimard, 1955), p. 29.

73 Vandromme, *op. cit.*, p. 34.

74 *Ibid.*, p. 39.

75 Frohock, *op. cit.*, p. 83.

76 Trotsky, *op. cit.*, p. 420.

77 André Brissaud, "Voyage au bout de la tendresse," *L'Herne*, No. 3, p. 226.

78 Céline's delight in leading not only his reader but also his friends astray, is well known. One critic even goes so far as suggesting that he was never trepanned, a fact reported by all his biographers. (See the startling article on this aspect of Céline by Marcel Brochard, "Céline à Rennes," *L'Herne*, No. 3, pp. 13–17).

79 Slochower, *op. cit.*, p. 92.

80 *Idem.*

81 *Ibid.*, p. 93.

82 Sartre, *Portrait* . . . , p. 476. It must be noted here that Sartre is referring mainly to those works of Céline (*Bagatelles pour un massacre, Ecole des cadavres, Les beaux draps*) in which Céline blames tendencies in our society that lead nations to war and unfortunately incarnates them in a figure of enormously evil, almost mythical proportions: "the Jew."

83 Vandromme, *op. cit.*, p. 17.

84 Brissaud, p. 230.

85 Pascal Pia, "Céline au bout de la nuit," *Carrefour* (February 13, 1963), p. 18.

86 André Parinaud, "Dernière interview avec Céline," *Arts* (August 12–18, 1961), 2; also *D'un château l'autre*, pp. 34, 35, 36.

87 Céline insists, in numerous statements, that he hates to write, would not have written a line had it not been for insomnia and lack of money, and also that he considers the craft of "écrivain" vulgar, narcissistic, absurd.

88 Medicine is frequently described as being a thankless, miserable, and sordid profession (see especially *Mort à crédit*, p. 518), a sadistic and exploitive one, especially in the case of surgery (see remarks in *D'un château l'autre*, pp. 226–27).

89 Letter to Milton Hindus, March 30, 1947, *Texas Quarterly*, V, No. 4 (1962) p. 25.

90 Vandromme, *op. cit.*, p. 64.

91 Opinion expressed by Marcel Aymé in an interview with the author of this study on September 10, 1962.

92 There is a startling description of the pamphlet written by Semmelweiss which sounds as though it were a comment on Céline's own pamphlets produced more than ten years later; it includes this statement: "although these truths were extremely pressing, nevertheless it was childish to proclaim them in this intolerable form. The hatred aroused by this pamphlet only represented the enlarged echo of the anger whose violence he had already felt ten years earlier." (*S.*, 111–12). Similarly, Céline presented what he considered a "truth" in an intolerable form, and his pamphlets elicited even more anger than his earlier work had done.

93 We should note that the name—and in Céline's work names are always significant—of the place where Robinson first joins Bardamu is Noirceur-sur-la-Lys (*Voyage*, p. 42).

94 Such outbursts are not dissimilar in nature from those which Céline himself will utter, stating: "I'll never be in favor, under any regime, I'm afraid!" (Statement made in a letter from Céline to Jeanne Carayon, written during the war. Quoted by Mme Carayon in an interview with her by the author of this study.)

95 As in the first 116 pages of *D'un château l'autre*, before the story of Siegmaringen finally begins.

96 Ole Vinding, "Vu par son ami Danois," *L'Herne*, No. 3, 69.

97 This is noted by as intimate an observer of Céline's work as his secretary, Marie Canavaggia (Interview, September 1962 with the author of this study). It is easily substantiated in one's reading, and may be due, in part, to the horrendous nature of the reality which is sufficiently black to need no alterations to suit it to Céline's literary vision.

The lack of transposition in the names of real characters has already resulted in a libel suit against *Nord* and necessitated a revised edition of the novel in which the names of persons and places have been changed.

98 No longer that "garçon sans importance collective. . . . tout juste un individu," of *L'Eglise* (p. 161), who had so intrigued the young Sartre that he used the phrase as the epigraph of his first novel, *La Nausée.*

99 The parallels with Villon, frequently suggested, find specific application here.

100 Robert Faurisson, "La leçon de Bardamu," *L'Herne*, No. 3, 311.

100 *Ibid.*

102 Statement made by Jeanne Carayon in my interview with her.

103 Ironically including even the dietary regime of "boiled noodles," on which Ferdinand subsisted and which Céline is subjected to at the end of his life, although in the latter case, it is dictated partly by poverty, partly by asceticism and partly by illness. (Information obtained from Céline's widow. See also *D'un château l'autre*, pp. 10, 11, 13, 102.)

104 Aymé, *L'Herne*, No. 3, 215–16.

105 Stromberg, *L'Herne*, No. 3, 270.

106 Hindus, *The Crippled Giant*, p. 79.

107 Slochower, *op. cit.*, pp. 92, 96.

108 Trotsky, *op. cit.*, p. 419.

109 Sperber, *op. cit.*, p. 18.

110 Serge Radine, *Lumières dans la nuit* (Paris: Editions du Vieux Colombier, 1956), p. 10.

111 Nadeau, *Littérature* . . . , p. 157.

112 Aymé, *L'Herne*, No. 3, 215.

113 Radine, *op. cit.*, p. 10.

114 Aymé, *L'Herne*, No. 3, 215.

115 Richard, *op. cit.*, p. 33.

116 *Ibid.*, p. 35.

117 *Ibid.*, p. 39.

118 *Ibid.*, p. 40.

119 Vandromme, *op. cit.*, p. 29.

120 An interesting connection between onanism and creativity might be suggested by Céline's humorous remark to a friend who dropped in while the former was writing. When asked what he was doing, Céline replied, "Tu vois, on se branle un petit peu!" (Lucien Rebatet, "D'un Céline l'autre," *L'Herne*, No. 3, 46) In French argot, *se branler* is to masturbate. The *Dictionnaire de l'Argot Moderne* also gives us this bit of additional information: *Miss Branlette* is a pseudonym for the imagination (p. 40).

121 Richard, *op. cit.*, p. 39.

122 Pierre Audinet, "Dernières rencontres avec Céline," *Les Nouvelles Littéraires* (July 6, 1961), p. 4.

123 Vandromme, *op. cit.*, p. 30. Note also Céline's phrase from *Mort à crédit*, "I piss on it all from a considerable height," quoted by Henry Miller on the last page of *The Red Notebook*, n.p.: Henry Miller, 1954.

124 Richard, *op. cit.*, p. 42.

125 Henri Clouard, *Histoire de la littérature française du symbolisme à nos jours, 1915–1960* (Paris: Albin Michel, 1962), II, p. 337.

2 · Humanism A Rebours

ECHOES OF SEMMELWEISS

"You could tell some pleasant stories . . . from time to time . . . . Life isn't always a dirty business," Ferdinand's friend suggests in *Mort à crédit* (505). One might make a similar remark to Céline himself. And despite all that was said in the preceding chapter, his answer would not necessarily be in the negative. For there *is* also a lighter, more pleasant, and even playful side to the author's character which sometimes affirms itself. This is shown in those delightful "ballets," [1] which contrast with his usual dark vision, and in the songs which Céline composed and wrote the lyrics for.[2] Many of his friends would attest that, in his private life, the author was capable of ribaldry, jets, lighthearted spoofing. It would be wrong to see Céline only in the guise of a thundering oracle of ugliness and death.

Had he not, in his first work, celebrated the worth of life and joy? The choice of his protagonist is significant. Céline says of him that he belonged to that "all-too-rare race of men who are able to love life in its simplest and most beautiful form: the very process of living." (*S.,* 30) Semmelweiss sought to preserve the most fundamental affirmation of life and battled fiercely for "the two great joys of existence: being young and giving life." (*S.,* 82)

The story of Semmelweiss is tinged with idealistic humanism.[3] It affirms that "a man's soul . . . will flower into a pity so great, into a bloom so magnificent, that the fate of humanity

85

will, as a result, be softened for ever." (20) The hero proceeds in this messianic mission driven on by a burning kind of
pity for humanity. His fight is directed against ugliness and
death, against all those things which attack man and prevent
him from living in dignity and joy. However—and here Céline's
dark vision is already taking form—the battle is doomed to
failure. There is a bitter irony in the fact that Semmelweiss,
who personifies compassion, health, and life, should be punished
by indifference, disease, and death.[4] It is as though nature or
society avenged any infraction upon its laws, destroying "the
man who had the unforgettable affrontery to challenge its
cruel order." (128–29) The price inflicted for daring to flaunt
its implacable rule of suffering is a terrible one: exile, madness,
disease, a long and excruciating agony.

The entire story is a warning. It demonstrates "the danger
of wishing men too well." (9) Its moral is quite explicit: "Everything must be expiated. Good as well as evil must be paid for,
sooner or later. The good of course demands a much higher
price" (10). "Goodness is only a minor mystical current
amongst others; its indiscretion is tolerated with great difficulty."
(115) Therefore, the cruel lesson that such indiscretion leads
to destruction is implicit. There is a deep pessimism in such a
stand, a terrible awareness that life and conscious existence will
necessarily be vanquished by death and chaos. We are assured
that "in the history of the world, life is only a moment of in-
toxication; the Truth is Death." (3) Man's most valued possession, his consciousness, is but a feeble thing, "only a small
light in the chaos of the universe, precious but fragile." (48)
Céline goes on to dishearten us with the warning: "One doesn't
light a volcano with a candle; one does not drive the earth into
the sky with the help of a hammer." (Idem)

The author whose calling will cause him to kindle vol-
canoes and to hammer at earth and sky alike, here admits the
helplessness of the human being, a creature possessing only
fragile weapons, a small supply of tallow candles, and beset by
dangers everywhere. Moreover, man is threatened by a fate not
unlike that which caused Semmelweiss to end his days "impotent among lunatics, more decayed than a corpse . . ." (129).
Will not the echo of these words ring throughout all of Céline's

work, and the madness of men, their state of "pourriture en suspens" (decay held in abeyance), or "mort à crédit" (corpse on the installment plan) become constantly more apparent?

One might venture the guess that *Semmelweiss* constitutes an important turning point in Céline's thought and a testing ground for many of his central themes. It seems as though the author reached several conclusions there which would be upheld during his entire literary career. The initial pity, involvement, and affirmation of life (incarnated in Semmelweiss), once understood as an admirable, but dangerous and even destructive, orientation, never again appear in their original form. Debrie-Panel has noted that *Semmelweiss* contains all the major themes of Céline's writings and that, while these themes will reappear throughout his work, they will only be present in a *negative* form. On the other hand, the initial themes of a pessimistic, sad, or grim nature will remain substantially the same. The other, more affirmative aspects—the celebration of goodness and beauty, of compassion and discovery, in short the "passion for life in all its forms" [5]—will never reappear in their native guise. They will be, in turn: angrily refuted, secretly experienced but carefully disguised, repressed to such a degree that they only rise to the surface at rare intervals.

Thus, while some have seen a "painful revolt against the inhuman" in Céline's work, as well as a "protest against death and all the ugly things that resemble or attract it," [6] his actual pronouncements take the form of a furious and pitiless denunciation of both human and inhuman, an almost continual evocation of death and ugliness. In the same manner, while it can be said that a "compassion as profound as it is secret forms his dominant inspiration," [7] the secret aspect of this compassion is so pronounced that the feeling often resembles indifference or even callousness. Moreover, if "Céline's virulence and insolence hide an authentic feeling of pity," [8] this pity is so well covered up that it only seldom appears in its true form. When it does, we find those rare displays of tenderness which resemble luminous points of light on a night firmament.

It is intriguing to think of this metamorphosis of Céline's original vision, by which existence is suddenly portrayed as if a dark filter had been interposed between the onlooker and his subject. Even if it is a restatement of early, positive beliefs in a diametrically opposed form, even if we can compare it to an echo effect in which only the last portion of an utterance (in this case, that portion being the grimmest) is repeated over and over again, the phenomenon is somewhat puzzling. For it is a profound change, one which goes beyond a simple flip of the literary coin to expose only the dark side of the same money. It might, with some likelihood, be the result of a serious upheaval that occurred in Céline during the interval which separates the beginnings of *Semmelweiss* from the pages of *Voyage au bout de la nuit.*

Not too much is known about this period of the author's life, except that it was a time of unrest, the breaking of conventional and familial ties, extensive travel, and work in the field of medicine. We might chance the guess that it is the last of these factors which had the most profound effect on Céline's view of existence. It is likely that the active confrontation with human misery and viciousness, which had already occurred during his war experiences, was reinforced and extended in the course of medical practice. Céline seems to suggest such an idea in a phrase of *Voyage au bout de la nuit:* "I cannot help questioning the idea that there are any other true insights into our deepest nature than war and illness, those two infinities of nightmare." (407) Having known both these states of suffering at first hand, Céline emerges from the experience with a vision which he consideres to be basic to human existence. It is also as though, in the course of the endless and often losing battle against death, chaos, and suffering—which Céline had described in *Semmelweiss* and in which he had now become himself engaged (although on a less grandiose scale than his hero)—he had become profoundly convinced of the validity of his grim conclusions. The writer, taking on the role of his protagonist, becomes himself the *"accoucheur* with black fingernails who discovered the germ of the disease from which today's world is dying." [9] Like Semmelweiss also, he passionately denounces these microbes, this fatal illness. Not content with pitying the patient or stopping at the expression of compassion, he diagnoses, describes the disease in all its manifestations, rails against its ravages, but admits that its dimensions are those of a plague.

As Céline's work progresses, the pessimism of *Semmelweiss* deepens. While in the former work, the author sided with life, and only noted sadly that death often triumphs, in *Voyage au bout de la nuit* he stated, "that's all life is, a bit of light which ends in night." (335) If one is capable of any lucidity at all, the only authentic choice is between "dying or lying," (200) for "the truth of this world is death," in this work just as in the preceding one. The difference in attitude between the two works lies in the embittered admission contained in the second. *Mort à crédit* goes further to state that to lie is a necessary step in the battle of existence, a fact which Bardamu had already noted when he realized that it was not so much a question of "life" as of "survival," and proceeded by a kind of "unreasoning animal instinct for physical survival." [10] Ferdinand in *D'un château l'autre* will insist that "life is a drive which one has to pretend one believes in . . . as if nothing were wrong" (151), and in his pronouncement echoes Bardamu, who had cried out "I don't want to die any more!" and had to add, "long live the madmen and the cowards! or rather, long may madmen and cowards survive!" (V., 66) While in Céline's first two works, the figures of Semmelweiss and Robinson are there to show that survival is not the supreme good and choose to die rather than to belie their beliefs, this affirmation disappears with *Voyage au bout de la nuit* (except for Courtial des Pereires of *Mort à crédit*, who stands halfway between the earlier and later protagonists, being "mad" but not "cowardly"). In the later works, authenticity is sacrificed for the preservation of life. In a world where violence and death are the rule of the day, madness or cowardice may be the only safe path. This becomes quite clear at the end of *Nord*: the strange chariot which carries the survivors to safety, is laden with the mad and the cowardly: the Kratzmuhl, Isis, the Countess Tulff-Tcheppe, the Revizor, Marie-Thérèse, and Nicolas (445–59).

It seems, indeed, as though we have come a long way from *Semmelweiss*, but if we think of the viewpoint fostered in the last works as a repression or an inversion of the dangerously idealistic pronouncements of the first, Céline's position becomes clearer. Humanism can only be expressed *à rebours* if it is to be kept alive. Moreover, we must be careful not to take the cover for the book, or the shell for the whole creature. If one equalled the other, if Céline felt only what looks like the prevailing vision of his novels, there would be no meaning in such phrases as the "prayer for vengeance," directed against life ruled by "a despairing God, as grumpy and sensual as a pig," which we find in V*oyage au bout de la nuit* (12) or in the further protests in the other novels which come closer to being "masses for vengeance," greater in scope than a simple prayer but containing similar refrains.

Pity then has turned to a desire for vindication, compassion to implacable denunciation. The futility of straightforward heroism, of human concern, of love for life has been so thoroughly proven that these must, as in a black mass, be presented in reversed fashion. In some instances, however, some of the original interpretation sticks to the ideas, and they become paradoxical or at least enigmatic. Thus, we note the phenomena of merciless pity, of cowardice that conceals heroism, of callousness that masks deep concern, of "inverted humanism," [11] of Life that equals Death.

The last of these paradoxes is especially intriguing. It is based on a distinction which Céline had already made in *Semmelweiss*: that of Life as a vital force, an *élan*, and that of life as the equivalent of everyday existence, a static and frequently revolting state. The same distinction continues to be made in all the work. While the first is exalted—whether in a direct or a hidden fashion—the second is decried and attacked. And if we examine the theme more closely, we find that it is in this *quotidien* realm of living—so frequently blackened by the author—that all of man's "rottenness" explodes. It is there also that one can only make two choices: "to die or to lie" (V., 200) and take the path of the hero or that of "madman" or "coward." Thus, it becomes clear that an affirmation of Life results in Death (as for Semmelweiss or Robinson), while the acceptance of life (that lesser form of *élan*) ends in a minor version of the same fate: apathy or death-in-life.[12]

It would be impossible to understand these and other basic aspects of Céline's vision without taking into consideration the original attitudes of the author expressed in *Semmelweiss*. Unaware of these, we could only note the results of the reversal which took place and not of the contrasting base of the work. Were only one side of Céline's literary coin known to us, we might easily conclude that it was counterfeit and had a hollow ring. Knowing, however, what had existed at the start, we see that the author, who would make it his task to expose the mud and blood which are at the roots of existence, had once also seen the healing virtue of mud and the life force which resides in blood. He who would speak of man as that hideous creature that is half worm and half devouring beast, had once seen him in all his possible splendor and celebrated him in the most profound terms: by affirming the value of his very life. Céline, the destroyer, was more than half creator. How else could he have said: "The inner life of any child contains the difficult harmony of a world in the process of creation." (*S.,* 22)

MERCILESS PITY

It might be said that Céline shares the "greatest fault of Semmelweiss: that of being brutal in everything, and most of all, to himself" (35). Certainly, his approach to the suffering that he depicts is not generally characterized by delicacy, *finesse,* or gentleness. But is this necessarily a fault? Just as the explorer cannot stop to consider whether his efforts will benefit the natives, or the *accoucheur* attend to the cries of the mother if the child is to be born, the artist must cut his vision from the immense matrix of existence and thrust his creation at us, brutally if necessary, in order for it to live. He cannot stop to pity either the reader or himself and avert the dangers of his work from them. If discovery (whether in medicine or in literature) necessitates brusqueness or brutality, it is because creativity cannot be genteel. It breaks—by its very nature—the boundaries of everyday nicety, of polite formulas; it takes the lid of caution from a boiling cauldron which is generally kept out of sight, or not alluded to. Once the cover is lifted, the scalding contents might escape and sear the hands of the onlooker. The risk is inevitable with a writer such as Céline. Yet, while he can be compared to "a volcano in the state of eruption, not a blast-furnace supervised by engineers," [13] his function is not to bury the world in ashes, but simply to thunder at it in bursts of flame, to spout fiery invectives at its guilty inhabitants.

In this task, Céline does not greatly differ from Semmel-weiss who, having discovered the germ which keeps life from flowering and creates horror where there should be joy, had to decry it, no matter the price. Cassandra is unwelcome in any garb. "It is not pleasant to live in an age of prophets." [14] Their words are ungraciously received, unless they are affirmative or consoling. But consolation is cheap in the eyes of both Semmel-weiss and his creator, for it is the twin of self-deception, the mark of an easy truce with existence. The only other means available is a violent denunciation which is too often interpreted as indifference or brutality but which, in reality, is the expression of profound feeling for man. "To spit in the face of our species because one despairs of being able to save it," [15] while not a pretty action, is an authentic response to a situation which is equally unpretty. For Céline, the world is " a kind of dis-grace; that's why he exhibits its infirmity in the market-place." [16] And, as if exhibiting it were not sufficient, he also condemns it to be publicly flogged and spat upon.

Significantly, Céline includes his own person among the disgraced, the shameful, the maimed, just as he had included himself in the ranks of the "salauds" and been intent on "blackening himself." Is it not possible also that "the man who wants to be a pitiless rock, a furious torrent, or devastating thunder: i.e., everything except a man," [17] does so because the term "man" is far from being a flattering designation? Actually, as we have already seen, the "human animal" is far from an ideal for him, but a target for violent attack. He is the creature who must be lapidated, treated pitilessly, assailed by a torrent of invectives, struck by punitive lightning. Yet, "behind the ferocious and irritating puppets of this Punch-and-Judy show for ogres, there hides an authentic friend of man," [18] a thunder-ing prophet who "respects nothing except the impatient pity which burns in his entrails." [19]

It is the impatient, ferocious, brutal aspect of Céline's pity which is so frequently misunderstood. Far removed from the code of "sweet compassion," from the comfortable reaction to a "tearjerker," where the kind Samaritan can feel superior to his unfortunate neighbor, Céline's variety of merciless pity is a much more authentic response to suffering. It is true that it

does not aim to salve anyone's conscience or allay hidden fears
for one's own skin. Rather than allowing the reader to remain
aloof and calmly superior, it attacks him in the nexus of the
emotions (of both fear and pity), sharply upsetting his equilibrium, pulling the complacent seating arrangement from under
him. It is as if he were thrown into the arena with the other
dying gladiators whom he had only come to contemplate. For
Céline believes that only then, in the blinding light of the
circular trap, in the midst of sand, cries, and blood can pity
truly be born. The moment of truth cannot be achieved outside the bull ring. The corrida must be experienced, the sword
penetrate one's own flank, if one is to really understand.[20] "Pity
develops in a peculiar way," Bardamu had already told us (V.,
27): by being oneself the prey, the hunted and tormented
beast in the jungle. Only through a trial by fear and pain can
one attain true compassion.

To understand, to probe beneath the surface of things,
even at the price of turning the scalpel against oneself without
pity, this is the real quest of Céline, and of his protagonists.
Thus, Bardamu must rouse himself from the warm, envelop-
ing resting place which is embodied in Molly, in order to continue his exploration of existence, to fulfill his journey. He
states, as if under a curse of having to wander about the earth,
without respite:

> I was always thinking . . . about not losing time and tender-
> ness, as if I wanted to keep it all, for I don't know what
> magnificent thing, something sublime, for later on, but not for
> Molly and not for this. As if life would rob me, hide from
> me, what I wanted to find out from it, from that life in the
> depths of blackness . . . and that I'd lose everything in the
> final analysis, through a lack of strength, that life would have
> deceived me, like all the others, Life, the true mistress of real
> men. (V., 231–32)

Thus, personal tenderness is sacrificed, the involvement
with one human being forsaken, for the search of a larger, more
"sublime," and darker union. The golden fleece is left untouched or only fleetingly caressed. The quest is for a prize of a
different hue: the black and matted fur clotted with the blood
of victims. And he who seeks this knowledge, who is "as one

sick with desire to always know more," must go on his explorations alone, as cruel to himself as to others. The departure is not easy. But its very pain brings with it understanding and a poignant pity. "I felt grief, real grief for once, for everybody, for me, for her [Molly], for everybody," Bardamu admits. He adds, "maybe that's what one looks for all throughout life, nothing more than that, the greatest pain possible, in order to become oneself, before dying." (V., 236)

It is not that Céline believes in a cult of suffering *per se* but simply that he feels that emotional or mental anguish is one of the deepest and most authentic of man's feelings and thus becomes one of the keys for the understanding of human existence. A similar idea is expressed in terms of Robinson, whose enigmatic figure haunts us, even before he appears on the scene: "I didn't see his face, but his voice was different from ours, sadder, and therefore more valid" (V., 44). He is, moreover, described as "that Robinson of all our misfortunes" (176), the explorer of all suffering, the shipwrecked hero whose existence resembles that of Semmelweiss "[who] seemed to exhaust all the possible expressions of unhappiness." (S., 54)

Not only do many protagonists of Céline seem to exhaust all the various misfortunes of existence, but they often seek experiences in which pain is a necessary component. Just as Bardamu had noted, in his departure from Molly, "a new kind of distress, something that bore a resemblance to real feeling" (V., 230), Ferdinand of *Mort à crédit* engages in similar explorations of grief. He watches his mother's grotesque torment with that implacable pity which characterizes many of Céline's narrators, and observes: "I didn't dare admit it, but nevertheless, at bottom I was still sort of curious." (69) Further on, in the same book, he makes a very revealing remark. Having listened to all the horror of his parents' existence, Ferdinand admits: "Sure I was sad . . . but I didn't feel grief that I was going to dribble about, in front of anyone!" (972) This refusal to whine, grieve openly, or exhibit one's compassion in the marketplace is the feeling which sometimes resembles brutality, but is actually one of pride, integrity, dignity.

Many of the incidents in Céline's novels which describe states that generally evoke pity are treated without obvious compassion. They are either reported in simple, descriptive terms or told in a terse, flat, almost indifferent tone, which might sound callous to the unattentive ear. Thus, for example, Bardamu's war experiences often contain matter-of-fact interjections which sum up the situation: "they were getting on line to go and croak," (V., 32) or flashes of grim humor: "they began to put the men in front of firing-squads to bolster their morale." (33) This tendency becomes most pronounced in Robinson's cruel remark to the dying captain who is calling for his mother: "Mama! She doesn't give a shit about you!" (38) Other examples include the description of the abusive treatment an old native receives from Lieutenant Grappa, which is couched in almost journalistic terms (153); the death of a young woman, which evokes only the comment: "Nothing to be done!" (262)

The incident that treats of Robinson's blindness is most interesting. Here Céline reveals the function of suffering, and thus, his real attitude concerning pity. The author says of Robinson, tracing the development of his feelings: "At the moment, he was still very busy, passionately interested in painting his soul with his distress and misery in a disgusting fashion. Later on, he would put some order into his unhappiness and only then would a really new life begin again for him . . ." (V., 325). Thus, Céline considers simple indulgence for suffering disgusting; only a lucid analysis has any value or dignity, even when this lucidity is painful. It becomes fairly evident that while the author does not glorify suffering or attribute any intrinsic worth to it, he does insist on its tutelary function. He had already indicated such an attitude at the beginning of *Voyage au bout de la nuit* when he stated: "in order for an imbecile to start mulling things over in his head, a lot of things and often some pretty cruel ones, have to happen to him." (3) He will continue to hold to similar convictions although, as the years pass and the shadows of a second world conflict fall on his late novels, the belief in man's ability to think or to learn through the experience of suffering will grow less strong. The misfortunes will be of such vast scope that no man will be able to order them to begin a new life, or any life. But even in the face of such impossibility, the author's demand for lucidity will remain constant, for one of the things that Céline decries most consistently is the use of hypocrisy, lies, pretenses, deceptions of any sort. He considers it abominable, for instance, to pretend, during a war when death is ever-present, that life will continue: "that lie is the one that's hardest to take" (V., 37); or when one knows that someone is dying of cancer to deceive oneself into believing that the disease can be cured, as does Lola (V., 220), and also Mme Armandine (C., 310–13). Most of all, it is the recognition that at certain times pity is useless, that there is nothing left to say. In that terrible moment "when one is completely alone, when one has come to the end of everything that can happen to one," when one has truly come to "the end of the world" (V., 323), it would be both absurd and the height of cruelty to speak in terms of consolation.

However—and here Céline is equally insistent—there are times when one must speak: not to console but to reveal. The necessity to tell the whole tale, no matter how dreadful, like some ancient mariner whose punishment and exorcism both reside in the telling, is made quite clear.

> There is nothing horrible in ourselves, on earth, and maybe in heaven, except what has not yet been said. We'll only have some peace once everything has been said, once and for all; then one will finally be able to keep still and be no longer afraid to keep one's mouth shut. It'll be done.[21] (V., 323)

Céline follows his own rule and proceeds to tell all that is terrible in us, on earth, and perhaps in heaven—although the last domain is dismissed rather than explored.

Such an action implies a brand of pity which goes much deeper than mere sympathy. It refuses to cloak misery or deny its existence, but becomes its spokesman and its accuser. Does it not also involve a feeling that goes beyond compassion—for compassion implies an inequality of suffering, a victim who is involved and an observer who is in some way superior because once-removed? Céline refutes such detachment and insists on a community of suffering which rules out the possibility of saving the "I" by dividing or shielding it from "the others." This is probably also the real reason for his emphasis on experiencing misery before being able to talk about it with any understanding. More even than having felt with one's own body the horrors of prison, of war, of disease, it is the knowledge gained from having lived as a "corpse on the installment plan," in a perpetual state of reprieve, on the border of extinction that allows one to grasp the truth about existence: "That postponed agony, during which one is lucid and in good health, when it is impossible to understand anything but absolute truths, one has to have endured *that* in order to know for always, what one is talking about" (V., 54).

The lack of pity, the refusal to spare oneself the full realization of "absolute truths" about existence, is what Céline demands. Having had the courage to speak, he expects the reader to hear him as courageously. In a sense, this demand or expectation is the truest affirmation of man, for it is to consider him capable of lucidity, or at least of being able to make an attempt in that direction. Céline is more than implacable. He implies an equal ability on our part.[22] It is a backhanded compliment to be sure, since it involves a confrontation of all our failings. Nevertheless, it denotes a belief in the existence of some recesses of dignity, worth, and integrity in the human being. For the ability to stand naked before the mirror without self-pity or sham is no small virtue.

CÉLINE AND "LE DOCTEUR DESTOUCHES"

It would be as limited to look at Céline without taking into account "le docteur Destouches" as it would be to disregard the medical background of a Rabelais or a Chekhov, for example. Entering literature rather late—Céline was thirty-eight when *Voyage au bout de la nuit* appeared—he had begun life as a doctor and continued to practice until his death. His was no superficial involvement, but a vocation which existed side by side with that of literature, so that if we wish to consider the writer we cannot ignore his double—the doctor.

Céline's work necessarily reflects his interest in medicine and his experience in that realm. In simplest terms, it means that the author has had intimate knowledge of disease, suffering, terror, death, and prolonged, first-hand contact with human beings sick in mind or body. It might well have led to the suspicion Dr. Knock had attempted to propagate, that even a healthy individual is "sick without knowing it,"[23] or a kind of "patient on the installment plan." A doctor, especially one who works in a poor neighborhood, as Céline did, sees an endless stream of miserable human beings parade before him who clamor for help, exhibit their failings. Could not Céline's description of Gustin (the disillusioned doctor of *Mort à crédit*) apply also to the author himself?

> Sufferers from eczema, albumen, diabetes, the fetid, the tremblers, the V.D. patients, the useless ones, all those who were "too much" or "not enough," the constipated, the repentant diarrhetics, the whole mess, the world of shifty murderers, had flowed together on his head, and moved like a waterfall in front of his spectacles for 30 years, morning, noon and night. . . . (518)

It is not a pretty picture of humanity, nor one that would induce genteel compassion or saccharine sympathy.

Céline's attitude is characterized by a gruff admission of commitment, a sharp denunciation of the causes of illness and the indifference which surrounds it. On the one hand, he bitterly refers to himself as "[the] good Samaritan of the concierge" (C., 74). On the other hand, however, he admits: "I can't keep myself from giving them a hand." (*Idem*) His lifelong involvement with medicine proves this to be no idle phrase. His writing shows this also: "Under the mask of turpitude and insults . . . [one can detect] the face of the doctor. He spits on his patients, but he cares for them." [24] Doctor Destouches seems to have been less stern in the handling of the sick; his severity is reserved for the denunciation of indifference toward illness, whether on the part of society or of medical practitioners themselves. Such an attitude was already apparent in *Voyage au bout de la nuit* and continues to be pronounced in the last works, especially in *D'un château l'autre*. In the first novel, we find those scathing descriptions of the military hospitals where war victims are abandoned to a fate of being either executed, confined in mental wards, or returned to the front (62–64, 67–71, 85–97). In the latter work, "the most upsetting spot" in the town of Siegmaringen, which is already a pretty devastating place, is a large store whose show windows are filled with the moribund of all ages, from babies to grandmothers: a whole "death-house" of forsaken victims (C., 193).

Céline had of course already decried fatalism and indifference
in the face of suffering in *Semmelweiss*; there he rails against
disease, that "dreadful divinity! so despicable! yet so much a
customary event!" which many people treat as though it were
"in the category of those inevitable, cosmic catastrophes." (55)
He denounces with equal vehemence the fact that "the hearts
of men contain not only war," but also stupidity, conservatism,
refusal of new ideas, which allow inertia to triumph (91). His
attack upon doctors guilty of such action, and upon patients
who passively accept or even welcome suffering, is extremely
severe. Surgeons and their all-too-willing victims are the special
targets of Céline's fury. This couple of torturer and tortured is
described in *D'un château l'autre*, as those "gilded sacrificial
priests," and their "delighted victims of vivisection," who both
revel in the horror of their situation (226–27). In the same
novel, there are echoes of a similar attitude concerning Mme
Niçoise and her friend Mme Armandine (309–13).

It is interesting to note that Céline's hatred of passivity—
especially in the face of suffering—appears in various ways in
those areas where he feels greatest involvement: literature and
medicine. It becomes quite obvious that he takes both profes-
sions quite seriously and has no patience or desire to accept or
be content with commiserating. Both as doctor and as writer he
tends to accuse rather than to spare, to disclose rather than to
gloss over or offer palliatives. While physicians no longer believe in purges and blood-letting and "le docteur Destouches"
certainly used more modern techniques, Céline, the writer, is
still given to the figurative use of these methods.

However, there are incidents in the writing in which active
compassion, pity, and even consolation are predominant in the
treatment of the sick. This is true for the pages in *Voyage au
bout de la nuit* which deal with Bébert's illness and depict the
desperate and futile efforts of Bardamu to prevent the boy from
dying, and his access of despair when he fails (273–88). The
passages of the same novel dealing with Robinson's blindness as
the result of his attempt to murder the old "Henrouille woman,"
are less marked by compassion, but they nevertheless reflect
devoted medical attention and great tact. Bardamu appears
twice a day to care for Robinson, attempts to spare him the

realization of his blindness, and to console him when the full horror of his fate has dawned upon him (321–23). At Robinson's death (585–87), compassion turns to a feeling of regret, helplessness, anger at one's own emotional poverty. In *Mort à crédit* the death of Mme Bérenge evokes feelings of devotion and sadness (501). On another occasion, an ill, destitute, nearsighted child is cared for and amused by the games Ferdinand invents for her (503–504), in the absence of any other means of changing her situation.

One might imagine that Gustin, of the same novel, had once shown the same kind of devotion for his patients, but has become so disillusioned, "so knocked out by circumstances, by his work, by drink, and by submission" (512), that his practice has come to resemble a factory in which drugs and treatments are dispensed with the full knowledge of their futility. At his door, the dregs of society have come to flounder, decay and die, full of reproaches, and doomed to total hopelessness. The fate of Ferdinand's parents is not too different: at the end of the book, we find the long catalogue presented by his mother of all the diseases, both mental and physical, from which she and his father suffer. It is one of the most detailed inventories of its kind in Céline's writing (M., 968–72). The narrator's response is a mixture of pity, horror, and disgust, reinforced by the inability to alter any of the suffering.

The reaction to unalterable misery can only be of two kinds: passive acceptance or active rebellion. Gustin takes the first road, Céline seems to indicate another. For there is a strong current in the works, sometimes voiced, sometimes silent and almost subterranean. It is the need to *stop* suffering: either by knowledge (discoveries such as those of Semmelweiss, or successful medical treatment), drugs, or—in the face of no other remedy—mercy killing. Here again, pessimism prevails, for there are few incidents in which knowledge succeeds. The other alternatives become necessary more frequently. Drugs occupy an extremely important place. Apparently, this is not only the case for the writing but also manifests itself in the practice of "le docteur Destouches." One of his colleagues states: "If need be, I could cite the ritual, almost sacral use he [Destouches] made of morphine when it came to his medical patients." [25] In the novels, there is more evidence of the use of drugs in the late works. Most striking are the references in *D'un château l'autre*, where morphine is frequently employed to induce rest, relief from pain, and even reduction of mental anguish. The "2 cc's" of morphine has all these uses: "I stopped by to give them some dreams, those who were suffering too much . . . 2 cc's!" (*C.*, 263); "For the sake of my craft and the great comfort of the dying! morphine! . . . morphine!" (17) Its main function though is to relieve the terror and suffering of the dying, to act in a more humane fashion toward their agony: "I wouldn't make them die all over again! No! Just watch me! . . . Quite the contrary! . . . gentleness! . . . Tebaic tenderness (opium extract) . . . 2 cc's!" (110) For Céline, who, in his profession, has "heard the death-rattle everywhere," and knows "all the stops of the organ *de profondis*," (109) is acquainted with the torment, the hideousness of dying and is understandably concerned with alleviating pain when all else is to no avail. We should note that Céline puts fear at the top of the list of torments. This becomes quite clear in relation to Bessy, a favorite dog: "She suffered in dying. . . . I didn't want to give her a shot though . . . even a little morphine . . . she would have been afraid of the needle. . . . I had never frightened her before . . ." (128). Thus the measure becomes one of superior concern, of greater kindness; only this makes the withholding of the drug more humane than its use.

Sometimes, however, suffering can only be ended by bringing about death as quickly and painlessly as possible. Euthanasia is already alluded to in *Mort à crédit*. There it applies to animals: the pigeons of Courtial des Pereires who would otherwise have died of starvation and are killed in the most merciful possible way by Ferdinand (910–11), after carefully considering the means by which this should be done: "I thought it over. . . . I pondered about it, as if it had been me" (910). In the late novels, similar considerations apply to human beings. In *D'un château l'autre*, there are frequent references to "cyanide" (258–59, 279). The quick poison has become a precious object, much in demand among those who live in constant dread of a more hideous kind of death. The narrator is the keeper of this terrible treasure and dispenses it to those who urgently seek it.

Thus, the role of the doctor becomes that of a guardian

of life and death, having their secrets in his possession. In a
sense this is a parallel position to that of the writer who reveals
the laws of existence which his vision permits him to see. It does
not seem true that Céline is bent on denigrating life and only
vindicates and "justifies himself with *Semmelweiss* or with his
medical practice." [26] His reactions go beyond mere justification:
they indicate profound involvement, and the most complete
engagement Céline was capable of. "Through medicine," he
states, "I had come closer to human beings, to animals, to
everything" (V., 240). The author actually seems to advance a
form of humanism—often misunderstood and interpreted as
misanthropy—which depicts man, not at the height of his glory
but in the depth of his misery, as the central figure of the literary universe. The role of medicine becomes that of a tool of
exploration and participation, a means for entering the domain
of man's central functions, for communicating with him on the
deepest level of his humanity: his suffering.

The suffering may be physical or mental. It has been said of
Céline that "his poetic work is the medical report of a specialist in mental illness, concerning contemporary man." [27] Indeed
he appears frequently preoccupied with various diseases of the
mind: feeblemindedness, severe neurosis, insanity. Psychiatry
holds great interest for him, and he seems fairly well versed in
the subject.[28] There are also indications that he himself would
have chosen the field to work in, the most direct of which is
contained in one of his last interviews. He states: "I wanted to
become a psychiatrist. . . . The work would have pleased me.
. . . The world of the asylum forms a sort of insulating layer.
It's perfect. . . ." [29] The pronouncement is an intriguing one,
since it contains several important notions: Céline's medical
and academic interest in the mentally ill; the fascination which
the world of the insane holds for the artist: the protective,
"insulating layer" which the asylum can provide and its value
for the disillusioned individual.[30] In the first instance, exploration of human suffering and alleviation of mental anguish seem
paramount, as they have in other medical concerns of which we
have already spoken. Céline had already indicated this in *Semmelweiss*, where he speaks of "the moving, pitiless labyrinth of
insanity" (120). As a doctor, he has no illusions about the

fascination of the state, for he insists that "the human being ends where the madman begins. The animal is on a higher level," (129) and that "madness represents decay, or decadence" in absolute terms.

In V*oyage au bout de la nuit*, however, the attitude tends to change and Céline seems more preoccupied with the second and third aspects of the question mentioned above: although there are quite a few references to the sufferings which Bardamu undergoes during his attacks of madness, the tendency to emphasize the advantages, the attractions even, of insanity and to consider the asylum a protective universe removed from the vicissitudes of life to which the disillusioned, the "alienated," the "estranged," the lunatics of all sorts can retreat. Thus, as we have already mentioned, Bardamu cries out: "Long live the cowards and the madmen!" who alone shall, not inherit the earth but at least survive. Toward the end of that novel, the scene is laid in the asylum of Dr. Baryton where many of the "lunatics" and "cowards" have finally landed (405–49). It is a strange place, run by a doctor who will himself shortly go mad, inhabited by his feebleminded daughter Aimée, and supervised by Bardamu, his friend Parapine who is more than a little eccentric, and Robinson. The inmates suffer from various kinds of delusions, hallucinations, phobias. Their strange and shapeless world of insanity is both a danger and an attraction to Bardamu who muses frequently about it:

> I didn't capsize [go under], but all the time felt in danger, as if they were surreptitiously drawing me into the inner sections of their unknown city. A city whose streets become softer and softer as one advanced among their oozing houses, the melting windows that shut badly upon those dubious noises inside. . . . The doors, the ground that constantly shifted. . . . Still the desire overcomes one to go a little further to find out if one really has the strength to regain one's sanity nevertheless, among all those ruins. (V., 417)

The ambivalence of Bardamu's feelings, as a result of which he is both repelled and attracted by insanity, is quite interesting to us. It echoes the fluctuating movement from the "hard" to the "soft" pole which is often in evidence in the writings and seems to form a fairly consistent pattern in the author's thoughts. More important though, it reveals two other factors: the tendency to explore to the fullest the dangerous and horrible aspects of existence, as already witnessed in Bardamu's attitude toward the courtyard of "unrelieved hideousness," and the systematic exposure to such experiences which all of Céline's novels subject us to; the attraction to a universe in the state of decomposition—in this case, that of dementia—where all is "soft," "oozing," "melting." In a sense, the last is an illustration of Céline's interest, as noted by Richard, in the falling apart, the liquefication, the melting away of the individual. It is also linked to "the quest for delirium" which has been emphasized as one of the leading components of his work.[31] In more general terms, however, it is a part of that first-hand exploration of all man's lower depths, physical or mental. Madness, whether institutionalized or allowed to run free, whether confined to the asylum or rampant in that open-air madhouse, which can be the inner courtyard of a tenement in the *banlieue* of Paris or the medieval castles of Germany, is one of the ends of night which must be illuminated.

The novels are filled with explorations of this nature. From *Semmelweiss* to *Nord,* there stretches an almost endless line of "madmen," "nuts," "imbeciles," and other creatures who are suffering from dementia, from alienation of one sort or another. It is, however, more than the description or analysis of madness that interests Céline. His medical orientation becomes evident in the fact that he also discusses its treatment. In doing so, the author's humane feelings come to the surface, if one only knows how to unmask them and does not allow oneself to be misguided by surface brusqueness or bitter humor. If the various incidents describing the treatment of the insane are analyzed, one finds that they fall into two categories: those in which the sick are in the hands of calloused men of science or vicious laymen; and those in which kindness and consideration are predominant. Among the first, we find "le professeur Bestombes" of *Voyage au bout de la nuit* (89) who uses electric shock treatment, ruthlessly experiments with his human guinea pigs, welcomes any situation—including war—which will permit him to probe their minds (93), ignores their real problems, and attempts to inject patriotism into his shell-shocked victims crazed with fear (94). In *Mort à crédit* there are incidents in which equally vicious treatment of emotionally upset or deranged individuals is depicted. Ferdinand himself is very roughly handled after the furious outbursts against his father; more brutal punishment still is meted out to the mad "priest" (933–35); it seems quite certain that Courtial des Pereires would have met with the same fate had he not committed suicide. Similarly, in *D'un château l'autre*, the madman who believes himself to be "the Bishop of Albi," (202–204) is removed to the death-chamber by Aïcha (205). In many of these instances, it is as though the insane (outsiders for whom a selfish society has no use) are viciously removed, treated as debris to be kicked out of the way. It is quite obvious—sometimes through oblique references, at other times through direct statements—that Céline does not approve of such action. This becomes most evident in the case of the mad "priest" in *Mort à crédit*, where the narrator expresses obvious sympathy for this victim (933–35).

At other times, Céline's demand for sympathetic treatment does not take the form of denunciation but simply that of a description of kindly care. This is the case for Baryton's asylum, whose director is neither stupid nor severe and does not mistreat his patients. While not much is done to improve their state, they are at least allowed·to vegetate in comparative comfort. In *Mort à crédit*, the greatest kindness is shown to Jonkind, whom Nora Merrywin cares for with infinite patience (729). In *D'un château l'autre* an old musician, Delaunys, "a bit looney from having been hit on the head" (231), is handled with great caution and gentleness. In a sense, the medical attitude is evident here, for the narrator seems to prescribe what should be done in the care of the mentally disturbed: "The main thing, with people who are a little nuts is never to shock them . . . not animals either! . . . Never surprise them!"[32] (233) This rule is put into effect in all the dealings with the narrator's friend, La Vigue,[33] who figures prominently in *Nord*, and is consistently treated with great skill and concern (124, 255, 297, 311–14, 338).

It becomes quite apparent that for Céline there are two kinds of madness: that of victim and that of torturer. For the first, he has compassion; for the second, he reserves a good deal of his anger. Thus, it is only half true that the author feels that "man in his illness is essentially malevolent," [34] since he castigates solely those sick individuals who are also vicious, and spares the harmless or innocent, even if they are mad. Interestingly enough, Céline's concern for the ill, whether in mind or body, goes so far that at the end of his life when the almost total loss of faith in human beings has caused him to reject them and turn away from them, he nevertheless reserved the medical domain for his only point of contact with men. Thus he is able to state that he feels "a physical and mental horror for ALL HUMAN CONTACT, except for medical purposes." [35] With the probing attitude of both the doctor and the writer he had elsewhere said of man: "His body and his music alone interest me. . . ." [36] Even when "his music," that is, man's imagination or creativity, seems no longer to hold any promise, his body continues to be of concern.

Although Céline might bitterly joke about "le docteur Destouches," [37] he cannot deny his double. His entire life is concentrated on the sufferings of mankind, both through medicine and through literature, and he cannot undo his training in either domain. For Destouches was no doctor in spite of himself, just as Céline—if we disregard his protests to the contrary —was no galley slave of literature. Both are profoundly tied to the object of their quest: the exploration of man in all his illness.[38] Neither can deny his devotion. For just as the gruffest of physicians is bound to his patient, even this most violently accusing of writers betrays a deep concern for humanity.

THE UNHEROIC HERO

"A man . . . after all, is nothing more than decay held in abeyance . . ." (V., 416). This realization, in the wake of medical exploration, might seem primarily a statement of man's mortality and vulnerability, but it is actually one of the clearest formulations of Céline's inverted humanism. Diametrically opposed to the humanistic ideal which places man on an ever-ascending stairway leading to the perfection of all his attributes, Céline's view emphasizes the downward path, the escalator going to a basement of impotence, futility, absurdity, decomposition. Essentially, the first sees man in a heroic fashion, while the second follows in the footsteps of Bardamu, "the hero of anti-heroism." [39] According to the former, man is lucid, creative, meaningful, capable of joy, dignity, perfectibility. According to Céline, he flees lucidity, is destructive, meaningless, absurd, capable of endless misery, cowardice, prone to continual decay and corruptibility.

In the beginning of his literary career, Céline had shown some leanings toward a humanistic point of view. We have already referred to this aspect of *Semmelweiss*, although the work also points to the futility of such an approach. Serge Doubrowsky noted during a lecture delivered at the Alliance Française of New York in March 1962 the "possibility of humanism as an outcome of the revolt expressed in *Voyage au bout de la nuit*," but had to admit the failure of that conjecture. It is as though all attempts in this direction are either cut short or proven to be fruitless by the author. The individual who stretches out his arm to attain the fruits of compassion, understanding, meaningfulness or joy, finds that the limb either withers because of his own failings or is lopped off through the viciousness of others. Essentially, this is the fate of both Semmelweiss and Bardamu and the lesson is so harsh that no such gestures are attempted in the future. In the novels in which these two protagonists appear we note a very clear development: a reaching out, followed by defeat in one form or another, which leads to a drawing back, dissolution, or apathy. Soon, however, even these ventures are abandoned: Doubrowsky states that Bardamu, whose early strivings were "like bridges stretched across his solitude," found that they were in actuality bridges impossible to cross. Realizing this, "he pulls them up as one would a drawbridge and remains a prisoner." It is this state of man as a captive in his own existence that Céline will depict in all his novels. The world becomes a jail, a trap, a disgrace, a sewer, or worse still, a meaningless and rotting corpse. Its inhabitant will have all the attributes of the inmate of such a place.

Besides being *noirci* and sullied—a process which, if it assumes gigantic proportions, might result in a heroic image of an almost satanic nature—man is also shown to be part of the throng of miserable creatures who are "too much," or "not enough," phrases used to describe the dregs of humanity that throng to the door of Gustin (M.C., 518). Céline's belief in "total gratuitousness" [40] leads him to consider men in the guise of absurd and meaningless creatures. He had already asked in *Semmelweiss:* "Does one have the right to underestimate the formidable power of the absurd?" (48) His answer remains a definite "No." Not content with only recognizing the power of the absurd or the "futile," Céline makes this the predominant element of existence. Thus, men are seen as "trinkets in a showcase," [41] meaningless, quite useless objects of slight value. More explicitly, "man is too small, weak and futile to ever be anything more than a pretentious knick-knack whose usefulness is quickly outmoded." [42] This quality, joined to the belief that man, allowed to be "simply, profoundly himself, that is to say, foul, monstrous, absurd" (V., 407), will also reveal himself in all his uselessness, makes the denunciation well-nigh complete. He becomes at the same time the object of hate, fear, and pity. The last adds a further dimension to his character: it is a step away from the grandiose position of the romantic hero, and the down-to-earth analyses of the naturalists. Man is seen in a different perspective, neither on a pedestal nor in a coal pit, but wandering on the outskirts of existence: a furtive, stray creature. Thus, Bardamu is much less "the last of the great prophets" [43] than he is "the meanest of men." A universal *clochard,* this "man from nowhere" [44] has no destination, no nesting place; his aimless journeys lead him from one *banlieue* to the other, always as an outsider, "a man in a state of total ruin and confusion, in a world just as lost as he." [45]

The story of Céline's heroes is an epic without grandeur, devoid of glorious exploits, conquests, or rewards. We might describe it as an epic *à rebours:* a tale in which all the qualities of a true epic are not only satirized but actually reversed. Thus, the life of the protagonist, far from being *ein Heldenleben,* depicts "misery without embellishments, without any subtleties, or apparent grandeur." [46] His death is usually just as ignominious. The last fact is perhaps even more striking than the first. For none of Céline's characters dies a hero's death, surrounded by glory, mystery, or even dignity. Usually, it is a messy, horrible affair, full of ugliness, occurring in humiliating or frankly disgusting circumstances. From the disembowled colonel in *Voyage au bout de la nuit* to the double amputee of *Nord*—drowned in a cesspool (391)—they die as awfully as they lived. For not even this last dignity is allowed them, not even their final refuge remains shrouded in any decency. Céline insists that man is born, lives, and dies unheroically, procreates and earns his bread in shame and sorrow, wakes and sleeps in terror. He has no aim, no quest, no hope for even the shabbiest fleece. Worst of all, he does not even have a companion for his misery.

The utter loneliness of man is probably the worst of his maledictions. It is not the loneliness of the hero, the isolation of greatness, but the lowly separateness of the shunned creature. Not only is he not formed in the image of any god or placed on earth for any purpose, but he does not even belong to a community of human beings and is thus truly without collective or even individual significance. An exile on the very globe on which he lives, he suffers from all the degradations that this state implies. "Of all the vexations inherent in exile, probably the most depressing one is having to excuse oneself . . . One does nothing but ask everyone's pardon . . . you are *de trop*, a burden in every way, to everyone, everywhere" (*N.*, 183). This feeling of being superfluous, unwanted, of having to ask forgiveness for being alive, pervades the existence of many of Céline's protagonists. It makes them more than mere pariahs. It qualifies them for the rank of lepers, of untouchables. Moreover, even among these lowest of outcasts, there is no communion in misery or the comfort of shared suffering. The adage "Every man for himself, the earth for all," (*V.*, 289) contains the ominous warning that life is utter loneliness, and that the only companionship possible is to be covered by the same earth after death, the only communion to be devoured by the worm that feeds on all corpses alike.

In a sense, almost all Céline's work is the "interminable rumination of a recluse," [47] an exploration of the impossibility of man to relate to man, of his inability to bridge the silence, to overcome the terror of his fellows. This becomes most clear in the case of Bardamu who, unable to feel, incapable of crossing the gulf of loneliness, remains a prisoner within his own tower, walled in not by ivory but by a muddy substance which is the essence of stagnation and fear. Removal from one's fellow beings does not in the least lessen the fear: "Solitude is not in opposition to fear. Instead, it serves to magnify it." [48] Thus, neither a movement toward or away from others brings any relief. The world becomes a total trap: man is caught both within and without. Aloneness then is no longer rational but absolute.[49] The exploration of the continents without, just as that of the worlds within, results only in an ever more complete realization of solitude, its presence in all geographical and emotional climes. Neither love nor hate, crime nor kindness, birth nor death, seem to establish even the most fleeting communion among human beings.

No salvation is possible, yet the search continues. In an almost obsessive fashion, man persists in his futile quest. Had not Bardamu already, in that citadel of loneliness, the hotel ironically named the "Laugh Calvin," found the lack of human contact so unbearable that he made a declaration to a waitress in one of those antiseptic New York restaurants where even the food is untouched by human hands, only to find that a guard "pushes him outdoors, justifiedly, simply, without the slightest insult or brutality, into the night, like a dog who has forgotten himself" (V., 208)? Repeatedly, the early heroes of Céline, like Bardamu, attempt to find a niche, a point "where all the forces of this world which rend, claw and kill, are neutralized or annulled." It is this place that they seek "in vain in the New World and the old . . . in the world of the maternal woman and in the domain of childhood." All of them find however that "there is no refuge. . . . One is forever thrown back into the very center of the slaughter," [50] and into the heart of loneliness. Paradoxically, this loneliness is also an incurable sickness from which man refuses to recover. Bardamu had realized that "one ought to find out why one stubbornly refuses to be cured of one's loneliness," (V., 370) but was never able to give an answer. It is though, once having started out "in the direction of *inquiétude* (anxiety)," (V., 229) man cannot veer from this path indicated by human existence and sinks more and more deeply into the ruts of the road.

It is a circular path: *inquiétude*, which leads man to wander from place to place and prevents any but the most fleeting of attachments, is also at the root of his search for a niche, a crack in the edifice of solitude. Mothlike, he throws himself continually against various walls of existence, fails, begins anew, until he is too exhausted to move. While he is still able to summon the strength, he attempts other maneuvers. Thus Bardamu, whose "dramatic leaps from one continent to another degenerate into a series of petty moves," [51] learns that he cannot escape life—which essentially is a confrontation with total aloneness —but turns towards various *évasions* designed to shut out conscious existence: dreams (ready-made or created), the cinema, the brothel. These are often the last resort of those who cannot find contact with other human beings. When, at the end of the novel, he loses that fellow-wanderer (Robinson) who had at least been a shadowy other self, Bardamu's isolation becomes complete and all efforts are abandoned. While the nervous laughter and the persistent uneasiness of former days at least gave sound and movement to his life, Bardamu now stands still and silent. He has come to that point where the paths of Céline's heroes often end, that mute center of stagnation which is despair. For while disquiet persists, or anguish drives them on, all is not lost. It is only at that static end of night, where not a breath stirs, that hope is relinquished.

For Céline, "despair is not . . . entertainment, or pretext for *romanesque* variations, but a fact of nature, a state of mind, the constant temptation of misery and absurdity. It is man's principal companion, on whose behalf he spends his entire life interceding." [52] The last part of this description is striking: for if we pause to consider it, we realize that it fits *Robinson*, that enigmatic figure who accompanies Bardamu on all his journeys. Is it not he who is the protagonist's principal companion, for whom he intercedes during the course of his life? In other words, does Robinson not symbolize *despair*,[53] which precedes us continually in our voyage into the night? We might suggest that it is not Bardamu who is the "demon of despair," but Robinson. While it is true that the former "reflects a universal state of mind . . . a specifically modern uneasiness," [54] it is the latter who embodies this uneasiness, this despair; he is the demon who must be exorcised if man is to recover.

Recovery, however, seems impossible, for Céline's heroes

do not have the necessary health, stamina, and ability to be saved or to save themselves. Bardamu had already realized that he was "a lost man" (V., 371). The author's other protagonists share that fate. While "the humanists and even those who criticize them still believe in man, L.-F. Céline goes much further in his despair. He states that there is no possible salvation for mankind." [55] Thus, man being neither a savior nor capable of being saved, he would seem to lose all possibility of heroism. Strangely enough though, he arises out of the ashes of his own destruction, a mangy sort of phoenix whose mottled coat and shabby appearance serve to create a new kind of hero figure: that of "l'homme vagabond," the failure, the wanderer, the tramp. Maimed in body and spirit, vulnerable, fallen, déchu, he is the prototype of that grotesque, pathetic, absurd hero who dominates an entire sector of modern literature.[56]

"Céline has seen contemporary man for what he really is: a sleepwalker without dreams," one critic has remarked.[57] We might enlarge this statement to say that the author places man at the edge of the rooftops of existence, sleepwalking in a dreamless state, thus having neither the advantage of lucidity nor that of self-delusion. In similar fashion, while Céline states that he has experienced "the same dread as Pascal . . . the sensation of the abyss," (Y., 99) he has not followed through with the latter's leap of faith, and is condemned to the continual act of cliff-hanging. This is clearly shown to be the fate of Céline's heroes, with despair as its inevitable result—not despair of grandiose proportions, but a silent desperation not unlike catatonia or paralysis, a state in which all movement, all speech have ceased. (V., 203) It might, in the case of a more active response, also lead to self-destruction, that is, suicide. In both instances, consciousness that is too painful is annihilated. A passive, vegetative state is the only alternative to total nonexistence or destruction. The apathetic, silenced Bardamu, the retreating Ferdinand, the drugged survivors of the last novels, the fleeing aged narrator who ends his life in almost total reclusion: all these are the embodiment of the state of despair. Their gestures, their slow and painful motion resemble a "ballet without music, people, or anything at all," [58] in which the dancers pass in a trancelike rhythm. For if consolation is impossible, consciousness implies suffering. The victim must shut out sight, perform a kind of frontal lobotomy upon himself, if he is not to succumb to despair. Thus, there are only two ways possible when one has come to the end of night: a state resembling death, or death itself.

While life exists—and in most of Céline's novels the central characters are forced to live until the end of the book —man must perform an endless series of experiments whose outcome he knows in advance. He is forced to repeat the gestures of the quest knowing full well their futility: "To go and convince oneself once more that fate is insurmountable, that one has to end up at the bottom of the wall each night, weighed down by the anguish of the morrow which is progressively more precarious and sordid." (V., 199) Anything less than this unending repetition of torment, this Tartarus which constitutes life, is abdication: "To feel grief isn't all: one must be able to start the music all over again, to go and look for more grief . . . bear even more." (V., 489) Céline's reader must listen and endure.

It is as if the author demanded true heroism from his audience rather than from his characters: the courage to contemplate the downfall of man, the destruction of his own treasured image, to bear the attack on his highest aspirations, on his frequently glorified attributes. While the protagonists of the novels are allowed to choose detachment, *évasion*, apathy, paralysis—the reader is not. He is trapped, snared by the work of art, fastened to his terrible reflection in the mirror, with eyes pried open. Actually, his is the most horrible fate. Céline's attack is directed primarily against him.[59]

Art then becomes both a cruel weapon and a profound affirmation of man. Even Bardamu, in his groping way, seemed to sense this, for did he not say that he had long searched for "an idea even bigger than [his] big head, bigger than the fear which was inside it, a beautiful idea." (V., 489) But while Bardamu has only found puny concepts which resemble "little candles that aren't proud at all, that flicker and tremble all one's life, in the midst of this awful world," (489) Robinson— probably the only truly "heroic" figure in all the novels of Céline [60]—has found "only a single idea, but that one such a splendid one, that it was altogether stronger than death" (V., 489). Only after having undertaken all the journeys without flinching before any revelation, any experience life has to offer, has he been allowed to acquiesce to his own death, to pronounce a modern version of the "so be it!" (the phrase "Fais comme tu veux!" [V., 484]) which will end suffering. In dying, he achieves a kind of calm, an almost mythical dimension. He becomes the guide for those who must survive: "It was as though he were trying to help *us* live now . . . he took us by the hand." Having gone out of life, "in one leap, as if he had taken off," the great adventurer seems to point the way for others, his outstretched arms beckoning them to continue (V., 487). It is as though Céline wished to say that only after having gone as far as Robinson does anyone earn the silence, the forgetfulness which are the sole rewards of death. Until then, the only heroism possible is to learn to see in the dark, to walk open-eyed even in one's own night.

"COINS DE TENDRESSE"

"Tenderness creates a lump in one's throat, not easy to swallow," Céline once stated.[61] At times, however, such an action becomes possible and we are allowed to peer into a world of warmth, sensitivity, subtlety, tenderness. Much has been said about the author's hard exterior shell developed to hide a vulnerable center, his defensive "bristling" to protect him from danger.[62] This view implies that there are two Célines: one who faces the outer world, armed and warriorlike, the other a gentle, poetic creature who withdraws and only rarely shows his face. Would it not be closer to the truth to consider him a many-sided artist, capable of the entire register of feelings, but who must concentrate mainly upon one end of the literary scale? In a society where sentiments so easily degenerate into sentimentality, expressing the first might risk connotations of the second. In this sense, Céline is a purist, preferring gruffness or brutality to anything resembling a cheap display of emotion, silence to overly effusive outpourings. He is not unlike Ferdinand's uncle Edouard in *Mort à crédit*: "He never spoke about feelings . . . that's what I respected about him" (812); "he understood all delicate matters perfectly . . .

he just didn't speak about them, that's all" (814). Céline *does* sometimes speak of what is delicate, or filled with emotion; when this happens, the incident or single phrase has the startling brilliance of a luminous stone against black cloth, a piercing point of light in otherwise total darkness. Their very rarity, their intensely lyrical quality, make these passages both striking and deeply moving.

In general, they seem like a momentary pause in the violent storm of invectives, a brief respite in the description of the vicious battle of existence. It is as though Céline, while unleashing the black *déluge* of his writing, set afloat a small ark of human beings and animals whom he will spare. In most cases, its inhabitants are the victims, the pitiful bystanders in the struggle of living. "Céline's wrath spares only the true innocents, the feeble who are destined for sacrifice: the children, the sick, and the invalids," [63] and, we might add, animals and prisoners (Céline's book, *Féerie pour une autre fois. I*, even bears the dedication: "Aux animaux, aux malades, aux prisonniers"). They are a small group, carefully chosen from the multitude of characters that throng his works. Among them we find: Alcide, Molly, and Bébert in *Voyage au bout de la nuit*; Nora, l'oncle Edouard, and Violette in *Mort à crédit*; Lili, Mme Bonnard, Papillon, and Clotilde in *D'un château l'autre*; Lili and La Vigue in *Nord*; Virginia in *Pont de Londres*; plus a host of animals (the horses, dogs, cats, birds, and other small creatures included among the dramatis personae of his books).

If we look at the human beings who evoke tenderness in Céline's writings, we find that they all have one thing in common: the ability to feel kindness or pity for others, or the need to be themselves pitied. Some have great sublety or finesse, a quiet beauty which amounts almost to an enchantment. This is especially true for the women: Nora, Lili, Mme Bonnard. Age does not seem to affect this quality, for Lili is less than twenty and Mme Bonnard ninety-six. While it is at times linked to eroticism, it does not necessarily depend on it, for "the famous female mystery doesn't reside between the thighs," Céline assures us, in speaking of Mme Bonnard, "it's on another wave-length, a much more subtle one" (*C.*, 218).

Even Nora, whom Ferdinand desires with all his youthful ardor, owes her enchantment not only to bodily beauty but also to that of feeling: "She always seemed happy, patient, untiring with the kids and the imbecile . . . they weren't always funny . . ." (*M.C.*, 729). The same is true for Virginia of *Pont de Londres*, the patient, youthful, "fairytale creature." Lili (also called Arlette, or Lucette), who continually appears in the last works, is the embodiment of charm, gentleness, patience, kindness, gaiety, courage. It is significant that it is also she who becomes the keeper of animals, their protectress, a trait which had also characterized Virginia (*P.L.*, 29–31).

Of all the women in his books though, it is Molly of *Voyage au bout de la nuit* who is the incarnation of warmth and tenderness. On the surface, her story might resemble that old, sentimental fiction of "the good whore." Actually, it has much deeper significance. Molly symbolizes many things: the triumph of a human being over an inhuman environment; [64] the sheltering spirit of the brothel where even the outcast is received without brutality (*V.*, 227). Above all, she inspires trust and is capable of genuine feeling. Bardamu is quick to sense this and to respond: "I soon experienced . . . an exceptional feeling of trust which, for frightened creatures, takes the place of love." (*V.*, 227) There are other overtones in the figure of Molly, more mythical in nature,[65] but in strictly human terms, she remains one of the foremost figures in Céline's works who elicits great affection and deep feeling. She herself is capable of these, for she shows selfless concern and true devotion. All her emotions are "truer, more real than in the rest of us" (235). As a result, she evokes geniune responses in Bardamu (236) and is able to pass the ability to feel on to him, a gift which will alter his whole life and persist long after her disappearance. Bardamu can say: "I am certain that I will never be quite as cold, evil or heavy as the others, so much kindness and dreams did Molly make me a gift of during those few months . . ." (236). Years later still, the memory has not been effaced. The image of Molly returns in all its simple beauty of feeling: "After all, when one's egotism slackens a little, when the time to end things has come, all one keeps as memories in one's heart are of women who really loved men a little, not just one man even if that one was you, but all of them . . ." (384).[66]

It is interesting that several of the women who show warmth or kindness to Céline's protagonists are prostitutes. Among them we find Molly, of course, as well as Violette of *Mort à crédit*, whose farewell scene with Ferdinand (967), although only a feeble echo of the one in which Molly figured, nevertheless has tinges of genuine feeling and significance. There is also Geneviève whom Ferdinand meets on his arrival in England and who shares many of the good qualities of the other two women: generosity, concern, understanding (*M.C.*, 696, 699–704). The fact that they are all prostitutes may or may not be very significant to their sympathetic portrayal, for there are as many women in more regularized circumstances who are described in this fashion: Nora, Lili, Mme Bonnard. One might venture the guess that Céline, having in his youth frequented the fascinating if shady milieu of London pimps and prostitutes [67] which he will describe in *Guignol's Band* and *Pont de Londres*, felt that women of such calling were interesting literary figures. But this attitude alone does not seem sufficient explanation.

It is also possible that, since Céline's heroes are essentially individuals who exist on the fringe of society, on the borders of existence, they would necessarily turn to women who are in a similar situation. More important, though, seems the consideration that the former are wanderers, creatures who do not make any permanently meaningful attachments, who live fundamentally on the basis of "mort à crédit." Would not love also tend to be obtained on the installment plan—a fragment of warmth, a brief moment of pleasure which must end swiftly, for fear that it might be corrupted or corrupt? There is one final factor, however, which is probably of greater significance than any of the others: the refusal of the object of his quest, which is characteristic of Céline's hero. This attitude is most apparent in the case of Molly, but it tinges the relations with other women of her calling. It is as though Bardamu or Ferdinand were possessed with a malady which causes them to reject their prize; as though, unlike Jason, they must throw away the Fleece and return forever empty-handed. The picture is consistent with the portrait Céline wishes to create: of the individual dispossessed, meaningless, disenchanted—an unheroic hero.

Yet, one of his characters can say: "I can't let anything go, neither a memory, nor a person," [68] and contradict the idea of any total detachment, just as he has ruled out the possibility of total attachment. In a paradoxical fashion, Céline emphasizes the rarity or impossibility of a certain experience, makes it the object of his hero's quest, only to have him abandon it almost instantly. It is as though both the unattainable and the attainable were equally untenable,[69] as though the hero had to remain suspended between them, in that difficult balance resembling the pose of tightrope walker which is the only movement possible in an existence in which safety nets have been ruled out.

The search continues although "people who have a heart . . . [are] infinitely rare!" (N., 166) Bardamu had already expressed his regret at such a lack, and thus shown—in a negative fashion—what is of value in others. He sadly recognizes that "he missed the quality which would make a man infinitely greater than his meager existence, the love for the life of those around him" (V., 486). The statement echoes the description of Molly (cited earlier) as one of those beings "who really loved men a little." It is this quality, more than any other, which characterizes all those who people the "coins de tendresse" (the recesses of tenderness) in Céline's novels. It does not matter that they appear only for an instant, or that their gifts are but briefly accepted. The "Love for the Life of those around them," creates a precious, if rare radiance which extends from *Semmelweiss* to *Nord*. Some of its keepers are minor figures: Alcide, slaving in the jungle to offer his crippled niece "the gift of years of torment, the annihilation of his poor life in this torrid monotony, without making conditions and without bargaining, uncalculating" (V., 159); Edouard, who appears like some male fairy godmother at every point of stress in *Mort à crédit* to save Ferdinand (770, 810, 814, 1082), who "asked nothing better than to give someone pleasure," (566) and does so, with great tact and no histrionics. Even Papillon—whose love affair with Clotilde is half pathetic and half grotesque—is capable of de-

votion and self-sacrifice (*C.*, 189–90, 194–205), qualities all
the more striking because they remain alive in a world where
almost all such feelings have disappeared, and only indifference,
cruelty, madness, and destruction reign.

The narrator himself is capable of such feelings and actions. Most often they are directed toward children or animals,
rather than adults. We have already mentioned that the basis
for such feelings is the harmlessness and comparative innocence
of these beings, but there is another cause as well. It becomes
apparent in a remark concerning Bébert, the young boy dying
of typhoid in *Voyage au bout de la nuit.* Bardamu notes that
on the child's livid face "danced that endless little smile of
pure affection which I could never forget . . . enough gaiety
for the whole universe" (242) which characterizes children and
animals. We note a similar gaiety in the young girl of *Pont
de Londres:* "She laughs! . . . She laughs! . . . Her laughter
rings! . . . A spring of live happiness! . . . leaps from her
laughter . . . fuses, cascades in the air all about! . . ." (84).
All these beings create joy and provide an affirmation of life
as well as consolation in hardship. In *Nord,* even though the
world is about to crumble, a robin redbreast has this power:
"During very difficult times . . . the best thing to do is to
think kindly of these really lovable small creatures" (269). In
the same manner, the thought of Molly, another "really lovable
being" has the power of consolation (325), as does the gentle
echo of her voice which seems to issue from the blues record,
"No More Worries," whose melody winds through the latter
part of *Voyage au bout de la nuit* (263 *et al.*).

The greatest tenderness however, is reserved for sick children and hurt animals. Incidents concerning them form a long
chain of compassionate fragments which spot the otherwise
harsh scene of the novels. They include those of *Voyage,* where
Bardamu invents a toy for a sick, nearsighted girl, commiserates
with Baryton's daughter Aimée who has been abandoned by
her father, and affectionately cares for Bébert; Ferdinand of
Mort à crédit sympathizes with "little André," with the idiot
Jonkind, and even shows regret at the departure of those wild
ruffians who swarm over Courtial des Pereires farm; in *D'un
château l'autre,* the narrator is in charge of a camp for sick

children and makes great efforts to save the lives of these unfortunates (120). If the attitude toward children is striking, the feeling for animals is almost startling. Bardamu had made the pronouncement: "I'd more easily feel grief for a dog in the process of dying than for Robinson, because a dog isn't malicious." (V., 486) One might connect this statement to another one in the same book: "I had a much greater desire to keep Bébert from dying than an adult. One is never too unhappy when an adult dies, it always means at least one less louse in the world." (279) It is, however, not only the preference for animals or children because they are less "malicious" or "lousy" which prompts such comments. It is also the recognition that they are more endearing, pitiful, worthy of compassion, capable of greater sincerity.

The last quality becomes especially pronounced at that ultimate moment which each creature has to face: his death agony. If we contrast the death scene of Robinson—who is already far above many of the other characters in terms of authenticity—with that of a hunting dog in *D'un château l'autre*, we find the man sadly lacking. In the first case, "the comedy of suffering tries to cross over from life into death itself" (487). In the second, the narrator states: "Oh, I've seen quite a few death-struggles . . . here . . . there . . . everwhere . . . but none by far as beautiful, discreet, faithful . . . the thing which lowers the agony of human beings is the song-and-dance. . . . Man is always on stage, no matter what . . . even the simplest" (129). At the same time, because of their artlessness and authenticity, the death throes of animals or of children are the most upsetting and painful to witness (C., 109).

The torment of animals evokes some of the most poignant responses in the works of Céline. From the wounded horses in *Voyage* whose festering sores make them bow in pain as the rider mounts (28), and the dreadfully tormented hog who provides amusement for his human audience by the futility of his terror (286–87), to the Rittmeister's dog, Iago, in *Nord*, whose death by purposeful starvation follows its course throughout the book (132, 214, 308, 309), animals are the victims of human indifference or willful cruelty. Their plight is frequently depicted with more intense compassion than that of their human counterparts. At other times, however, we note an almost parallel course between the sufferings of animals and men. Thus, in *Voyage* the torture of the hog occurs in passages inserted between accounts of Bébert's losing battle with death; the wounded horses share the fate of their masters in the war; the limping dog, too frightened to be saved, arrives on the scene after the description of the sick daughter of drunken parents; in *Mort à crédit* Mme Bérenge's squinting old mongrel will be taken to the pound after she is buried.

The most important animal companion—and one of the few truly heroic creatures in Céline's work—is of course Bébert the cat, who figures prominently in the last novels. He shares the plight of Ferdine, Lili, and La Vigue during their wanderings through a Germany in flames, uncomplaining, faithful, courageous in the face of deprivation and destruction.[70] It might be worth noting that the name Bébert which the cat now bears, had once belonged to the child in *Voyage au bout de la nuit* for whom Bardamu showed such concern. It is not conclusive evidence, but certainly a possible indication of the fact that the affection for an innocent creature has been transferred from a human being to an animal. Or that, like Lili in *Nord*, the author has become immune to the sufferings of men and has relegated his feelings to animals, whose misery generally passes unnoticed (*N.*, 328–29). It is also possible that in the face of the enormity of the struggle, and the grotesque, almost unreal nature of world conflict, the torments of men are beyond the reach of feeling or the bounds of tenderness. Only a few simple creatures can still evoke or profit from such emotions, for it is they who are the only vestiges of a less insane or chaotic existence.

The "coins de tendresse" grow smaller and further removed from the human realm as the work of the author progresses. Is it only a case of increasing misanthropy, or also the result of a growing tendency to conceal valuable experiences from harm, to shield them from the dangers of exposure? Any fragile, delicate feeling, whether in a person or a work of art, is both difficult to capture and easily soiled or destroyed. "[It's] a kind of subterranean music. . . . Oh, one which can't be captured . . . just like that!" (*C.*, 218) "It's not that easy

. . . it's as fragile as butterflies. At the slightest touch, it falls apart, sullies you . . ." (M.C., 513). In other words, experiences characterized by delicacy, elusiveness, tenderness, belong and must remain in a subterranean realm. The writer who is so concerned with "blackening" will not risk defacement or vandalism in those few areas which shed an inward light.

THE CULT OF PERFECT FORMS

"Her body was a joy without end to me," says Bardamu, lauding those "fundamental revelations of a biological nature," which Lola was able to offer him when, worn out by the terrors and fatigue of battle experience, he faced the fate of a "murder-victim on momentary reprieve" (V., 54–55). The quest of other bodies "just as audacious in their grace" seems suddenly imperative. He decides to embark on a pilgrimage to the country which produces such wonders. The cult of feminine beauty and perfect forms has begun. In it, we find a side of Céline's vision which portrays the human being—or at least the female of a certain body type—in all its splendor, celebrates its joy, beauty, and perfection. Throughout all the novels, its presence will provide a positive image to pit against that of ugliness, misery, imperfection. The otherwise unrelieved picture of deformity in mind and body is thus balanced in some measure, and hideousness need then not be considered absolute.

Céline is as implacable in his standards of form as he is about everything else. Nothing short of perfection is admissible. Paradoxically, the earthly paradise of female beauty is located in a country which he has otherwise treated in sardonic and devastating terms: America. Bardamu, upon his arrival there, is overwhelmed by "a sudden avalanche of absolutely beautiful women. . . . [A] supernatural aesthetic revelation. . . ." The vision is so extraordinary in its grace, harmony and perfection, that the hero asks, as if dazed: "Could it be ancient Greece . . . resurrected?" (V., 193) The women, generally as unattainable as even the most reticent of Greek goddesses, constitute "a long, palpable temptation," (196) and pass into the realm of erotic meditation. There are, however, more accessible creatures of their sex available: the women of the Detroit brothel whom Molly exceeds in physical perfection.

As is often the case in his writings, Céline concentrates mainly on the beauty of Molly's legs, "her long blond legs, magnificently slim, supple, and muscular, noble legs"; for, he insists, "true human aristocracy, despite everything that's said, is unquestionably conferred by the legs." (V., 228–29) The same kind of royalty is attributed to Madelon, who also has "firm and supple legs," well-shaped feet and ankles, "to add to her other perfections" (378). Sophie, in the same novel, possesses a related treasure, beauty of movement expressed in her "winged walk, so supple and precise," (463) just as Nora of *Mort à crédit* who in turn "emanated total harmony, whose every movement was exquisite," (729) or Virginia in *Pont de Londres,* "the most graceful one . . . Ah! what a delicate walk! . . . Ah! what a gentle majesty!" (86)

The exploration—both physical and aesthetic—of perfect female forms becomes as important and absorbing as any ritual. Bardamu had already said of Sophie: "I couldn't stop admiring her. I proceeded muscle by muscle, in anatomical groupings." (V., 462) He had studied the effects of lantern light on Madelon's body with equally rapt attention, noting "the sculptured reliefs which move the length of the leg" (379). Something aside from pure eroticism is involved here: for we witness the search for palpable beauty, for a glimpse of "the era of living joy, of great undeniable harmonies, physiological ones" (V., 462). At the same time, it is a celebration of the human body in its most admirable state: that of health, physical well-being, youth, and joyful optimism. Among those who incarnate these virtues, we find Molly, Lola, Sophie. All of them have the youth, vigor, grace, and "light-heartedness" which Céline demands from his women. Each one is a creature in a class with Sophie, "whose flesh, supple and tender carriage, divine health, seemed to us, I must admit, irresistible." (V., 462)

The narrator of *Mort à crédit* had already admitted that he was "living on [his] aesthetic capital." (508) Céline himself is prone to the same penchant, for he writes: "I love the physical perfections of women almost to the point of madness. It's a truth I reveal to you. It governs all the others." [71] At a much later date, he will once again state: "I'm choosy and *raffiné,* alas! I'm willing to admit it! I have the tastes of a grand-duke,

an Emir, of one who raises thoroughbreds . . . all right . . .
we all have our little weaknesses." (C., 173) Of course, the
involvement with perfection of forms is more than "a weakness." It is also a cult which has the strength of an addiction:
"Compared to this vice of perfect forms, cocaine is nothing
but a hobby for station-masters . . ." (V., 462). More than
anything else, it is the affirmation of aesthetic purity, refinement
of movement, bodily grace.

All these qualities are achieved in the figure which is a
dominant theme in Céline's writing: *la danseuse*.[72] In V*oyage
au bout de la nuit*, she is only indirectly present: in the dedication to Elizabeth Craig and the references to the muscular
perfection and aristocracy of women's legs, which indicate descriptions of dancers. While Nora (*M.C.*) and Virginia (*P.L.*)
also have the attributes which would qualify them for a role
in Céline's ballet of women, there is no actual reference to the
dance as an art in these novels. In *L'Eglise*, however, we find
several dancers, and among them one named Elizabeth Gaige
(a thin disguise for Craig). The many dancers of the "ballets"
Céline composed, culminate in Lili or Arlette of the last novels.
She incarnates perfection of the art of the dance, physical
beauty, harmony, youth, as well as bravery, joyfulness, love of
adventure, of danger.[73]

Céline makes a very revealing remark in one of his novels
when he states: "I love the physiology of human beings . . .
their pathology makes me sad . . ." (*F. II*, 154). It is a paradoxical phrase, coming from an author who is so bent on describing pathology, but also one which sheds light on his delight
in the beauty of man's physical being. The perfection it implies
cuts through that which is problematic, failing, moth-eaten,
bent, and ugly. Especially when centered in a woman's body,
physical beauty becomes a life force close to the simple and
true domain of the emotions which interest Céline. This realm
is both delightful and troubling to those whose lives have dried
up, whose instincts have lost their strength. Thus, the band of
disillusioned men living in Baryton's asylum are enchanted by
Sophie "so much more beautiful and so much less conscious"
than they, full of "that strength which is at the same time
lively, precise and gentle," so different from their own tired and

harsh reactions. Sophie herself, who drifts like some Greek goddess among these all-too-mortal creatures, has "the walk of those great beings of the future whom life carries ambitious, lightly toward ever new kinds of adventures." (V., 463) One of the loveliest descriptions in all of Céline's writing is the one of her awakening: drowsy and still somewhat heavy with sleep, "she was funny and ridiculous like everyone else. She staggered from happiness for another few minutes, and then all the light of day flowed back over her as after the passage of a very heavy cloud, and she took her flight once more, glorious, delivered. . . ." This is the moment in which the sublime arises from the ridiculous, that instant "when matter turns into life." (464)

If anywhere in Céline's work there is a glimpse of hope and beauty, of sun and joy, it is in the sight of such women. In a world falling to ruin, where pathology seems rampant, only the physical perfection of a woman, an animal, a gesture, can offer affirmation or a momentary respite from horror. In the midst of the holocaust, during the flight from Sodom and Gomorrah, only the backward look has any power; the look toward a small eden of perfect forms in which health, laughter and freedom reign. Even in this most appalling vision of man and of the universe, there is a chink from which the light breaks into the darkness: the haunting odor of the sea which penetrates the foul smelling dungeon, the memory of a state of fragile perfection in a time when "all of youth reaches the glorious beach, at the edge of the waters, there where women seem finally free and are so beautiful that they no longer even need the lie of our dreams . . ." (V., 370).

Notes

1 The principal collection of these, *Ballets sans musique, sans personne, sans rien* (Paris: Gallimard, 1959), contains four works in a light, fantastical, often satirical vein.

2 Two of these songs were recorded by Paul Chambrillon, during a spontaneous performance by the author. They are obtainable on "Pacific" L.D.P.-F199 (Paris).

3 The definition of humanism as it applies to discussions in this book is based on the concepts contained in the Latin statement, "Nothing concerning man do I deem alien to myself," or Michelet's definition of

"the discovery of man by man." It is also the affirmation of man's powers, abilities, potentialities, and the belief that he is capable of self-fulfillment.

4 We must note that Semmelweiss is the first of Céline's victim figures in an evolution which proceeds from martyr to scapegoat. This phenomenon will be discussed in greater detail in Chapter IV of this study.

5 Nicole Debrie-Panel, *Céline* (Lyon: E. Vitte, 1961), p. 27.

6 Pierre-Henri Simon, "L'Aurore est au bout de la nuit," *L'Herne*, No. 3, 292.

7 Mondor, "Avant-propos. . . ," Pléiade edition of Céline, p. ix.

8 *Ibid.*, p. XV.

9 Yvan Audouard, "Que dites-vous de Céline," *Le Nouveau Candide* (6–13 Juillet, 1961), 16. It must also be noted that other, more direct echoes of *Semmelweiss* are to be found in *D'un château l'autre* (p. 300, etc.) in connection with obstetrics. Céline himself reportedly dreaded "accouchements," unable to remain unmoved by the pain of childbirth. (Information obtained in my interview with Jeanne Carayon.) This fact throws some light on the author's interest in Semmelweiss, whose work on puerperal fever diminished the horrors of childbirth. It also adds insights concerning the author's attitude in the incidents connected with childbearing in *Voyage au bout de la nuit* (pp. 258–62; 296–300) which on the surface resembles indifference or callousness in the face of misery. Is it not more likely that the feeling conveyed is mainly one of unspoken or inverted compassion? Similar feelings of concern are shown in *D'un château l'autre* (pp. 300, 301, 303).

10 Germaine Brée and Margaret Guiton, *An Age of Fiction* (New Brunswick, N.J.: Rutgers University Press, 1957), p. 166.

11 Slochower, *No Voice Is Wholly Lost. Writers and Thinkers in War and Peace* (London: D. Dobson, 1946), p. 93.

12 Céline will state: "We're all dedicated to boredom. Our life is nothing but a sort of death without *élan*." (Pollet, August 1933, *L'Herne*, No. 3, 100).

13 Walter Orlando, "Grandeurs et Misères de Bardamu," *La Table Ronde*, No. 57 (1952), 173.

14 *Ibid.*, p. 174.

15 *Idem.*

16 Pol Vandromme, *Céline* (Paris: Editions Universitaires, 1963) p. 34.

17 Jean-Paul Sartre, *Réfléxions sur la question juive* (Paris: Paul Norihieu, 1947), p. 68.

18 Orlando, *op. cit.*, p. 174

19 Poulet, *La Lanterne magique* (Paris: Nouvelles Editions Debresse), p. 27.

20 A similar emphasis on direct experience also enters into Céline's notions on style. We have already cited his insistence that, in order to write well, "you have to plunge in, with your nerves all raw (exposed) . . ." Many of his other comments indicate that he demands a similar involvement on the part of his reader and works at achieving this by means of his particular stylistic devices (see Chapter I, "Se Noircir," of this study for a more detailed analysis).

21 The relationship between Céline and Samuel Beckett, previously mentioned, becomes strikingly precise in this instance. An almost parallel utterance to that of Céline appears in Beckett's *The Unnamable* (New

York: Grove Press, 1958), and constitutes an equally fundamental statement for both writers: "Perhaps I've said the thing that had to be said that gives me the right to be done with speech" (p. 149).

22 Although he often retracts such a view, and accuses men of wishing continually to drug themselves, to lie, to deceive, to hide, to run, in order to escape the truth. (See especially: Marc Hanrez, "Céline au magnétophone," *Le Nouveau Candide* (November 23, 1961), 14.

23 The reference is to Jules Romains' well-known play, *Knock*, in which the hero is a charlatan who plays on the fear and gullibility of human beings for his personal gain.

24 André Suarès, "A Propos de Céline." *La Nouvelle Revue Française* IX, No. 104, 328.

25 Christian Dedet, "La condition médicale de Louis-Ferdinand Céline," *L'Herne*, No. 3, 313.

26 Slochower, *op. cit.*, p. 93.

27 Karl Epting, *Frankreich im Widerspruch* (Hamburg: Hanseatische Verlagsanstalt, 1943), p. 53.

28 In a letter to E. Pollet, dated July 1933 (*L'Herne*, No. 3, 99), Céline criticizes Dr. Allendy, and lauds Freud for the perspicacity of his works.

29 Claude Bonnefoy, "Dernier adieu à sa jeunesse," *Arts*, No. 833 (August 3–9, 1961), 5.

30 We again note a *rapprochement* with the work of Beckett, who frequently alludes to the protective nature of the asylum, its function of isolating one from life. One of his protagonists, Murphy, in the novel by the same name, spends a large part of his life as an attendant in an asylum, as does Bardamu in *Voyage au bout de la nuit*.

31 In an outstanding study by Michel Beaujour, "La quête du délire," *L'Herne*, No. 3, 279–88.

32 It is interesting that Céline makes a connection between the sick man and the animal, who are both members of the victim group for whom Céline expresses sympathy. See the section entitled "Coins de tendresse" for further discussion.

33 In actuality, Le Vigan, the famous French actor who starred in *Goupil Mains Rouges* and was a close friend of Céline.

34 W. M. Frohock, "Céline's Quest for Love," *Accent*, II, No. 2, p. 83.

35 Letter to Albert Paraz, July 1951 (*L'Herne*, No. 3, 151).

36 Letter to Dr. Camus (not to be confused with Albert Camus, the writer), September 21, 1948, *Ecrits de Paris*, XCIII (October, 1961), p. 108.

37 In *D'un château l'autre*, for example, Céline informs us that his patients mock him for being poor, for having no car or servants (p. 15), and that they actually consider him to be "lower than Bovary" (p. 62). Had he not already called "Medicine, that shit" (*M.C.*, p. 501)?

38 It has been said that all Céline's works are "the books of a doctor," which describe "the inescapable suffering of living; they thrive on it, as doctors do on the dying, and at the same time jeer at it. . ." (Suarès, *op. cit.*, p. 328).

39 César Magrini, "Céline et Lautréamont," *L'Herne*, No. 3, 300.

40 Magrini, *op. cit.*, p. 298.

41 Letter to Dr. Camus, June 29, 1949, *Ecrits de Paris*, 109.

42 Letter to E. Bendz, *L'Herne*, No. 3, 128. It has been noted by

quite a few critics (see for example, Brodin, p. 193) that Céline's explorations of man's futility and absurdity occurred some time before that of the Existentialists.

43 Robert Brasillach, "Céline prophète," *Les quatre jeudis, Images d'avant guerre* (Paris: Editions Balzac, 1944), p. 235.

44 Vandromme, *op. cit.*, p. 41.

45 Marcel Arland, *Essais et nouveaux essais critiques* (Paris: Gallimard, 1952), p. 229.

46 *Ibid.*, p. 229.

47 Vandromme, *op. cit.*, p. 16.

48 Letter to Eugène Dabit (n.d.), *L'Herne*, No. 3, 87.

49 Slochower, *op. cit.*, p. 89.

50 Nadeau, *Littérature* . . . , p. 157.

51 Brée and Guiton, *op. cit.*, p. 166

52 Vandromme, *op cit.*, p. 29

53 Rather than evil as has been suggested by one critic (Slochower, *op. cit.*, p. 91), or loneliness, since his name is reminiscent of Robinson Crusoe, that other traveler "who experiences . . . what total solitude means in this world." (Milton Hindus, "Dire, redire . . ," p. 245.)

54 Robert Poulet, "Ou l'on retrouve Bardamu," *La Meuse* (28 September, 1933), n.p.

55 Brodin, *op. cit.*, p. 193

56 The forebears of such a hero exist among the characters of writers like Flaubert, Laforgue, etc. and find their contemporaries in some of the figures portrayed by Charlie Chaplin, or those that appear in works of Cocteau, E. M. Forster, Beckett, Ionesco, Adamov, the young Camus, Robbe-Grillet, and others.

57 Pol Vandromme, "L'Esprit des pamphlets," *L'Herne*, No. 3, 276.

58 Paradoxically, this desolate phrase is (it will be remembered) the title of the delightful collection of tales mentioned earlier in this study.

59 Interesting comparisons might here be drawn with the "theater of cruelty" of Antonin Artaud and with certain concepts of Jean Genet which emphasize the attack on the spectator by means of the work of art.

60 For he is a symbol of lucidity, refusing to be blind but stretching his arms into the darkness as far as he can reach, "as if to touch the very bottom" (*V.*, 323). The same gesture is repeated when he has fulfilled his quest and has died, this time to point the way for others. His journey duplicates that of the traditional mythical hero who goes forth into night, away from men, only to return among them to impart his message. (See *V.*, 323–24; 335–36 for detailed examples, and the pattern of the entire novel for the larger structure of the hero-voyage).

61 Brissaud, *op. cit.*, p. 230.

62 Debrie-Panel, Poulet, Stromberg, *et al.*

63 Vandromme, "L'esprit . . . ," p. 273.

64 Note Henry Miller's comment in *Sunday after the War* (Norfolk, Conn., New Directions, 1944): "The beautiful and surprising thing about Céline's chapter on Detroit is that he makes the body of a whore triumph over the soul of the machine." (pp. 23–24)

65 These will be discussed in the section of this study dealing with "l'érotico-mysticism" of Céline (Chap. V).

66 Céline here plays on the role of the prostitute which causes Molly

to "love" all men, but the implication is much bigger, having to do with a love of humanity which goes beyond the physical realm alone.

67 See the interesting article of Georges Geoffroy, "Céline en Angleterre," *L'Herne*, No. 3, 11–12, for an account of this aspect of Céline's early life.

68 Manuscript copy of *D'un château l'autre:* "Brouillons" (unpublished), IV, 492. (Collection of Michel Bolloré.)

69 One is here reminded of the characters in Beckett's *Endgame*, one of whom cannot sit, while the other cannot stand.

70 Including extermination as a result of a German edict demanding the killing of animals that are of "impure race" or "non-reproductive" (*Nord*, p. 46). A similar edict was of course applied to human beings by the Nazis, a fact to which Céline does *not* choose to allude and about which he expresses no outrage.

71 Letter to Eveline Pollet, February 1933, *L'Herne*, No. 3, p. 96. He also admits to having been, in his youth, a "priapique terrible," when it came to dancers and the perfection of their bodies (Poulet, *Entretiens . . .* , p. 14).

72 Céline's predilection for dancers is well known. Among them we find Elizabeth Craig, the American dancer who was the author's mistress for a number of years; several others less well-known, including one Scandinavian named Karen; finally, Lucette Almanzor, who appears in the last novels as Lili or Arlette.

73 *Féerie pour une autre fois. I*, p. 325; *Féerie pour une autre fois. II. Normance*, pp. 45, 77.

3 · Totentanz

THE MUSE OF DEATH

"No art is possible without a dance with death." Céline is categorical on this point. He goes on to elaborate: "Whatever is not 'tuned' by death is worthless and will always ring false. . . ." [1] What does the author mean when speaking of death as a kind of dancing master without whose tapping foot the round falters and halts, a piano tuner without whose intervention the music falls flat and has no tone? It is not merely the conviction that death is an ever-present factor in human existence, that "all thoughts lead to death" (V., 322), or that its contemplation constitutes "the primary concern of man." [2] The question is more complicated; it is also paradoxical. For while it is true that Céline has an immense hatred for death, which leads him to deride or mock it, he also tends to be haunted, almost anguished by its presence, a feeling against which he alternately defends himself by laughter or confronts with brutal clarity. However, if in Céline's universe "death occupies the place that the devil holds in a Christian world," [3] the author's task is to exorcise this demon by means of his art. "The truth is death," he states, "I've fought nicely against it [death] as long as I could . . . danced with it, festooned it, waltzed it around . . . decorated it with streamers, titillated it . . ." (P.L., 33–34). This treatment gives way to another method of exorcism of death; by plunging into the total exploration of every one of its aspects, a meditation on its worst facets. Céline then turns into "the chronicler of all agonies," [4] and makes death a major theme of his entire art.

More than a short phrase, a faint note sounded here and there in the works, it becomes a *leitmotif* which predominates, accompanies, disappears only to assert itself again, is always part of the orchestration. As the author states, "You have to hear, underneath all kinds of music, the song without notes, written for us, the song of Death" (V., 293). It is an ominous melody which is never absent either in human existence or in the writings of Céline. Man cannot be free of its presence, or the nagging thought of his mortality, especially if he is lucid. For, while "most people don't die until the very last moment . . . others begin and work at it twenty years in advance and sometimes even more. Those are the unhappy ones of this earth" (V., 39). For the thoughtful person, or the artist, it becomes an especially agonizing realization, for "when one has no imagination, dying is a small matter, but for the imaginative man, dying is too much" (V., 22–23). Céline seems to speak mainly for those "unhappy ones" who are afflicted with lucidity or imagination. Their lives are one long agony, a slow dance before death, an endless wait in the ante-chamber of destruction. If one believes that it is in this domain where human existence plays out its end game, the work of art—if it is to possess any authenticity—must deal with its enactment. Besides, if one considers "life the true mistress of real men" (V., 232) and realizes at the same time that "the basic truth of life is death" (200), then it is impossible to speak of the first without continual involvement with the second. As a result, the work of art takes on the character of a long contemplation, a veritable meditation on death, which is continuous.[5] The search for this fundamental reality of existence is soon accomplished; its explication is endless and only terminates with the author's own demise.

While Céline expresses anguish in the face of death, alternating with mockery or grim derision and the resolute confrontation of its terrors, he also makes it his muse. He speaks of it as of a dancing partner whom the artist must embrace so that, from their union, the work of art might spring. Alternately leading and following, the writer and his horrid muse—for

Céline has known death too intimately to think of it in any more romantic way [6]—wind their way through the dance of creation. The character of the dance changes as the writing evolves: from the measured pavane of *Semmelweiss*, and the *pas de deux* of *Voyage au bout de la nuit*, to the grotesque jig of *Mort à crédit*, the sarabande of *Pont de Londres*, and the witches' round of *D'un château l'autre* and *Nord*. In turn, each beats the tune: sometimes death guides the choice of themes, the key, or dictates the shaping of the work; sometimes the artist makes her his handmaiden, mocking or lauding her performance. At first, he treats her as a dark goddess, implacable and mysterious, vengeful of any infraction upon her domain (*Semmelweiss*); later, he addresses her with "a song of death" [7] which resembles an angry requiem (*Voyage au bout de la nuit*); this turns to derision, mockery so severe that death is displaced from her throne and becomes a bogey creature: "La Blême" ("The Paleface," *Mort à crédit*); finally, she is portrayed in almost medieval terms: grinning, utterly hideous, gigantic beyond all comprehension or the reaches of individual terror (*D'un château l'autre* and *Nord*).

At all times, however, death remains on the scene. Hers is the largest role in the play of man. Nothing escapes her clutches, neither beings, things, nor words. In the endless round of creation and destruction, all must continually perish. Without the hope of resurrection though (abolished in atheistic thought), only the law of diminishing returns applies. The world is in a state of progressive decay, and all participates in the slow germination of death. Is not "the Célinean night, [that] ultimate state toward which everything returns, where it drowns, and asphyxiates itself in the all," [8] actually the domain of death? It is in this inescapable circle that leads from original to final darkness, this closed trap in which man is caught and permitted to struggle, that the work of art is located. All things then become equal, and the writer goes about demonstrating "the algebra of our century: flight from death equals flight to death," [9] and providing us with the most eloquent proof of his equation.

The same algebra, interestingly enough, also applies to the work of art itself. While creation might seem to be the very opposite of destruction, and composition the converse of decomposition, Céline does not feel this way. For him, "a book is already a kind of death," [10] because of its inevitable fixity, its finality resembling rigor mortis.[11] He knows that words die as soon as they are uttered, musical phrases fade when played, the dancer's motion is lost within the space where it is traced. He also realizes that his writing contains the seed of its own destruction, and moreover, "searches for a form of expression which will wear itself out in an instant . . . his phrases live only for the space of a gesture." [12] Thus, a book, once completed, is "fixed," entombed as if dead. Yet, while the author himself lives, resurrection is possible for his work. The process of anabolism and catabolism can repeat itself. The muse of death, however, is unrelentingly awake. She guards the realm of art with a monster's watchfulness, presides over the hoard with her dreadful gorgon's face. Unable to be slain, victim to no modern Perseus, she can only be won by a prolonged embrace.

THE PASSING OF THINGS

Céline, like his hero Bardamu, often seems to be standing on the banks of a river watching the relentless flow of the waters, of life, passing and being swept away. At the end of *Voyage au bout de la nuit* the sound of a boat horn had already called people, objects, the city itself to their dissolution in that element which is both the beginning and the end of life: the sea.

> From far, the tug whistled, its call passed the bridge, an arch, still another, the locks, another bridge, further on. . . . It called towards it all the barges on the river, all, and the whole city, and the sky, and the countryside and us, it swept everything along, the Seine also, everything. . . . (V., 493)

Stranded on the shores of existence, Bardamu—like so many other figures in Céline—watches time, beings, things fade, abandon him, die. Witness to man's mortality, they feel both anguish and disgust for all that passes, vanishes, returns no more. Their conviction that "the 'never again' is a judgment which spares no one and no thing," [13] is an ever-deepening one. Céline's cry of "Nevermore," which he utters at the conclusion

of each chapter of existence, is not unlike that of Poe's croaking bird, both in sound and meaning.[14]

All that perishes absorbs him: the human body, feelings,
objects, everything that weakens or decays. Sometimes, this
feeling takes on a form as violent as in Ferdinand's mad uncle
Rodolphe who practices necrophilia, because "He didn't understand that things could die . . ." (M.C., 548). At other
times, the preoccupation with decay or the disappearance of
things is expressed in less extreme terms. Often it is voiced
simply as nostalgia: the faint sigh of "she is gone!" which
terminates the description of Mme Bonnard (C., 219), the
query "where are they now?" concerning old friends who have
been dispersed over the years (M.C., 501), the sad realization
that "children are like the years, one never sees them again"
(M.C., 1034). All the various ways of passing are painful, sad,
and disgusting whether they occur through death, departure,
or the passage of time.[15] The sense of loss that results is one of
the most difficult of the fundamental aspects of human existence.

Loss is a constant theme in the works of Céline. In Voyage
au bout de la nuit the entire architecture of the novel is based
upon a series of explorations, each of which results in a loss:
the abandonment of Molly and the return from "the other
world"; the death of Bébert; the passing of Robinson. But there
are other losses as well: of youth, adventure, joy and pain,
tenderness, finally of all that is alive. Memory fails, youth
passes, one's companions are abandoned or disappear. Some
fade into a kind of death-in-life. Thus Robinson seems to walk
about with his deathmask already on his face. Something unknown "had come over his face, a sort of portrait one might
say, covered his very features already with oblivion, and with
silence all around." (V., 440) Fixity freezes people and objects
into death, oblivion, torpor. Corruption taints everything that
lives.

It is quite true that Céline "is obsessed not merely with
the inexorability of death but even more with the vision of
putrefactions." [16] These do not necessarily have to be physical
in nature, for he is just as concerned with the decaying of experience, the weakening of the past. Thus, "even memories
have their youth . . . they turn sour as soon as one lets them

grow moldy, become disgusting ghosts that ooze egotism, vanity, lies . . . they rot like apples." (V., 326) When they do not putrefy, they fade, disappear as people do: "All gone . . . the memories too! . . . so quietly and slowly." (C., 137) Joys pass, youth is gone, almost as soon as experienced. It is hard to reconcile oneself to their loss. The knowledge of "what one is losing with each passing hour" does not give one "the necessary strength or wisdom to stop dead in the track of time," to abdicate, to let one's youth go, and perish (V., 284).

Mort à crédit begins with the words: "Here we are, alone again," emphasizing the sense of loss, the passing of life. Ferdinand looks back at his past and sighs "All this is so slow, so heavy, so sad. . . . Soon I'll be old. And it will finally all be over." (M.C., 501) The regret turns into a wish for the cessation of this pattern, the desire that it all be over with, "that the spring return no more." The feeling is not too different from that of Bardamu who, worn out and despairing, wishes to fall asleep in his own night, "that coffin," because he is "so tired of walking and never finding anything" (V., 288). Having wandered and found nothing, or only things that fade almost as soon as they are touched, the individual rejects experience as too painful. Yet, while one can still feel and yearn, one tends to clutch at the slipping fragments of existence, to repeatedly bruise one's hands in the attempt. Rebellion at the futility of living then takes on a violent form. We need only look at Ferdinand's reaction to the loss of his friend, "little André," and all those whom he will not see again, to realize this:

> Maybe I'd never see him again . . . and he'd left for good . . . had passed body and soul into the stories they tell. . . . Ah, it's terrible nevertheless . . . despite one's youth one realizes for the first time . . . how one loses people on the way . . . pals one never sees again . . . never . . . that they have disappeared like dreams . . . that it's finished . . . faded away . . . that one will oneself disappear and be lost . . . on a day still far away in time . . . but still . . . lost in the whole dreadful torrent of things . . . of people . . . of days . . . of forms which pass . . . which never stop. . . . (M.C., 883)

In an impulse growing out of the panic of this revelation, Ferdinand throws himself at the passersby and attempts to hold them back by force, screaming: "Make them stop . . . don't

let them move anymore at all. . . . There, make them freeze
. . . once and for all! . . . So that they won't disappear any
more!" (M.C., 883–84)

But the "dreadful torrent" continues to sweep along and
cannot be held back—things and events turn into their shadows,
people into phantoms, day into night, life into death. Finally,
the dizzy round of the living, the maelstrom of things, the years
swept by gusts of time stand still. The losing battle against
decay is over. Putrefaction has triumphed over objects and men.
The first, like Courtial des Pereires' incredible balloon, fall to
rot after a long battle to preserve them, almost as desperate
as a human being's fight for life (M.C., 864–65, 887, 890).
People die and memories decay. At the still point, when time
has stopped, words are dead, things hollow and experience stale;
only the ghosts of men and objects remain.[17]

Then, that "lousy penchant for ghosts," which Bardamu
had recognized in himself (V., 235), becomes a necessity rather
than a mere predilection. The shades of things replace their
daylight image; sham and emptiness predominate; the world is
full of hollow men. Events become a mere shell, like the amusement park through which Bardamu wanders after the war,
where there is:

> Mechanical music which falls from the wooden horses, from
> the cars which aren't cars, from the mountains that aren't
> Russian at all, the platform of the wrestler who has no biceps
> and doesn't come from Marseilles, from the woman who has
> no beard, from the cuckolded magician, from the organ not
> made of gold, from behind the shooting gallery with empty
> eggs. . . . (V., 307)

In this half-lit world, where even the hero is transparent, in-
visible, almost a phantom, where meetings with his shadowy
alter ego often have the character of an encounter in limbo,
where paths never truly cross or human beings touch for more
than an instant, where a night in which there is "no longer any
road or light" (V., 335) prevails, the inhabitants are the dead
or the near-dead.

This state exists in all of the novels of Céline we are considering. The narrator in D'un château l'autre states: "Wherever I turn . . . the dead! . . . the dead!" (101) The strange

and horrible hordes of ghosts which crowd toward Charon's boat (93) are only the enlarged visions that follow in the wake of similar hallucinatory scenes, in *Voyage au bout de la nuit*, of the numberless dead who dance in macabre fashion across the sky of Montmartre (359–62). In the second instance also it has become clear that the hero has arrived "at the end of the world." "One could go no further, because after that, all that was left were the dead." (362) All those beings he has known in his own lifetime, the dead of the ages, pass in procession before him. But even these phantoms vanish, and man is left alone once more. Not even the shadows of things or people are his to keep. Only the ebbing away, the disappearance and decay, are constants. The backwash of existence is the only movement of its waters that he is allowed to contemplate.

THE QUICK, THE MAIMED, AND THE DEAD

> I've seen them croak everywhere, in the tropics, in the ice, in misery, in opulence, in prison, in full power, with honors, as leprous convicts, during revolutions, in the midst of peacetime, during artillery barrages, under a shower of confetti, I know all the stops of the organ *de profondis* [*sic*]. (C., 109)

The map of agonies which Céline draws for us covers the entire globe. It stretches like a pall over all of experience. Like the grinning figure of Death in medieval frescoes who dances his *pas de deux* with men of all callings, or Charon in *D'un château l'autre* who looms over "the rich! the poor! the mothers! the babes in arms" (93), the author seems now to conduct the dismal round, now to stand at the bedside of the dying. All the while, one can hear the pronouncement of doom on his lips, the refrain pervades his lines: "The penalty for life is death, and the penalty for braving death is agony." [18] Giving a dusty answer to most queries about existence, he assures us that death is the only dependable rule, that if there is anything certain under the stars, it is the dissolution of beings and things.

Céline indeed sounds "all the tones of the organ *de profondis*" and makes it accompany the long funeral cortège which stretches from his first novel to his last. Even the mourners, however, are not immune from death, nor intact in body

and spirit. The dead are followed to the burial ground by pall-
bearers who are halt, maimed, or themselves dying. Céline
seems convinced that the only role to play is that of undertaker
or corpse. But even the undertaker is not sound. Often, he is
simply decaying on the installment plan, a man whose death
has not yet reached its term. Sometimes, Céline's "croque-mort"
is as merry as the gravediggers in *Hamlet*, as rowdy as a mourner
at an Irish wake. Sometimes, his laments achieve the shrill and
barbaric sound of keening or the brutal indifference of remarks
that might accompany the burial of plague victims in a common grave.

   In the gigantic catacombs whose labyrinthine ways Céline
illuminates for us, he has heaped not only the dead, but also
the dying, the living dead, and those who thrust death from
their sight.[19] Almost all the characters in his works are a continual reminder of man's mortality. They disintegrate, die, or
are about to die. This is their "tragic" flaw. The imminence of
death and the various stages of decay which pursue Céline's
characters cause all of his works, not only the last novel, to
deal with "a world of tragedy" (*N.*, 150). In this kind of universe, victim and executioner alike are subject to the same fate.
The quick, the maimed, and the dying are equally on the verge
of doom. The quick destroy the maimed. The maimed slowly
or quickly die. A horde of furies—not of divine origin but bred
of strictly terrestrial horror—pursues them all, attacks without
cause and without reference to any supernatural design. The
oracles are more than silent; they have been razed to the ground.
Even the small gods are dead. Only gratuitous existence over-
shadowed by the constant threat of meaningless death remains.

   No wonder then that the odor of putrefaction hangs over
everything. It is present in the places where food is prepared
(*M.C.*, 549), the mouths of people (*V.*, 332), decaying objects
(*M.C.*, 890), the wounds of the sick, the mounds of offal, the
masses of phantoms. Even mummies dead for over five hundred
years still emit "their odor of dust and ashes" (*V.*, 381). The
stench of death becomes overwhelming as it rises from the
cesspool which provides the focal point for the activity of *Nord*,
and in which stagnation and decay are dramatically centralized.

For it is in this "liquid manure pit" that Schertz suffers death by drowning (N., 394–95).

Schertz is the epitome of the maimed creatures who appear in Céline's works. What interests us is that such a person is already partially dead, being no longer sound, intact. His body or his mind has lost part of its life function. Death has already claimed some portion of his being. We have formerly spoken of the emotional maiming which occurs in Céline's typical hero: his inability to feel, to communicate, to achieve any meaningful relation to existence, to resolve terror into anything but apathy or self-destruction. We have also mentioned the long line of those who are ill in mind or body which stretches across the novels. We must add those who function fairly well, but who are maimed in some manner or in whom the life-force has been reduced in a drastic fashion. These include Mme des Pereires who, as a result of a hysterectomy, had turned into a grotesque creature, half man, half woman (M.C., 891–905); Ferdinand's mother, who hobbles through the long pages of *Mort à crédit* on her crippled legs; the strange satyr without legs who dominates the two volumes of *Féerie pour une autre fois*, and is the forerunner of Schertz, who will appear in *Nord*.

The figure of the wounded hero includes that of the narrator himself, who refers continually to the fact that he is disabled, "75 per cent mutilated," (C., 12, 29) hobbles through *Nord* supported by canes (45, *et al.*), and alludes to his further reduction to an invalid state in Danish prisons. In *Nord*, we also come across an entire store which specializes in various merchandise for the use of "the disabled" (43). It is a kind of supermarket stocked with canes, crutches, false limbs, wheel chairs, platforms for double amputees. The candidate for such a platform—although he prefers riding on the shoulders of a giant Russian prisoner—is that most mutilated of Céline's creatures, the epileptic *cul-de-jatte* who circulates in a world in ruins, torn apart by bombardments, and who dies by drowning in a cesspool. He portrays the high point of Céline's growing awareness of the progressive decay in life which lops off limbs, atrophies the mind and the body, mutilates man almost completely.[20] The relentless movement toward death and destruction proceeds with accelerated speed. The descent is continually steeper, accidents become more frequent and increasingly more terrible. "Everything always takes a wrong, a filthy turn. . . . Man staggers from one mishap to another, from one bankruptcy to the next," [21] from partial to total mutilation and death.

To add to the dilemma, the narrator's double in the novels of Céline also becomes progressively more maimed. Robinson, who had been trepanned in Flanders—like Bardamu—and suffered from temporary blindness, changes into a more severely crippled creature in the last work. In *Nord*, Ferdine proceeds "to walk around with a double, a sort of corpse, a corpse with canes and troubles who would kill him, get him sent back to the cemetery which he never ought to have left" (62). While Robinson had been "a kind of sickness" for Bardamu (V., 268) and symbolized a maiming by despair, the double of the later novel signifies full-fledged despair, a sickness unto death. Just as the narrator's companion grows increasingly decrepit, the decor of the story more and more closely approaches the state of total decomposition. Thus, while the early novels were set in the various *faubourgs* of cities or of life, the last works take place within the ruins, the rubble heaps. We find places like war-torn Berlin which is "a city which is nothing more than a stage-set . . . whole streets of mere façades, with all the interiors destroyed, fallen into holes" (N., 45). Their state resembles that of the human beings who wander through them.

The author himself seems to have lost his strength, his furious power to attack of former days. One of his friends and close observers has noted: "He no longer dominates, he doesn't sink his claws into the flesh of the reader any more. The monster has lost his incredible agility; he can only bite unceasingly in the same spot, with the formidable and disenchanted chawing motion of the sick lion. . . ." [22] It is true that, while the early works partake of the spirit of a furious, energetic wrestler, the last are the pronouncements of an invalid, of a *grand malade*. They are the sad rehashing of tales of terror, the redundancies of old age and illness, the digressions and gaps in the memory,[23] the fragments of a story punctuated by death: the death of masses of people, of one's companions and friends, of one's own self, which seems just around the bend.

It is certainly fitting that an author who himself suffers from various afflictions should describe a world so prone to the same fate. Ironically, the last two novels take place in Germany, a country where the sick, the maimed, the "non-reproductive," those who are considered "imperfect" in any way, were almost ritually exterminated to preserve a race of mythical supermen. Yet, the place itself is full of creatures of this kind, for all the characters of *Nord* are afflicted in some way. From the mad La Vigue and Delaunys, to the senile Rittmeister and the monstrous Schertz, no one is whole or wholesome. Reproduction has been supplanted by destruction. Only deformity could be engendered in such a setting. Aberration is rampant, both on a small and on a large scale. It is an all-pervasive quality, affecting people as well as buildings, actions as well as thoughts. Women assume the shape of witches, bacchantes, or mad whores; men are crippled, rent in pieces, castrated (*C.*, 274) or otherwise mutilated; children are allowed to roam about, with bloated bellies and starving mouths. The earth itself is continually torn asunder, the sky trembles with bombardments. Nothing is left intact; piecemeal death is doled out everywhere. While Céline does not necessarily believe that there is no other "solution except collective suicide, non-procreation, or death," [24] he certainly depicts this state of affairs as a reality.

While death of the major characters does not occur in the last novels as it sometimes does in the first, a more general form of dying takes place. We find mass destruction which happens mostly offstage, behind the scenes, and seems more ominous for this reason.[25] Individual deaths would mean little or nothing in the enormous collective suicide which involves entire nations.

Only at an earlier stage in his career, when Céline was still concerned with single human beings—even when in themselves they had no "collective importance"—did he use his art to describe their particular agency. Thus, we find a number of incidents of this kind in *Voyage au bout de la nuit* and *Mort à crédit*. In the first novel, aside from the war scenes, there is the death battle of M. Henrouille, described in graphic terms, and in that terse, matter-of-fact tone which we have referred to earlier: "His goose was cooked." Soon he would "begin to rot, with his heart all juicy and red, oozing like an old crushed pomegranate." While the images might be fitting for a horror movie, the awful struggle of the human animal in his death throes has a much more realistic terror. At the end of the battle, the victim "fought as hard against life as against death," unable to find peace in either state, or even to obtain release from pain (V., 366). The second agony described in some detail is that of Robinson, which is of a far different nature. Taken out of the realm of the ordinary, his last moments have a more legendary quality: "It was a business in which everything was novel, the sighs and the eyes and everything" (485). "He was not like an ordinary patient, one didn't know how to behave in front of him" (487). His death is a kind of *élan*, almost an ascension. Even his corpse remains in a startling position, its gesture like a sign to the living who will stay behind: "We freed ourselves from his hands. They remained in the air, those hands, quite stiff, sticking up all yellow and blue in the lamplight." The survivors are cowed, awed by his presence: "It seemed as if there was a stranger in the room now, who had come from a dreadful country and to whom one no longer dared to speak." (487) Other *rites de passage* which lead to that dreadful country of death are related in the various novels. In *Mort à crédit*, the death scene of Ferdinand's grandmother predominates. It is once again described with great realism and quite a bit of harshness. The narrator relates the quality of her death rattle: "She was breathing hard, she was gasping, making an awful racket. . . ." He adds a description of the waxlike face about to fall into decay: "Her face was all yellow now with a lot of sweat on it, like a mask that's in the process of melting." (M.C., 586)

After the technicolor horror of such scenes, we proceed to the last novels where all agonies of any importance are collective ones, and are evoked rather than described in minute detail. The death scenes depicted are those of the countless victims in the store windows of Siegmaringen, the cancer ward in which Ferdine was forced to work as an attendant by the Danes, the passengers of the shipwrecked "Chella," the children dying in the camp at Cissen, that "Nursery Grand-Guignol" (C. 120).

The dying, lined up in long numbers, are reminiscent of those parades of phantoms who had appeared in *Voyage au bout de la nuit*, and would again arise in *D'un château l'autre*. If we compare the two scenes in which this imaginary resurrection of the dead occurs, we find that both are a summary of past experiences of the narrator, a review of all those whom he has seen "croaking everywhere" (C., 109). However, we note that an evolution in the author's point of view has taken place. In the earlier work, the crowds of the dead are mainly individuals whom the narrator has known during their lifetime. In the later one, they are rather unidentifiable hordes of human beings. In the former case, sadness mingled with some spoofing characterizes the account, in the latter, brutality and grotesque horror prevail. Thus Bardamu watches as they pass before him, Bébert, "the pale, pale girl, finally aborted"—both of whom he has cared for as a doctor—the old negro flogged by Grappa, the Spaniard living in the African jungle, and many others. Finally, as the vision becomes enlarged, it goes back in time to include "les communards," La Pérouse, the cossack troups, and all the epic heroes of the past, who battle with each other, one century pitted against the next. At last, the ghosts flee and disappear, leaving behind them only a gigantic sorceress who hangs over the British Isles, brewing tea in the hull of a ship and stirring the mixture with an enormous oar. Silence falls, her fire goes out: "There's no more life to feed the flames . . . no more life in the world for anyone . . . and everything is almost over" (V., 360–62).

Ferdine in *D'un château l'autre* experiences a similar "onslaught of phantoms." Interesting differences become evident when we compare it with the vision described above. The dead throng to a ghost ship that resembles an old *bâteau-mouche* which the narrator remembers from his youth. Its conductor, Le Vigan, is disguised as a gaucho and sports a white beard. He crowds the phantoms—who are mostly victims of the second world war—into the ship. Charon himself is an immense creature with the head of a monkey and the body of a tiger, dressed in a kind of redingote and an admiral's cap. The monster hits his passengers on the head with an enormous oar and plunges his fingers into their brains. The grotesque horror of the vision only stops with the arrival of Lili and her dog. The *danse macabre* ends with the barking of Frieda, not the crowing of the cock (*C.*, 82–94).

In both descriptions, Céline seems to say that the fate of the dead is not unlike that of the living: in the first instance, he depicts an assembly of "crooks," drunkards, "bastards," which ends in a "terrible fight" and in the disappearance of the phantoms "by way of a big hole which they made by puncturing the night." (*V.*, 360–61) We recognize there the behavior and characteristics of the living who appear in V*oyage au bout de la nuit*: their sadness, viciousness, cantankerousness, and forward flight into the night while an indifferent divinity of uncertain grandeur sits brewing tea.

In the second passage, the ghosts and their masters are of a somewhat different nature. They include the grotesque figure of Le Vigan, Emile, who has been lynched by a Parisian mob after his arrest for alleged collaboration, and is so badly mutilated that he resembles "an insect-monster" (*C.*, 87); Charon, that hideous torturer-executioner of gigantic proportions and features which combine the most terrible aspects of the underworld gods of Greek and Egyptian mythology, who proceeds in the "décervelage" (braining) of all alike.[26] All of them resemble figures in that enormous and grotesque catastrophe which occurred in Europe, players in the tragedy during which civilians and soldiers, old and young, guilty and innocent were tortured and killed without distinction and with total savagery. While, in the earlier vision, the sorceress presides over the last vestiges of life during the peaceful, almost domestic task of brewing tea in a boat hull and stirring it with an oar, the latter one presents a much more terrifying picture. A monster now holds sway; the boat which served as teapot has become the ominous "bark of Charon," the oar which had been an innocuous spoon has turned into an instrument of torture with which the monster proceeds to "remassacrer" the phantoms of the dead.

It becomes clear that Céline traces, in his work, a long and dreary procession on its way to decomposition and death. It includes the quick who are all "cadavers on reprieve . . . living by chance and for a moment only," [27] and either drug them-selves into oblivion or start dying many years before their actual decease. There are also the maimed who are one step further along the path to destruction, experiencing partial annihilation of mind or body even during their lifetime; the dying who suffer through the terrible hours of their agony; and the dead who, even in the phantom realm, must endure all the horrors of hu-man existence. It is a progression from one kind of hell to an-other, with almost no surcease in the suffering involved, and no dignity or grandeur at any point. We have already seen how severely Céline blackens the quick, what disgust and terror man arouses when he is well and able. His crippled or mutilated brother generally evokes no greater sympathy and only slightly less fear.[28] The dying are usually hideous and grotesque in their suffering, and inflict pain on their family and friends. Even after death, Céline allows for no immunity from harsh por-trayals, for he then depicts man as worm food, revolting carrion, or a tormented and tormenting phantom.

However, the author goes still further to rob death itself of any dignity or mystery. He makes a mockery of its secrets and denies it its most ancient role: that of an awe-inspiring force in man's existence.

FROM "LA COMÉDIE DE LA MORT" TO TRAGEDY

"Here's what one must not forget: my *danse macabre* amuses me as much as an enormous farce," Céline reminds us, in case we forget that in the tragicomedy of existence, "the world is comical, death is comical." [29] Similarly, Bardamu had assured us that "death is there . . . full of stench, next to you all the time . . . and less mysterious than 'une belotte' " (V., 448). In reducing the tragic or mysterious nature of death to the low humor of a farce or the level of an insipid card game ("une belotte"), Céline makes some very interesting statements. Death is thus not only valueless as a bridge to the afterlife (although this idea is common to all atheists), it is not even that puzzling cessation of life which has given pause to many men's thoughts, nor a resting place that provides unending calm after the strife of living. It becomes simply the gateway to that kingdom of corruption of which man had been partially a citizen before, as foul as his life, as ridiculous, and just as devoid of meaning.

Céline had not always expressed such an attitude, nor is it consistent throughout *Voyage au bout de la nuit*. If we analyze the evolution which takes place in Céline's outlook on death, during his literary career, we shall find some fairly extensive changes. In *Semmelweiss* its image is at its most grandiose. The meditation on death, which Céline will engage in, begins with an impressive fanfare. *La Mort*—capitalized—is one of the most important actors in the drama of the unfortunate hero, a personification rather than a concept, a force as important as that of Life against which it is pitted. Death avenges the infraction upon its kingdom made by the hero and destroys him in an-eye-for-an-eye struggle. Her vengeful gesture annihilates him, but nevertheless, "he enters the realm of peace" (131). This, incidentally, is the only time in the work of Céline that peace is mentioned in connection with death, or that the latter takes on almost the form of a divinity, a fitting opponent for a force of equal importance, that of Life. We might guess that while Life is considered to have value and is worth being affirmed, Death will have equal weight and grandeur. When the first becomes absurd, futile, grotesque, the second—its opposite pole—will suffer the same degradation and to a correspondingly greater degree.

In *Voyage au bout de la nuit*, the theme of death undergoes many variations. On the one hand, it is disparaged. From the grotesque death scenes during the war and Bardamu's medical career, to the denigration by which death loses all mystery and dignity, is only a short step. At the same time, the final moments of Robinson's life are filled with some grandeur, in contrast with which Bardamu shamefacedly admits: "Me, I wasn't great like death" (486). Another interesting idea presented is that of different kinds of death—some acceptable and worthy of the human being, others to be rejected because unworthy. Death in war is definitely in the second category, as is that which is the result of the kind of accident which Robinson suffers. Bardamu explains, in connection with the latter: "All in all, death is a bit like a marriage. That particular death didn't appeal to him at all. . . . Robinson wasn't ready to die in the circumstances which were proposed to him. Perhaps presented in another manner, it would have pleased him a lot" (V., 325). Indeed this is the case, for when Robinson is ready, he chooses his own kind of death—to be executed by Madelon —and insists upon its being accomplished. After dying, an experience in the course of which he retains much of his dignity (which is rather rare for one of Céline's heroes), Robinson continues to be a grandiose figure, an awe-inspiring spectacle.

In *Mort à crédit*, the picture changes drastically; so much so, that the novel has been described as "a caricature of death." [30] The work is truly "a sort of blasphemy," [31] if one believes in the sanctity of death, a mockery of what is often considered the saddest of all events. Much more interesting than these, though, is the concept that the work "is the successor to the tragedy of death, its comedy." [32] In other words, we might compare it to the satyr-play which followed a Greek tragedy, the juxtaposition of broad burlesque or grotesque horseplay and high tragedy. Such a notion already appears in the title of this novel, which is "terrible and buffoonish at the same time." [33] It is apparent in the very name given to death. For, while in the past it had been referred to as "la mort"—sometimes capitalized as in a morality play—it now becomes "La Blême" ("Paleface," M.C., 527), a title both disparaging and slangy at the same time. One should also note that the place where death appears in all its horror—the town in which Courtial des Pereires takes his life in so hideous a fashion—is aptly named "Blême-le-Petit" (M.C., 976). The whole novel, as even such a minor detail indicates, is both "more sinister and gayer than *Voyage*." [34] The sinister side is characteristic of the site of des Pereires' death. It is located in the country, in the midst of that nature for which the author has such misgivings. The eeriness of the place is exaggerated by the only inhabitants of the property, two old, deaf, and almost blind beggars who live in the midst of their own offal, and constitute the only sign of life in the place. Owls, the strange night creatures whose ominous cries pervade the whole last part of the novel, infest the countryside. Corruption seems rampant even before des Pereires spreads the putrefaction both of his agricultural experiments and his suicide. The latter is certainly described as both hideous and grotesque, an act which results in a monstrously deformed bundle of flesh, wrapped in a winding sheet indicative of all his human folly: the remnants of his first balloon.

The grotesque nature of death, the mockery of its horrors, are of course not limited to *Mort à crédit*. We have already seen an excellent example of this nature in the mummies of Sainte-Eponime, for which Robinson and his would-be murder victim, "Mother Henrouille" have the concession. These "old dead" are subject to terrible buffoonery. Dragged out of the quicklime in which they have lain for hundreds of years, they are now exhibited in their filthy state, decrepit and absurd, as well as horrifying. They are lined up, as if in a parade, and constitute a ridiculous and macabre crew:

> Women with bonnets perched on top of their skeletons, a hunchback, a giant, and even a baby who was all decked out too, with a sort of lace bib around his minute shriveled neck, if you please, and a little shred of a shirt. (V., 380)

Adding to the black humor of the situation is the fact that Mme Henrouille, who herself came close to being as much a phantom as these creatures, is the one who "made the dead perform, just like in a circus." "They're not sad at all," she insists, in speaking of the members of her sinister sideshow and to prove it, pounds the shriveled skin of their bellies eliciting a drumlike sound to amuse the customers and collect their money (381).

This, however, is one of the rare instances in *Voyage au bout de la nuit* where one can allude to a "comedy of death," unless one wishes to include the related mention of the "comedy of suffering," which Céline speaks of in connection with the death throes of most human beings (V., 487). Both concepts become much more pronounced in *Mort à crédit* where they even extend to objects. Thus, we find the remarkable passages dealing with the decay and death of Courtial des Pereires' balloon, and the futile attempts to save its life (863, 865, 871, 1038). The human actors in this comedy of death and misfortune are Ferdinand's parents, whose grotesque and progressive "falling apart" reaches its high point at the end of the book. More important, though, is Mme des Pereires, who has deteriorated into a monstrous and pathetic creature, as a result of her operation. One of the most remarkable figures of this genre in Céline's writings, she exemplifies sudden decay, a change from beauty to ogrelike hideousness, from health to illness, from life to its corruption. Like a swift change of scene, the transformation is accomplished. "All that wiped out in the space of a day! . . . with a scalpel! I can't believe it!" her husband moans (905). His own fate, however, will be no less hideous or absurd. He will die in a revolting manner, come to resemble nothing more than a bloody placenta, and (in a final, humiliating revelation), be deprived even of the small dignity of his name.[35] Both M. and Mme des Pereires are the forerunners of a long line of actors who will appear in the later works of Céline, and figure in the grotesque "comedies of death" which are to be played there.

One of the most striking examples is to be found in *Pont de Londres* where death takes on the guise of a grotesque entertainer named "*Mille-Pattes*" ("The Centipede"). During several hallucinatory episodes he appears as a Spanish dancer equipped with perfect castanets (in the form of rattling bones), as a seducer of young girls, and finally as the catalyst of an enormous and maniacal orgy (155–60, 263–65, *et al.*).

In the last novels, everything contributes to a performance of a grotesque "comedy of death." The settings are those of gothic horror-tale castles, full of dungeons, secret passages, and underground tunnels. The ogres who inhabit them come from a long and well-known lineage, like those of the Hohenzollern in *D'un château l'autre* whose portraits line the walls. The narrator wanders among galleries containing "faces without shame, horrible, ferocious . . . increasingly more sly, cruel, greedy . . . more monstrous!" (122–23) Of course, these devilish creatures from the past have their equally horrid contemporary counterparts: Frau Frucht, von Raumnitz, the mad surgeon, the "Bishop of Albi," and, principal among them, Aïcha the female monster accompanied by a whole host of apprentice demons.

In *Nord*, we find an equally unholy crew: Matchke, the Rittmeister, the Kratzmühl couple, Isis Schertz[36] and her maimed husband, the whores turned maenads. Death—in this work especially—becomes a totally grotesque event. While in

D'un château l'autre violence to individuals was only rarely
described in detail (as in the case of Papillon), and the doomed
victims were simply made to disappear into the ominous "room
no. 36," in *Nord* it becomes a major part of the action. As its
frequency increases, so does the terrible buffoonery which accompanies it. Thus Isis, who plans to murder her crippled husband with the help of drugs which she attempts to coerce
Ferdine into getting (*N.*, 291), asks him at the same time and
with almost equal urgency to procure her some hard-to-come-by
disposable sanitary napkins (295). Frau Kratzmühl plays a
strange role. Maddened by the death of her two sons, she en-
acts her "comedy of suffering" with such skill and devotion
that she almost loses her life in the process (314–15). Grim
humor also appears in the incident in which the *Revizor* and
the *Rittmeister* have been wounded and killed, respectively, by
the prostitutes who have gone wild. Ferdine suggests that these
women have moved on to ravage the countryside, where they
will probably find food in the guise of "a little horse! or maybe
a policeman . . . on a spit! . . .," but his remark fails to make
Matchke of the S. S. laugh (358). Other events tinged with
similar *humour noir* include the celebration under the aegis
of "Kraft durch Freude" which stars a troupe of gypsies. During this performance, the Landrat Semmelring is drowned in
the cesspool (390–92) which will later also disclose the body
of the crippled Schertz (392–95). The description of the latter's
corpse has that sardonic quality which characterizes many of
the most devastating incidents in the book. The cadaver is
brought to the surface of the fetid water, "huddled together,
the fat trunk and atrophied legs, covered with manure, all
black and yellow, smeared as if with paint, plastered over . . ."
(395). The three victims in the novel (including the masochistic Rittmeister murdered by the prostitutes) are given a
weird burial, complete with drummers to precede the cortège
and a pastor to read the services. A group of ill-assorted mourners follows the coffins, initialed in red for easier identification,
and the dead are buried to shouts of "Honig" (honey) from
the hooting populace (413–16). The ritual is a mixture of
operatic grandeur and maniacal humor (tinged with what might

be a satirical take-off on classical funeral offerings) which qualify it for a mock-tragedy.

However—and here the most interesting phenomenon takes place—as the buffoonery surrounding death increases, the terror also mounts. This becomes most evident in the last works where the comedy of death and suffering reaches such dimensions that it breaks the bounds of its initial form. It seems to flood the theater and inundate the spectators who have come to revel there. One can no longer observe it as one would a comedy, feeling slightly removed and superior, calmly watching the humorous although grotesque playacting of the performers. Their antics have take on a more threatening note. The terror—if not the pity—becomes so pronounced that the result is a kind of tragedy.

It is not traditional tragedy in which we contemplate the downfall of a heroic figure, but in many ways Céline is right, evoking in his last novels a comparison with the universe of Greek tragedy (N., 150). Only a few elements have been changed. Fate, formerly decreed by the gods, has become a destiny determined by the stupidity and viciousness of man; the struggles of the hero have turned into the contortions of the victim or the executioner. Essentially, it is the enormity of the catastrophe, in the light of which individual suffering becomes small yet remains worth contemplating, that merits the title of tragedy. For while the death of a single human being becomes—after the first two of the author's works—a ludicrous or grotesque event, the annihilation of entire peoples takes on truly great proportions. Not that such mass destruction has any quality of dignity or mythical grandeur, but it does evoke the terror which is a necessary part of the tragic experience.

In this drama of human degradation, it is the fall rather than the ascension, the befouling rather than the purification through suffering, which we are forced to witness. Nevertheless, the purging by pity and terror takes place. This, however, is not followed by any ennobling vision. In a sense, Céline's is a truncated tragedy in which the spectator is not uplifted by a contemplation of the hero's grandeur, but only allowed to view his torment, his downfall. It is as though Oedipus were to terminate his role by appearing on stage with gouged-out eyes, or the *Oresteia* to end with the degrading murder of Agamemnon. But is not such a view of tragedy fitting to our world? In an age where the great god Pan is dead, can Dionysus still be celebrated by the offering of *tragos*?

Notes

1 Letter to Dr. Camus (not to be confused with Albert Camus, the writer), June 29, 1949, *Les Ecrits de Paris*, XCIII (October 1961), 109.

2 Marc Hanrez, *Céline* (Paris: Gallimard, 1961), p. 277.

3 Pol Vandromme, *Céline* (Paris: Editions Universitaires, 1963), p. 63.

4 *Ibid.*, p. 60.

5 Nicole Debrie-Panel, *Céline* (Lyon: E. Vitte, 1961), p. 171.

6 As he stated: "I knew very well how one dies. It makes one suffer enormously" (V., p. 381). His medical experience of course provided him with first-hand knowledge of death and all its aspects.

7 Debrie-Panel, *op. cit.*, p. 137

8 Jean-Pierre Richard, "La Nausée de Céline," *La Nouvelle Revue Française*, X, No. 115, 44.

9 Irving Howe, "Céline: The Sod Beneath the Skin—I," *The New Republic* (July 20, 1963), 21.

10 Letter from Céline to Eveline Pollet (March 1933), *L'Herne*, No. 3, 97.

11 In the same letter to E. Pollet, Céline states that he hates everything that "congeals life." This idea seems to have determined the author's refusal to go over publisher's proofs or even read his work, once it was completed. (Information obtained in my interviews with the author's secretary Marie Canavaggia, and his editor, the late Roger Nimier.)

12 Debrie-Panel, *op. cit.*, p. 127.

13 Hanrez, *Céline*, p. 80

14 Indeed, ravens and other birds of ill omen are heard calling from *Mort à crédit* to *Nord* (pp. 385, 358, etc.).

15 "The scrapings of time are sad . . . disgusting, and ugly," as Ferdinand says (*M.C.*, p. 541).

16 Howe, *op. cit.*, p. 21

17 Céline, quoting Shakespeare, refers to men as "walking shadows" (Poulet, *Entretiens . . .* , p. 98).

18 W. M. Frohock, "Céline's Quest for Love," *Accent*, II, No. 2, 82.

19 See the author's remarks on this subject in Poulet's *Entretiens . . .* , pp. 98–99.

20 It is striking that the ascension of the maimed hero is paralleled by his opposite: the dancer.

21 Karl Epting, *Frankreich im Widerspruch* (Hamburg: Hanseatische Verlagsanstalt, 1943), p. 52.

22 Robert Poulet, *La Lanterne magique* (Paris: Nouvelles Editions Debresse, 1956), p. 58.

23 These are often referred to by Céline himself: See *D'un château l'autre*, pp. 37, 77, 125, 127, 129, for examples.

24 Sartre, "Portrait de L'Antisemite," *Les Temps Modernes*, I, No. 3, 462.

25 One is here reminded of A. Adamov's play, *La grande et la petite manoeuvre*.

26 One might also draw some parallels with Alfred Jarry's *Roi Ubu* here, in which "La Chanson du Décervelage" figures prominently.

27 Robert Poulet, *Entretiens familiers avec Louis-Ferdinand Céline* (Paris: Plon, 1958), p. 97.

28 Certainly, that most maimed creature, the double amputee of *Féerie pour une autre fois* and *Nord*, is revolting, and vicious, and dangerous.

29 Poulet, *Entretiens . . .* , p. 99.

30 Debrie-Panel, *op. cit.*, p. 142.

31 *Ibid.*, p. 140.

32 *Ibid.*, p. 141.

33 André Suarès, "A propos de Céline," *La Nouvelle Revue Française*, IX, No. 104, 327.

34 Debrie-Panel, *op. cit.*, p. 140.

35 His real name proves to be Léon Charles Punais! (M.C., p. 1030). The feminine form, "punaise," means bedbug.

36 As stated in the Introduction, due to libel suits *Nord* has had to be revised. In the "definitive edition," the following name changes must be noted: Matchke = Kracht; the Kratzmühls = the Kretzers; Schertz = von Leiden.

Part II   Nox Irae

4 · The Horseman of the Apocalypse

THE SOUND OF THE FIRST TRUMPET

"I am the thunder, the cataclysms . . . ," rages the aging Céline,[1] like one of the avenging angels in the Book of Revelation. The prophecy and chronicle of doom has been central to his literary task from the very beginning. Had not Ferdinand of *Mort à crédit* already cried out: "I am manufacturing the opera of the deluge," (526) and Bardamu embarked on an "apocalyptic crusade" (V., 17)? The setting of a world about to end, the atmosphere of impending or unleashed catastrophe characterize almost all of Céline's works. It is as though the cavalry officer Destouches, riding courageously into the battles of World War I with plumed helmet and flashing eyes, had been transformed into one of the dread horsemen of the Apocalypse when he exchanged his rifle for a pen. It is a long leap, but not an inexplicable one.

War, the first and foremost of all terrestrial "cataclysms," apparently touched Céline very deeply, effecting that deflowering of confidence and destruction of a stable or affirmative feeling about existence which seem at the basis of his literary vision. In the first five pages he wrote and published, we already find a swift chronicle of the disasters of war and revolution, culminating in a description of "those monstrous years when blood flows, when life gushes forth and dissolves in a thousand breasts at a time, when backs are harvested and crushed by war like so many grapes in a wine press. . . ." (S., 14) His last work will describe essentially the same kind of catastrophic epoch, only this time the theme which was only sketched in *Semmel-weiss* will become the mainstay of the entire architecture of *Nord*. If in the first case he spoke of the tempest of wars in years past, in the last novels he will speak of the present peril and prophesy the destruction which will overrun the world when the Chinese threat becomes manifest. Whether the danger comes from men who are yellow, black or white, "youtres" or "boches," (as Céline disparagingly refers to Jews and Germans in his various writings) Céline is there to point out its presence. It is as though he wished to proclaim the fact that a continual threat hangs over existence from start to finish, that destruction is imminent at every instant. Individuals are, as we have seen, doomed from birth. It is useless for them to act "as if the worm of decay were not already inside them, having been born together with their first cry." [2] Civilizations, also, will founder, fail, or stand on the verge of crumbling. And the author is there to herald their fall. More dismal than the gadfly, Céline stands with his book at the gates of annihilation. He announces the coming of the holocaust, a bitter laugh bursting from his lips. "The angel of destruction" [3] grimaces sharply, there is a moment of silence, and he lifts the trumpet of doom to his lips.

The malediction, which has lain like a pall over existence since the beginning of his works, is finally released in its full force. The various stages of the Apocalypse unfold before us. Céline seems to be echoing T. S. Eliot's refrain: "This is the way the world ends," but he does not join his contemporary across the Channel in the religious leap which the latter chose to make. Indeed, Céline shows us a strange kind of Apocalypse, just as he has given us a tragedy of odd description, for one is as truncated as the other. Once again, we are shown devastation without ascension, judgment without vindication. Only the end of the world is made evident. There is no resurrection of the dead, no triumph of the just over the unjust. Guilty and innocent alike are hurled into hell fires. No new reign is promised. All is endlessly damned; the world falls into ashes not to rise again. The prophecy of the triumph of original chaos, made in *Semmelweiss*, is fulfilled in *Nord*. Nor can it be otherwise in a universe in which man is a vicious, destructive creature who craves the annihilation of his fellows,[4] and where God is more than dead, for he is an object of derision, as unimportant as a broken mechanical toy.

We become, once again, aware of Céline's need to blacken everything he touches with his pen. For he has shown us a vision close to the biblical description of the day of wrath which ends the world, but has only chosen the darkest aspects of the event. It is as impossible for Céline to give us the redeeming side of the picture as it would be for an avenging angel to wander through a sunny and fruitful countryside, or for the apocalyptic beast not to graze in regions of a starker nature. Neither can walk lightly; their relentless tread brings waste and devastation to the earth. Even before their dread figures appear on the horizon, one can feel the trembling of the ground and hear the ominous call which summons them. Its sound is heard here and there in all the works of Céline, sometimes as faint as the notes of a horn or disguised as a grotesque, humorous discord, sometimes resounding in all its threatening diapason.

Apocalyptic visions are conjured up, sometimes facetiously, as in Ferdinand's father's reprimand of his behavior as "infernal . . . Apocalyptic!" (*M.C.*, 721) but often with more serious overtones. Thus, Bardamu describes his experiences in the war as "an apocalyptical crusade," (*V.*, 17) a phrase which succinctly states the essential characteristics of the event. In the two early major works, Céline's attitude concerning annihilation is close to that of a prophet of coming events, a preacher who attempts to terrify the guilty—comparable to the medieval *sermonneur* who uses humor, anecdote, colloquial speech, even vulgarity, to sway his audience. In the last novels the resemblance is to a St. John who, horrified, is forced to watch the apocalyptic vision unfurl before him. In this sense, it is true that "the relationship between Céline's first and last works is comparable to the progression from the Gospels to the Book of the Apocalypse." [5] At the same time, Céline is also present during the holocaust, like some early *chroniqueur*, a living witness to the desolation, as well as a victim. He not only describes what he is seeing; the earth also opens at *his* feet. The world about to end spells terminus for him as well. Thus,

Siegmaringen, which has become a kind of graveyard for all the shipwrecked of Europe, shelters a narrator who is as marooned as any of his fellow travelers. And in the last work, *Nord*, where the monstrous predominates and suffering has become grotesque, the trio of protagonists finds that hardship has so altered their faces that they themselves resemble monsters, that their appearance is as distorted as that of the world at large.

The last works are situated on the brink of annihilation. All signs announce the coming end. It is evident that in *Nord* "the often heralded Apocalypse" (168) is about to take place. The author even evokes "the *Four Horsemen* of Dürer," (*N.*, 143) those dread riders whom he himself seems to join. All of them are there, spreading famine, plague, madness, death. And wrath—although strictly man-made and spread by human decree—seems to encompass the universe as completely as in any biblical rendition of the last day. The narrator in these works wanders through the desolate landscape, a feeble creature attempting to abate the flood of misery and terror with the aid of a stethoscope and a few syringes full of morphine. A description by the German critic, Karl Epting, fittingly sums up the universe depicted in Céline's last works:

> An apocalyptic glow hangs over the figures. Devils and witches dance around man. . . . Nightmare demons sink their claws into the living flesh of men and suck the blood from their veins. And even the doctor, that present-day wizard, is unable to put a halt to their carryings-on.[6]

Not only can he not check the nightmare forces, but he is himself a participant in this underworld. The realm of devils and witches has become his terrain. He had already played a part in that infernal ballet, depicted in *Féerie pour une autre fois. II*, over which a ghoulish creature presides, that double amputee who seems to incarnate evil in his love of horror and his endless hatred. In the last two novels, however, the narrator plays an even more important part in the vast and hellish choreography. He is both performer and onlooker. As a result, the Apocalypse seems announced not by the avenging angels, but by one of its victims, described from *within* rather than from without. Yet, this role is somewhat more complicated still, for the author himself has the function of one of those demon guardians of cathedrals who are destined to ward off evil forces by the hideousness of their grimaces. The action has been described as one familiar to artists of the Middle Ages and consists of the "exorcism of terror by outstripping it," [7] of fighting horror with greater horror still. It is also the belief that since the world is in a state of delirium, it can only be coped with in its own terms.

The exorcism of terror by terror is an old method, primitive perhaps, but not to be underestimated or relegated to the distant past. While we no longer attempt to use torture to draw demons from the bodies of those possessed, nor try the insane for witchcraft, other "time-honored" practices persist. They are often equally medieval in concept and in form. Scapegoats still roam bleating along deserted and stony paths, witches are burnt in crematoriums rather than bound to the stake, *autos da fé* claim whole cities, the rain of fire has mechanical origins but falls nevertheless on the parched and wasted land. The horror is unchanged. The Horsemen of the Apocalypse simply ride through the sky in newer garb.

It matters little that the angel's trumpet has changed its sound to that of the siren. While at its first note, once

> there followed hail and fire mingled with blood, and they were cast upon the earth: and the third part of the trees was burnt up and all green grass was burnt up. . . . (Revelation, 8)

so now is the earth devastated by equally powerful human means.

Céline's last works take place in a universe awaiting the first trumpet call of destruction. The awful moment, when the seventh seal has been opened and there is silence in heaven for the space of half an hour, becomes the tortured instant of eternity which lasts for nearly a thousand pages. All actions are played out in this space of time, spotlighted in the eery light which precedes the holocaust. Suspended at the edge of annihilation, every gesture casts a gigantic shadow, every word calls forth an echo of doom. The contortions of the victims, the desperate motions of the damned, the hideous grimaces of the human and inhuman alike, the macabre jests of the condemned, and the laughter which has a demonic sound, are all that is left to describe. Céline does not reject this harsh task.

DER SÜNDENBOCK

The practices which arise out of despair are manifold. The threat of annihilation calls forth strange and often horrendous measures. The processions of self-flagellants, the long streams of victims toward the various bloody altars, the myriad forms of sacrifice to propitiate the angry gods, to raise the wind, to avert disaster, to hold off the day of wrath—all these are only too well known. Among the oddest, yet most clearly motivated of these customs, is the one which involves the creature known alternately as the scapegoat, der *Sündenbock, le bouc émissaire.* Familiar to many lands, his lot is to be weighed down with the sins and misfortunes of the community and then sent into the wilderness, bearing its misery with him and thus freeing it. Sometimes this role—now that it is no longer practiced in its primitive form involving an actual animal victim —is played by an entire group, sometimes it is one individual who must bear the burden. In either case though, the roots of persecution are blind terror in the face of adversity, and the inability to tolerate the reality of the threat. The outgrowth is the incarnation of guilt and crime in a chosen victim who is then disposed of, in the hope that adversity will be wiped out with him. It is not surprising that Céline, whose last works deal with a world in the throes of desperation, struggling in vain against annihilation, evokes the scapegoat so frequently.

It follows that, once having shown that the sacrifice of *tragos* (or *le bouc*) is no longer valid, just as tragedy that has its origins in this ancient practice can no longer depict man's present condition, Céline goes on to establish the cult of "le bouc émissaire." In the latter, the victim is no longer a sanctified creature, but a shunned, beaten, accursed animal. He is the pariah who is driven out of the human domain to end his life ignominiously in shame and isolation. No longer afflicted with a tragic flaw, but laden with all the stains and humiliations of his fellowmen, he becomes that most hated of creatures, the palpable image of their own failings.

The attempts at exorcism might fail, but the scapegoat who

has been their instrument has not outlived his usefulness. He continues to be necessary as the object on which all fury can be vented, the whipping boy, the lightning rod which continues to receive flashes of wrath even though the house has already burnt down. A figure of this kind plays a part in all of Céline's writings. A procession of protagonists in his works can be formed on this basis alone. They can be aligned in a descending order, from Dr. Semmelweiss to Ferdine of *Nord*, in terms of diminishing stature. In the first novel, while the victim is the butt of the anger, vindictiveness, and stupidity of his contemporaries, he has the romantic grandeur of the persecuted hero. However, even there we find traces of ignominy: Semmelweiss' career ends in madness which, we are told, reduces man to a state lower than that of animals; his life is terminated by slow dissolution, a state during which he is "more decayed than a corpse" (S., 129). In general, however, the protagonist remains a figure of tragic dimensions and his malediction is of a lofty nature. In V*oyage au bout de la nuit*, the picture changes drastically: Bardamu belongs to the world of hostages, of lowly victims, who are reduced to the state of "meat destined for sacrifice . . ." (97). He realizes that he is a member of that society of victims which the world has clamored for during ages past and present. "In the time of corridas . . . I was 'it' [the animal]," (118) states Bardamu, concerning his fate on the "Amiral Bragueton." [8] Had he not already identified himself also as "that indispensable, foul and repulsive dirty dog, the 'disgrace of the human species' who is singled out everywhere in the course of the centuries," (114) in other words, the well-known figure of the scapegoat? Even when he is not designated as the guilty one by others, Bardamu has to contend with his conscience, which strives to accuse him. The feeling of guilt is so highly developed that he admits: "I could never manage to feel blameless for the disasters which happened." (275) *Mort à crédit*, which has been described as "the drama of the guilty conscience," [9] continues and emphasizes this tendency. Ferdinand, the protagonist, has so successfully internalized the guilt heaped upon him that he speaks of himself as "the scapegoat for all blighted hopes . . ." (566). He fullfills his mission admirably. Céline has painted him as a truly abject creature, shameful, repulsive, laden with every possible taint, every imaginable misery. So worn out by his role that he does not have to be driven out of human society, he offers voluntarily to go into exile, to enter the desert of army life, to disappear, even to die.

We must disgress for a moment to consider another of Ferdinand's realizations in *Mort à crédit*. While part of his guilt stems simply from the original sin of having been born, the other crime for which he is persecuted is that of having spoken. The conviction that to voice one's thoughts, to express one's ideas, constitutes a grave danger continues to preoccupy his author as well. Just as Ferdinand had understood that "to confess brings on disaster" (583), so Céline will reiterate the complaint that his writings have been the cause of his own persecution. This becomes especially pronounced in the last novels, where the author makes such statements as: "My books have done me enormous harm," (C., 227) or: "It's *Voyage* which has caused me all the trouble . . . no one has forgiven me for *Voyage*" (*ibid.*, 59). Sometimes he has the insight to place the blame where it objectively belongs. This is the case when he refers to *Bagatelles pour un massacre*—one of his most violent pamphlets, which brought on accusations of anti-semitism, pronazi sentiment, and even collaboration, as "the book of the scapegoat—the one who's slaughtered, cut to pieces!" (C., 228).

In tracing the progression of the scapegoat theme in the works of Céline, we note that a switch occurs after *Mort à crédit*. While the early novels seem to speak for the underling, the outcast, the hunted—in the person of Bardamu or Ferdinand—the author seems suddenly to turn his rage and his black invectives against a group currently persecuted in Germany: the Jews. His enormously violent pamphlets, *Ecole des cadavres*, *Bagatelles pour un massacre*, and *Les beaux draps*, all written at the time when the Nazis were in the process of carrying out their abominations against this and other groups of scapegoats,[10] are indeed material for rather severe criticism or indictment. Whether one subscribes to the view of a writer's *engagement* and responsibility to his society or not, one cannot help but be struck by the admittedly objectionable point of view expressed in these pamphlets, nor deny the propaganda value which their very titles imply. They are undoubtedly dangerous, if not downright lethal utterances,[11] especially when one considers the historical setting in which they must be placed.

The reasons underlying the writing of these works are far from clear and would demand much careful and impartial research before they could be elucidated with some objectivity. Although it is not within the scope of this study to treat the pamphlets in any detail, we must attempt to understand the shift in Céline's point of view—if it was truly a shift—concerning the victim, which these works seem to imply. One can partially agree with the view of one of Céline's critics who states that the author, having previously sympathized with human suffering, with the advent of the pamphlets "reacts against his own nature and attacks the weak . . . the tortured one thus becomes the tormentor." [12] It is very likely that Céline encompasses the two aspects of that couple familiar to such thinkers as Hegel, Baudelaire, and Freud—that of victim and torturer—both in his personal life and in his literary works. However, in the case of the pamphlets, other things must also be taken into consideration. First of all, Céline does *not* consider the objects of his attack "the weak." On the contrary, he is lashing out against what he believes to be, rightly or wrongly, a power group. The Jews had already appeared to him in this light at the time when—concomitantly with *Voyage au bout de la nuit* in which he sympathizes with the sufferings of the underdog in the form of Bardamü—he wrote *L'Eglise*. In this play, the League of Nations is shown to be dominated by "Yudenzweck & Co.," who are involved in a conspiracy very like the one for which he will attack "les youtres" in his pamphlets. His main accusation in the pamphlets is that Zionist groups are plotting a Second World War for their own ends, and against the interests of other groups. While it is conceivable that Céline, whose horror of war was so extreme that it could have unleashed the most savage invectives against any group that he suspected of fostering it, thought he was writing the pamphlets to prevent the possibility of suffering on a worldwide scale, the fact remains that the group he chose to put the blame on was already one which had traditionally played the role of scapegoat. It was also one which was being severely victimized (at least in Germany) at the time of his attacks. In this sense, Céline has joined the ranks of those who, seeing disaster surround them, resort to the rather primitive means of exorcism which relegates guilt to a specific group or individual, and then clamors for the destruction of the guilty one.

Céline has said in *Mort à crédit* that to avow one's thoughts and feelings brings about disaster. He has also realized that his work—often an avowal of ideas so incendiary that they might unleash a furious response from others—will bring about his personal ruin. Had not the narrator in that novel stated: "I will tell such [stories] that they'll return expressly, from the four corners of the earth, in order to kill me . . ." (M.C., 502)? Nevertheless, he proceeds to tell just such tales. Alternately aware and unaware, lucid and blind, he expresses hurt and surprise when the retaliation becomes manifest. The last works of "that bleeding genius, who drags his broken wings," [13] show a narrator full of self-pity, of almost whining complaints. There are numerous remarks in these novels of Céline which take on this tone. Thus we find: "I can no longer count on anyone or anything . . . I've been victimized everywhere . . . . What gifts I had, which I've wasted! thrown to the swine! . . . what strings on my bow!" (C., 306) While Céline often insists that it is his literary career that has brought about his suffering,[14] he is not always able to pinpoint its causes in this manner. Like the hunted animal which twists and turns, trying this path and that in an effort to escape, the author attributes now to art, now to some vague malediction, the fate which he has encountered. Thus, he alternately states that he has been victimized for the past twenty years, in 1956,[15] which would make the beginning of the attacks date from 1936 (the year of the publication of *Mort à crédit*), and that he has been victimized for thirty-five years (C., 265), thus making persecutions date back to a period which precedes the publication of his first work *Semmelweiss*. At the same time he feels that he is a marked man, doomed to be singled out for hatred no matter what his actions are. It is as if he bore the mark of Cain, even before the attack on his brother. He insists: "I've got the face for being blamed for everything! I'm made for it! . . . how happy everyone is that I'm so dumb, that I'm getting it in the neck, that all possible horrors are heaped upon me" (C., 180). An object of horror and ridicule both, he becomes "the old clown" who must jump through fiery hoops, do abject tricks, fall on his face in order to survive—a buffoon who slips on deadly banana peels.

The attacks on the scapegoat are not limited to himself alone, but include members of his family: his wife, his mother. Paradoxically, Céline—so often considered an arch-destroyer of convention—seems to feel the sting of persecution most keenly in terms of his family, an institution which he had so severely derided in his early works. We find several references to the fact that his mother's name, Marguerite Céline,[16] does not appear on her tomb because it has become "a shameful name" following her son's disgrace (C., 30). The rankling nature of this event is shown by a similar mention in Céline's next novel (N., 18). In this instance, the author goes on to add that his grave will be nameless, for "they won't dare put my monicker on my tombstone." [17]

Nord etches the portrait of the victim, the self-image of the scapegoat, with acid humor and even harsher lines. Having sprung the trap of hostility, Céline places himself in it, at dead center. Hated by left, right, and those in the middle, he states that he is doomed to be accused of all things (N., 279), guilty of all crimes (344) from murder to treason, from having been responsible for the death of Frau Kratzmühl's sons to the selling out of the Maginot line (N., 343). While he is at times reduced to the role of whipping boy, of "the dope who pays for everybody," (N., 124) he is often even more severely ostracized. He summarizes his fate in such remarks as: "I've got the talent, no matter which side I'm on, to get myself excommunicated, treated like the lowest untouchable," (N., 275) or: "There always has to be *one* who's the most execrable, the most foul, it's you . . . . there! . . . You're *it*! . . ." (N., 350). The choice of the victim for the sacrifice, the animal for the *corrida*, Céline suggests, is as random yet as unerring as the selection made in Blind Man's Buff. The protagonist of all his works is "it." Only the victim changes from Bardamu or Ferdinand of the early works, to an abstraction called "the Jew" of the pamphlets, to the narrator himself in the last works. The heavy sentence passed upon the scapegoat cannot be commuted. Bardamu had attempted to slink away on the path of "cowardice," Ferdinand had taken that of silence and indifference. In the later works, however, no escape seems possible, no ruse can win the day. Slowly, unwillingly the narrator accepts his state of guilty leper: "You get used to it, but it takes quite a while—to thinking that you're in the way, no matter where you are, that you exude an unbearable stench, that you're really meant to be liquidated." (N., 268)

Only at the very end of his literary career do the works of Céline show the author in a posture—already hinted at by some of his protagonists of former novels—which denotes "that very special bearing . . . of a man who has already given up everything. . . ."[18] It is as though the writer who has seen the world as a mixture of asylum and slaughterhouse, and suffered both from its insanity and bloodthirstiness, has finally chosen removal and indifference as his last retreat. His heroes had already done so: Semmelweiss dies; *Voyage au bout de la nuit* ends with the plea, "Let's talk no more about it!" (493); *L'Eglise* concludes with the words "Curtain/slowly/on all that" (263); *Mort à crédit* terminates in a tired "No!" addressed to the only human being who has shown any concern for its protagonist. The "No" of the last works is wearier, more disjointed, all-pervasive. As the scapegoat, beaten, accursed, humiliated, and laden with crimes, might in the end prefer the silence of suffering alone and welcome the desert, so does the narrator of the last works choose to withdraw into that sphere which is inhabited by all those who have forsaken existence even before the advent of physical death.

And yet, even though everything has been abandoned, the author's voice continues to ring out for a while longer. Whether its phrases are as fragmentary, splintered, ill-fitting as the world they describe, whether its sound is as weary or harsh as the braying of a forsaken animal, or has the hollow tone of a discourse from beyond the grave, its owner must keep speaking till the last moment, until the twitching convulsions of life have stopped, and the grotesque contortions of madmen and butchers, victims and torturers finally are still.

THE WORLD OF GOYA, BOSCH, AND BRUEGHEL

"I only rejoice in the grotesque on the brink of death," [19] Céline states in one of his characteristically paradoxical pronouncements. His remark, made with reference to one of Brueghel's paintings, *Madmen's Feast*, which the author singles out as being the closest parallel with his own vision of existence, is quite significant. He admits that for him, just as for the Flemish master, there exists a central preoccupation with depicting a world in which terror and buffoonery are mingled to produce what he had already described as "horror and laughs" (*C.*, 82). We must add that if Céline sees himself as being "quite Brueghel-like by instinct," [20] it is also because both artists are involved in depicting the absurd and hideous aspect of man, revealed as soon as he is more closely examined, the moment one penetrates the surface manifestations of his existence. This is true even for those areas of life which one likes to think of as idyllic—such as childhood. We need only think of Brueghel's *Children's Games* and Céline's *Mort à crédit* to have an illustration of this concept. What is even more central, though, is the common concern of the two artists with capturing the moment which precedes destruction of one kind or another. We realize that both men are fundamentally describing a madmen's fair in which the convulsions of victims, the lunacy of crowds, the diseases and infirmities of men, the macabre jests of the onlookers or the tormentors are depicted on a gigantic canvas before us, with crude and harsh realism as well as through artistic transposition of the subjects portrayed.

Clarification of Céline's vision (which is the central aim of any comparisons made with the pictorial art of the three painters in question) might also be gained from a *rapprochement* with the work of another artist—Goya. Certainly, his series of etchings on war alone would be a perfect match for some of Céline's most unforgettable writing: that is to say, the pages the author devotes to warfare to be found in *Voyage au bout de la nuit, D'un château l'autre*, or *Nord*. The dreadful and precise notation of abominations, sadness, and torment is carried out with bitter humor and exacting craftsmanship. While the ribald laughter and the down-to-earth obscenity of Brueghel seem to fit in better with Céline's earlier works, the

sharper and more tormented portrayal of Goya has closer
affinities with Céline's last novels. Etched in even somberer
tones, these prose-canvases have an effect as corrosive as the
statements in acid of the Spanish artist.

In the later stages of his literary career Céline himself
links his vision most closely to that of Hieronymus Bosch and
insists that he sees existence as unfolding mainly in "a universe
à la Bosch . . . torture and jocularity . . . ." [21] Indeed, if we
examine the two artists' conception of the world surrounding
them, we find that they depict it as filled with nightmare
creatures, grotesque torments, laughter inextricably linked to
terror—an almost archetypal image of hell. This is especially
true for those portions of Bosch's paintings which treat the
world of the condemned, and the plight of its inhabitants
damned to eternal torment. The desolate landscapes peopled
with demons, monsters, phantoms create an end-of-the-world
ambiance. Eery lighting, flashes of sulphur from bombs and
grenades or hellfire, thunder divine or man-made, dread silence
broken now and then by the shrill cries of victims or the diabolical laughter of their tormentors, sudden outbursts of moans
or curses: these all create the almost palpable terror of both
the paintings and the writings in question. Barring the religious
overtones present in the work of Bosch, the two visions are
almost synonymous. This is not so surprising, since both artists
—of similar sensibility, although separated by time and background—are dealing with subject matter essentially the same,
if we admit that global warfare has apocalyptical proportions.
The fact that in Bosch's universe horror is often lodged in
supernatural creatures and that in Céline's vision we find a series
of lay monsters and beasts, simply connotes a difference in belief concerning the origins of the disaster. Its manifestations,
however, are almost identical, since both artists labor to make
terror and the grotesque incarnate and allow it to totter on the
brink of world annihilation.

Common to the artists evoked here is a predilection which
Céline shares: the linkage of two elements often considered
antithetical—dread and laughter. The startling description of
the author, given by one critic, as "the angel of destruction
[who] is convulsed with laughter," [22] is indeed a fitting one

and only seems paradoxical in an epoch where we do not usually laugh uproariously at physical or mental anguish (or at least the grotesque manifestations of this anguish).[23]

Laughter associated with dread can have several connotations. It may be the only affirmative sign in the midst of destruction; the involuntary grimace of a tormented being, an hysterical outburst that has lost all meaning; a kind of sigh of relief if one is among the survivors, of superiority if one has been spared. The author and his reader, the painter and his spectator, all have the advantage of having survived the holocaust described in the works. Their emotion then is one of dread mixed with relieved or superior laughter. However, in each instance the artist has created great uneasiness in the onlooker by showing him how close he is to being among the victims and how imminent his own annihilation is. The grotesque nature of the spectacle is thus no protection; it simply agitates him all the more by calling forth opposite emotions and creating a greater feeling of participation by engulfing him or forcing him to react with two major forces of his psyche.

If we turn to scrutinize Céline's last works, we find a universe in which all the artists mentioned could easily wend their way among familiar landmarks. The grotesque, which in the early works such as *Voyage*, had consisted of an approximately equal mixture of dread and laughter, in *Mort à crédit* already begins to move toward a predominant mood of nausea and horror. In the final novels, the grotesque takes on a different and much more hideous shade. In *D'un château l'autre*, the scene is almost totally dominated by the dread castle of Siegmaringen with its labyrinthine passageways, subterranean hideouts, secret cupboards and catacombs. It sports that fantastic portrait gallery of the Hohenzollerns which contains an entire family tree of monsters fit to grace any Gothic horror tale. The last living survivor, the ultimate flowering of this hideous clan, is a weird creature, half witch and half mole, who emerges from her subterranean haunt under the castle armed with a pink sunshade; she converses in the midst of bombardments and strafing machine-gun fire for a moment, only to disappear into the earth again forever (C., 133). Other beings, just as weird but more nightmarish in nature, wander about in

this setting of medieval horror. They include the madman who
believes himself the Bishop of Albi and is certain that the
persecution begun in 1209 has not yet ceased (*C.*, 202–203);
Orphize, a movie director, and his starlet who have come to
make a film of life at Siegmaringen, as cheerfully as if they
were producing a soap opera (221–23); an insane surgeon and
the victim upon whom he is about to operate by force and
without benefit of anesthesia (150). The grotesque terror of
the last scene is increased by the fact that the surgeon has an
approving and enthusiastic audience that cries for blood and
urges him on to the sacrifice (161–62). The whole novel is
crowded with a swarming mass of human beings, themselves
victims of one sort or another, herded together in the corridors
of a dilapidated hotel. It demolishes everything in its way,
copulates, defecates, screams for violence, rages for destruction,
insists on scapegoats. Only a more demonic apparition can put
an end to this hellish round: it is provided by Aïcha, the sultry
female executioner who stalks through the novel in blood-red
boots, with Great Danes at her heels, and presides over the
jaws of hell, "la chambre no. 36," where the damned are
dragged to their destruction (162–64).

Hallucinatory scenes such as these, reminiscent of the
diableries of medieval drama, in which the tormenting demons
have ghoulish grins on their faces and the laughter evoked is
strongly mingled with anguish, alternate with somewhat more
humorously grotesque happenings which resemble the antics
of condemned clowns. Among these we find the description of
the ministers' constitutional, during which they relieve themselves in the course of a bombardment, only to proceed once
again on their walk, with absurd dignity and thinly disguised
terror (*C.*, 139–46). Another scene involves an S. S. man whose
Hitler mustache is really fake and has been glued on to give the
desired effect, but can be removed at will should the necessity
arise (*N.*, 265). The almost Chaplinesque quality of this fragment also extends to other incidents in the last novels, such as
the menacing flock of geese which drives a group of German
officials into a nettle patch while they are in search of a
secluded place on a farm to relieve themselves after a hearty
rural repast (*N.*, 264–65); or the excursion of dignitaries to

attend the funeral of one of their group. In the latter instance, the ministers, decking themselves out in yards of filmy material found in the railroad car they are using for their trip and which had originally been built to transport a Shah, dance about in their costumes as if at a Mardi Gras. (C., 289–91) Their outburst of hysterical glee seems to reflect Céline's statement quoted earlier: "I only rejoice in the grotesque at the brink of death."

These books, set on the edge of total destruction, are filled with actors whose contortions are meaningless, and resound with laughter that resembles a madman's cackle or the croaking peal of the trumpet of doom. Their scene is the open-air madhouse of Europe, with Germany in flames as its focal point. Life and sanity end here. The padded doors are shut. The movements of the inmates are as grotesque and haphazard as those of creatures crazed with fear, or prisoners condemned to dance before their execution. And dance they do, with the author there to record the tune, notate the pattern of every move, attentive down to their last convulsive step.

Fear is the spur which urges on their movements and dictates the round. Yet this is not the same fear that Céline had once shown to be a valuable aid in survival, for it has lost all efficacy of that kind. No longer directed toward a useful or hopeful end, it runs rampant and manifests itself in a series of aimless, convulsive moves as futile and absurd as the twitching of a frog's limbs after its head has been severed. Céline had already shown us scenes of this kind—we need only recall the unforgettable passage in *Voyage au bout de la nuit* which depicts the struggles of a tormented hog, surrounded by his tormentors, unable to escape or hide, who knows that he is doomed but cannot cease to grunt, moan, pull at his rope, urinate in terror, attempt to crawl under the bit of straw he has left at his feet (V., 286–87). In the last works, the animal butcher changes to the executioner, the tormented beast is now a human victim, the spectators are as callous as before, however, as they watch with glee the grotesque struggles of the condemned. This is most clearly shown in the passage dealing with the insane surgeon and his victim, alluded to before (C., 161–62). The difference, however, lies in the fact

that the onlookers—and even the tormentors—are themselves
doomed and contemplate the spectacle of their own imminent
destruction. Annihilation is no longer a spectator sport in which
the privileged can with impunity watch the contortions of
their victims. All are caught within one and the same arena,
the circular trap from which none can escape. Fear, then, has
turned to utter and widespread despair.

Céline's hatred of passivity is so great, however, that even
despair cannot be silent. It must express itself in horrendous
ranting or in the grimmest possible form of humor. The laughter
of the last novels no longer resembles the bitter smirk or
macabre jokes of his earlier works. Death itself seems to have
been forced to grin. A vengeful irony twists the faces of the
victims into grimaces resembling laughter, forces the death
masks to smirk. The laugh itself comes close to a hysterical
cackle, a maniacal shriek which bears only a distorted resemblance to its benign counterpart. It is a sound fit only to be
heard in the midst of violence and hate, accompanied by the
rending noises of destruction.

Hate, which had earlier appeared only sporadically or in
the more salutary form of anger, is now unleashed in its full
force. As the world comes to ruin, all dams are removed: the
original blackness within man, within the universe, floods over
everything. In this deluge of apocalyptic dimensions, man is
pitted against himself, against his fellows, and is powerless before the vast forces of annihilation which are as impersonal
as they are horrendous.

The last works of Céline are visions of a hell in which
powers as mechanical as the metallic monsters of Bosch inflict
torment impartially, absurdly. This is no day of judgment, for
man is universally damned. Retribution becomes devoid of
meaning, since the ranks of the just are so thin and their
behavior so unusual that they appear almost as anomalies. No
justice, divine or human, is allowed to reign. Reason, order,
meaning have all long been abandoned. Only the absurd, chaos,
and chance remain. We are now truly confronted by a gigantic
"night epic peopled with mechanical incubi, in which an ogre
periodically appears, who tortures, rends the flesh, and kills." [24]
The tormenting ogre is no supernatural being, however, nor an
agent of divine justice, but man himself, vicious, blind, im-

potent, evil, acting in a meaningless conspiracy directed against life itself. The indictment of him is all the more terrible for Céline's black humor and grotesque portrayal.

The creature who incarnates man in this role is Schertz,[25] the mutilated, insane, and evil being who appears in *Nord*. Epileptic, deprived of both lower limbs, destructive to all those around him, he is man at his ugliest and lowest point. His death by drowning in a cesspool is a fitting comment in this chronicle of growing grimness and desperate laughter.

In the process of annihilation, whether individual or general, hatred is shown to be the principal catalyst. Once the gigantic doomsday machinery has been set in motion, its action is self-perpetuating. Hatred engenders more hatred, until total destruction is achieved by a process as involuntary as a reflex action. Céline phrases it this way: "It appears to me like a dreadful and gigantic skin disease . . . one scratches scratches scratches oneself . . . ."[26] The image suggests several things: the revolting spectacle of a diseased individual or society, mangy, scrofulous, which scratches itself bloody in a vain attempt to gain relief, only to succeed in spreading the disease and killing the sufferer: at the same time, the illness itself is of an ignominious nature, shameful and grotesquely humorous. Both point once again to a view of man as dying ingloriously and essentially by his own hand.

All the elements we have considered lead us to what appears to be the central theme of Céline's last novels: that of gigantic, all-encompassing delirium. It is of course true that the threads of this idea can already be picked up in the earlier works, as the emphasis on madness and mental aberration in all the author's novels has shown. Now, however, it is no longer a case of describing individuals suffering from such a condition, but of entire nations and even continents. All of existence seems depicted as though seen through the bloodshot eyes or the frozen stare of madness. From nightmares, we proceed to full-fledged hallucinations, from the asylum-shelter of *Voyage au bout de la nuit* to the general bedlam of the last novels, from the relatively harmless ravings of mental patients to the vastly more ominous display of hordes of furious maniacs sweeping over the countryside. Sometimes concentrated on the insanity of individuals, sometimes depicting the madness of crowds, the theme of "delirium" threads its way through the numberless scenes of *D'un château l'autre* and *Nord*. We need only leaf through the novels to find illustrations by the dozen: the former lawyer who has gone berserk and has visual hallucinations concerning Hitler (*N.*, 67); the epileptic fits of Schertz (203, *et al.*); the grotesque breakdown of Frau Kratzmühl (*N.*, 250); the senile dementia of the Rittmeister who, tiring of sessions of flagellation, rides off in a final flourish of Prussian glory to fight a phantom horde of Russians (319); the growing insanity of Le Vigan, whose stages are traced throughout the book (311, 380, 381) and include states of catatonia, wild ravings and self-accusation of a crime which he did not commit and which is punishable by death (409). Violence and delirium increase when entire groups go berserk: when the Munich whores turn bacchantes (353–57); a series of murders are committed with seeming lack of logic (391, 394); the entire estate threatens to go up in flames by the work of a group of pyromaniacs (423). Chaotic violence and mass dementia serve as a backdrop for both the last novels, and the behavior of individuals or groups only highlights and pinpoints what is a more general and therefore more amorphous action of the same nature.

In this infernal and grotesque round which is performed on the edge of the abyss, we are aware of the double function of the dance. This had been so even for Céline's early novels, where the author "made his characters play a buffoonish mime, without ever forgetting that the comic deliverance was valid only for the fictional universe and that elsewhere an infinitely more terrible drama was being acted out." [27] While it is true that we still grimace in a way which resembles laughter and find some grimly comic relief in the late works, the buffoonery has come to resemble the antics of madness. The infinitely more dreadful drama is no longer played elsewhere; it is before our eyes and all around us, revealing itself in all its full-blown terror.

At the same time that this unity is achieved, both man and his universe become incoherent, fragmentary, disjointed in every sense of the word. We find ourselves in a world rent to pieces, ready to fall asunder, to crumble, dissolve, return to ashes, to original chaos.

SOLVET SAECLUM IN FAVILLA

From the mummies of Sainte-Eponime in *Voyage au bout
de la nuit* and Courtial des Pereires' balloon in *Mort à crédit*,
objects, places, people in Céline's novels have fallen to dust.
Dissolution, decomposition, disintegration has attacked everything in sight: human emotions, language, memory, beliefs,
traditions, institutions. The last novels will show us this rotting,
crumbling, falling apart in terms of the world at large.

Everything is set for the final scene. The reader finds himself in the center of Europe, in one of those landlocked places
from which there is no exit, caught in a gigantic fiery trap. The
sky has become the lid of a cauldron pressing down. At times,
it opens to admit spurts of flame and other missiles of destruction. Within the trap, aimless and vicious movement, a few
last convulsive twitchings of the victims which result in the
death of their fellow sufferers, is all that is left to be observed.
The feeling of doom is all-pervasive. It is a world about to end.
Everything appears suspended, ready to fall, to be dissolved,
consumed.

It is as if one were to view a filmstrip of the Apocalypse in
slow motion, stopped now and then to allow one to contemplate
it, to study in detail every one of its horrors. The décor, which
had already trembled and fallen to partial ruin in *Féerie pour
une autre fois*, is, in the last works, one of fragmented or
totally desolate nature. The setting is that of the center of
destruction—Germany just before its defeat—with cities razed
to the ground or resembling necropolises, with broken signs
as the only indication of former human habitation, and rivers
that are only fit to run in the shadowy world of the dead.
Berlin, in the core of this devastated landscape, is a ghost city.
It is as meaningless as a cardboard stage set built on a river
that is equally terrifying: "The Spree, the Styx of the Teutons,
. . . how slowly, inexorably it flows by, muddy, black" (*N.*, 46).
The few houses which still remain standing resemble ruins in
surrealist paintings:

> A floor, in a house opposite us, as if suspended between the
> columns of the building . . . like a hammock . . . the floors
> above and below it were no longer there . . . blown away!

> . . . nothing existed any longer in this house except an airy
> mezzanine . . . and its great staircase. . . . (N., 63)

The Zenith Hotel—which would more aptly be named the
Nadir—where the narrator and his fellow travelers live, is
equally on the verge of disintegration: its walls crumble at the
slightest touch, its hallways end at every turning in chasms seven
stories deep (N., 54–55). Everything is about to fall into oblivion: "Soon, there would be nothing left of the houses . . .
only a bit of dust and bomb-craters . . ." (59). But these are
only the more immediate and minor signs of devastation. The
precarious state of the material world is matched by the near-
death and growing disintegration of those who inhabit it.

Both individual personalities and groups of people undergo
a process of fragmentation, progressive decay, and dissolution.
In D'un château l'autre, Siegmaringen is a kind of graveyard,
"[a] harbor for all the shipwrecks of Europe" (261), in which
the outcasts of various countries are deposited like flotsam at
low tide. In physical terms, the survivors of the last two novels
are rapidly deteriorating. They are, almost without exception,
ill, maimed, or mutilated to such a point that they no longer
resemble men but vestigial forms of life—such as Emile in D'un
château l'autre and Schertz in Nord. The narrator himself drags
his infirm body along on canes, and seems close to death at
several points in the story. One of the few remaining stores
specializes in prostheses and various objects for the crippled and
maimed, and even its salesmen are all mutilated (N., 43). The
emotional wreckage is even greater. Nearly all the individuals
seem on the verge of insanity or mental disintegration. Most
end in this way.

The falling apart occurs in every realm and in all possible
directions. Consciousness recedes or is blotted out by drugs,
madness, death. Societies founder; all moral codes are abolished;
values no longer even have the function of façades. The structure of the world is about to cave in, bombarded by explosives,
but also by other missiles: those of fear, hatred, pain. The last
works, and especially Nord, describe the moment—an excru-
ciatingly long moment—before the world falls to total ruin. All
signs foretell the coming end. The dread Horsemen who announce its advent are advancing from the corners of the earth.

The pounding hooves of the beasts on which they ride tear everything asunder. Places, objects, bodies, minds, even words crumble before them.

It is evident that the splintering, rending process, to which everything is subjected in Céline's last works, must be reflected in the style itself. It becomes increasingly fragmented, disjointed, thus giving us at times halting, almost incoherent passages or monologues that pursue each other but do not meet. It is as though the words were filtered through the chaos they describe. They come at us, like a shower of intermittent missiles—phrases that crack, break, gasp, perish. If they are to reflect "the lack of coherence in the fragmented universe of minds that have lost all sanity," [28] this is the form—or formlessness—they must assume. Then, words, which for Céline serve more than just to describe the world around him but make it palpable, must become as much a part of this world as possible: they must incarnate it, resemble its very shape. Thus, they become one with the decor, with those "façades which stand, gape, float, fall apart, are scattered, peeled away by the wind" (*N.*, 59); or with those fear-crazed, disintegrating individuals who are themselves only damaged façades, about to sink and founder into oblivion. The narrator himself, who is present in the holocaust both as chronicler and victim, barely survives to tell his story. He speaks with the halting voice of the "grand malade," knowing full well that the tale he tells is fragmented, disjointed. "Don't blame me if I tell everything in disorderly fashion . . . the end before the beginning!" (15) Elsewhere, he entreats the reader to take the shreds of his *récit* and to piece them together, to reweave the worn fabric which depicts the world ending: "Treat this bunch of anecdotes like so many fragments of a tapestry . . . you go ahead and patch them, fit them together as well as you can. . . ." [29]

Céline, in his last works, is the chronicler of events without order, coherence, structure. In a world in a state of chaos, in which at every moment all can be overturned, reversed, blown to bits, atomized, how can the chronicler be any more fixed and ordered than the subject he is treating? If the writer is more than a mere eyewitness, but a sounding board for the events he describes, then he must vibrate with his subject in

order to render an authentic sound, although it is a distorted
and chaotic one.

In order to get the ultimate vision of the abyss which
Céline describes, we will probably have to await the publication
of his last novel, which forms the third panel in the triptych
describing the Western Apocalypse. The first two panels, *D'un
château l'autre* and *Nord*, described the foundering world so
completely that it is hard to imagine how much further the
author can go. We have already partaken in a journey which
leads no longer only to the end of night, but to the end of
existence itself. As they stand, these last two works depict an
almost total eclipse of sanity, well-being, joy, and meaning in
human existence. The Fall, not from some sort of earthly
paradise but into terrestrial hell, has been made manifest. The
desolate, tortured landscapes, the contorted, moribund individuals, the raving masses sweeping over everything on their
way to annihilation, the faltering voice of the narrator which
fails, stops, weakly drones on—all speak of imminent doom.
The writer himself, no longer an angry prophet but a broken
one, shouts in a pained tone the shame and terror of the
sinking world in which he, also, must go down. Like some
ancient mariner, he fixes his piercing Breton eyes upon us,
clutches us with his bony hand, and as though under a curse
which will not let him be still, croaks in his dreadful voice the
tale of an albatross as large as the world and equally hideous.

Notes

1 "Je suis la foudre, les cataclysses" (popular deformation of "cata-
clysmes"). Manuscript copy of *D'un château l'autre*, Vol. IV, "Brouillons"
(unpublished, in the private collection of Michel Bolloré, Paris), p. 21.

2 Robert Poulet, *Entretiens familiers avec Louis-Ferdinand Céline*
(Paris: Plon, 1958), p. 98.

3 *Ibid.*, p. 2

4 An unpublished manuscript which appears to be an early version of
D'un château l'autre, refers to men as "crocodiles with big ideas!" (p. 396)
and states that "there is only one heartfelt cry which they utter in unison:
'let the others croak!' " (p. 397) See note 29.

5 Maurice Clavel, "Trois Ecrivains Parlent de Céline . . . ," *Arts*,
LCCCXVII (July 1961), 3.

6 Karl Epting, *Frankreich im Widerspruch* (Hamburg: Hanseatische
Verlagsanstalt, 1946), pp. 52–53.

7 Nicole Debrie-Panel, *Céline* (Lyon: E. Vitte, 1961), p. 143.

8 The theme of the sacrificial victim seems to pervade all of Céline's writing. This becomes again apparent in the projected title of his last, unpublished novel which was to be "Colin-Maillard," or blindman's buff— a game dating back to ancient customs of choosing a human sacrificial victim—until Céline decided on its present title of "Rigodon." (Information obtained during an interview with Céline's editor, the late Roger Nimier, in September 1961).

9 Poulet, *Entretiens* . . . , p. 75. In connection with this point, Poulet quotes Céline as saying: "Even as a child, I had a very clear feeling of culpability," indicating that the preoccupation with guilt was deeply ingrained in the author's own personality.

10 One should remember that the publication dates for the pamphlets were the following: *Bagatelles pour un massacre*, Paris, Denoël, 1937; *L'Ecole des cadavres*, Paris, Denoël, 1938; *Les beaux draps*, Paris, Nouvelles Editions Françaises, 1941.

11 Even one of Céline's friends, the painter Vlaminck, exclaimed on reading *Bagatelles pour un massacre*, "It's an invitation to a Saint-Barthélémy [massacre] ! ! ! [*sic*]" Letter from Vlaminck to Lucien Descaves, January 19, 1938. Private collection of J.-C. Descaves.

12 E. Kaminski, *Céline en chemise brune ou Le Mal du présent* (Paris: Les Nouvelles Editions Excelsior, 1938), p. 27.

13 Poulet, *Entretiens* . . . , p. 67.

14 The idea that the artist who is genuine or sincere in his work will necessarily be hated and persecuted by society is expressed on numerous occasions in Céline's work. The most concentrated elucidation of this idea can be found in his *Entretiens avec le Professeur Y* (see especially pp. 9, 10, 29, 32, 33, 44, 70).

15 Letter to Albert Paraz, June 4, 1956, *Le Menuet du haricot* (Geneva, 1958), p. 49.

16 Whose name the author had chosen for his pseudonym.

17 Facts do not bear this out: although Céline's burial was of an almost clandestine nature, his tombstone carries the two names under which he lived: "Louis-Ferdinand Céline / Le Docteur Destouches." His wife's name figures beneath. The grave itself is in a small but well-kept cemetery at Meudon, outside of Paris.

18 Dr. Quentin-Ritzen, "Trois Ecrivains . . . ," p. 3.

19 Letter to Léon Daudet, 1932. *L'Herne*, No. 3, 92.

20 *Idem.*

21 Letter to Ernst Bendz, *L'Herne*, No. 3, 124.

22 Poulet, *Entretiens* . . . , p. 2.

23 This would not be at all the case for the Middle Ages, for example. We might here point to the medieval spirit which seems frequently present in Céline's work and is best exemplified in his penchant for opposites, his belief in the vileness of man, his preoccupation with death and disease, etc.

24 Nadeau, *Littérature présente* (Paris: Corréa, 1952), p. 159.

25 The name Schertz is in itself an example of Céline's black humor, for it means "joke" in German—a rather dreadful pun, considering the characteristics of the creature the name designates. As has already been mentioned, in the new edition of *Nord* the names are changed: there, Schertz has become von Leiden, the Baroness Tchulf-Tscheppe has been

renamed Thor Thorfels, etc. Much of the humor is lost, since Céline was not alive to make the revisions and name the characters himself in his inimitable fashion.

26 Letter to Lucien Descaves, Denmark, 1948; in the private collection of J.-C. Descaves, Paris (unpublished).

27 Michel Beaujour, "La Quête du délire," *L'Herne*, No. 3, 284.

28 *Idem*.

29 Unpublished manuscript of what the author of this study judges to be an early sketch for *D'un château l'autre*, p. 442. Originally in the private collection of J.-C. Descaves, Paris; recently acquired by the New York University Libraries (Special Manuscript Collection).

5 · L'Autre Côté de la vie

> Our voyage is entirely imaginary. Therein lies its
> strength. It leads from life to death. Men, animals,
> cities, things, everything is imagined. . . . It suffices
> to close one's eyes. One is on the other side of life.
> *(Voyage au bout de la nuit)*

METAMORPHOSES

Céline's journey, which has led us to the edge of life, does
not end there. Having explored every recess of a world in
shadow and flames until we have reached the very limit of night
terrors, knowing that we can go no further along this path unless it is to plunge into total annihilation, we must turn back.
Not along the same road, for nothing but utter chaos awaits us
there. The downward path has been so well traveled, so clearly
shown to lead to a dead end, that one might suggest an ascend-
ing voyage. While Céline's vision is not totally nihilistic as
has often been suggested,[1] he would tend to disparage such a
move or compare it to the grotesque efforts of Courtial des
Pereires in *Mort à crédit* to make his ascensions in the balloon
which was so tattered and worn out that it could only serve as
a winding sheet. Only one road remains open. It is a detour,
full of hazards and hard to travel, but there is no other way to
turn. When all has been denied, besmirched, blackened and
reduced to ashes, one can shut one's eyes to the dreadful
spectacle or interpose a lens which magnifies and alters it.
Céline admits this quite openly: "For me, real objective life
is impossible, *unbearable*. It drives me crazy—makes me furious
it's so ghastly. So I transpose it as I go along, without breaking
my stride. I suppose it's more or less the world's pervasive illness we call poetry." [2] Of course, what Céline terms an illness is also the only drug remaining when all other remedies
have failed. It is close to the "2 cc's of morphine" which offers

solace to the desperate crew that peoples the last novels. Art, poetry, dream, hallucination, myth provide the only possible detour. This realm—beyond the paroxysms of hatred, ugliness, and suffering—has served as a last retreat to many writers sickened by the aspect of reality. Céline takes his place among them.

The cry of "Oh, to leave this world!" so reminiscent of Flaubert, of Baudelaire, already resounded in *Voyage au bout de la nuit*. It will grow more plaintive in tone in *Mort à crédit* and finally develop into a desperate scream in the last novels. It reflects the realization that in a totally impossible world there are only two choices: to go under or to get out. The way out, in Céline's terms, is neither easy, graceful, nor heroic. One may have to crawl, lie, cheat, or hack one's way through a wilderness of animate and inanimate obstacles. Nor does one attain a utopia as a result of this struggle. In simplest terms, all one can hope for is a shelter from ugliness, misery, and terror. The realm of art is a thorny one, and the artist himself a man condemned to hard labor. Céline realized this early in his literary career. He writes: "I am nothing more than an instrument of work and treat myself as such. Existence is much too heavy and monotonous to bear without continual artifice . . . ." [3] At the end of his life, when existence has taken on an even grimmer form, Céline's work—although frequently disparaged by him—remains the only possible reason for making any assertive efforts at all. While both the world of the everyday and the realm of art are a torture, a torment, artifice or the transfiguration of reality is the sole remaining gesture of any validity or significance.

The problem is more complex, however. There is no simple juxtaposition of art and reality, of the poetic and the *quotidien*. Nor is Céline suggesting mere flight into the aesthetic realm. The futility of various types of flight has been fully explored in the novels of Céline: Bardamu flees in vain from continent to continent, unable to come to terms with either the old world or the new; Ferdinand shows that there is no escape into the past, even into childhood dreams; Courtial des Pereires' flights of fancy and dreams of lighter-than-air vehicles end in destruction; even the genius of Semmelweiss could not soar above the jagged peaks of reality. This reality, which in Céline has only the vilest connotations, continually intrudes or forces its way into the realms of the imagination, of fantasy, of art.

In the last works, however, we find a development of a trend already visible in the early novels: reality takes on such a hallucinatory aspect that it is hard to separate it from the realm of fantasy. We witness what has been described as "incantational delirium." [4] The implacable exploration of this delirious reality, as well as the attempts to overcome it by a kind of exorcism, create an important part of the dynamism of these works of Céline. At the same time, one may also note a quest for delirium, as an escape from time, failure, horror. This has already been true for such works as *Voyage* and *Mort à crédit*, where "delirium . . . provides a brief moment of reconciliation with fate." [5] In the last novels it is no longer even a momentary truce of this kind, but the briefest of respites, a sudden—if brutal—removal from reality. In the first writing of Céline as in the last, it is clear that one must take the leap if one wishes to turn one's back on existence: "In order to truly flee, one has to pass through the mirror, into the domain of dream or madness." [6]

On the far side of the mirror, however, lie not only the dream, madness, or death, but also fantasy, poetry, and myth. When all has been tried and done, when the sullied mirror has been held up to the entire world—the only remaining step is to shatter the glass and recreate a new image from its splintered parts. While for the characters of the novels only apathy, madness, or death seem to be the result, their author has the path of recreation open to him. He becomes the artist who sees beyond reality or transfigures it, Céline "the visionary or the 'creator of mirages.'" [7] Comparable to the alchemist who has taken metal and proven it to be dross, he then proceeds to transform it into a new and marvelous form.[8] More than any of these, however, Céline is a powerful juggler of reality and unreality, of rational and irrational alike, a true *maître ès métamorphoses*.

Sometimes his sleight-of-hand tricks are comical: they plant a mustache on an elderly lady or change doughnut-eating into a major patriotic activity, turn Vichy ministers into a flock of

honking geese or Lavalle into a guardian of the virtue of
German maidens. At other times, the transformations occur on
a more grandiose scale. Immigrant ships turn into galleys embarked on voyages of an epic nature; the Bois de Boulogne
becomes the scene of a vast and horrendous orgy; a London
night spot turns into Death's amusement center; an old
bateau-mouche takes on the mythical shape of Charon's barge
which ferries the souls of the dead to the underworld. Sometimes we are witness to disappearing acts: Robinson in V*oyage*,
who enters suddenly upon the scene, vanishes just as swiftly,
only to turn up again, furtive, unpredictable, phantomlike. The
author himself plays a part in this act: he wears a series of
masks, ducks in and out of his works, present and absent in
turn, mystifying, leading the reader astray. Often, we seem to
be watching a shadow play in the course of which Céline creates
"magical transformations of beings and things which produce effects that are sometimes tragic, sometimes comic." [9]
Reality melts into the fantastic, expands, stretches, swells until
it attains the gigantic proportions of a fairy tale or myth: the
customer in *Mort à crédit* changes in size like Alice, touching
the clouds, sweeping the whole city along with the hem of her
petticoat (575–81); the mass attack of the inventors on the
offices of the "Genitron" takes on the guise of storming a
citadel (940–43); the channel crossing in the same novel turns
into a scene of titanic vomiting, of almost superhuman retching
(610–13). Finally, the metamorphoses become frankly hallucinatory. The transfigurations no longer belong in the realm of
former fever-dreams or nightmares. They are now closer to the
visions of the mentally deranged. In *Mort à crédit* already,
Ferdinand, crazed with disgust and terror, had seen the dead
Courtial des Pereires reappear before him (1067–68). A similar,
but even more terrible vision pursues the narrator of *D'un
château l'autre*, taking on the form of a "hallucination," in
which the ferryman of the dead and his crew appear in threatening guise (76–97); just as in *Pont de Londres* death suddenly
grimaces from under the sombrero of a Spanish dancer (263).

The world of changing realities—whether in humble form
or in grandiose garb—greatly preoccupies Céline. Thus, we
find that an ordinary voyage undergoes a change through which

we glimpse "a ridiculous little infinite . . . a small vertigo for imbeciles" (V., 214); however, we are also allowed to witness gigantic adventures in which neither the infinite nor the vertigo assume mean proportions. Such voyages may lead the human being to the ends of reason and of life; he may wander "in the absolute, in those glacial solitudes where the passions no longer awaken any echoes, where our human heart, terrified, beating to the breaking-point on the road to the Void, is nothing more than a lost and stupid animal." (S., 121) Sometimes this heady sensation of emptiness is the result of the most extreme loneliness, such as that experienced by Bardamu in his hotel, the "Laugh Calvin." The Void becomes manifest. It seems to stand within his reach: "At that moment I became as if dissolved. I felt quite close to simply not existing any longer." (V., 203) The moment the present scene disappears, the instant the warm, noisy, although revolting and vicious movement of existence ceases, we are confronted with a no-man's-land of silence, a void, which borders on the terrifying reaches of the absolute. "Céline takes us beyond those safety rails which we habitually fear to cross." [10] Outside of these barriers, beyond the frontier of the habitual scene, lies the realm of delirium —but also that of art, of legend, and of myth.

It is neither a safe nor a careful place. The dangers are great for those who enter and those who dwell there. Nor does our guide reassure us and promise protection from monsters and strange beasts. There are no guard rails, no life preservers on the ship which he steers through a nightworld as treacherous as the seas encountered by any mythical hero. Once the dividing line between reality and unreality is broken, once the personal and the impersonal merge, the rational and the irrational combine, the mirror has been traversed—and we find ourselves "on the other side of life."

Yet, the eclipse is never total; the metamorphosis is not complete. The worlds on either side of the mirror cannot be kept apart. Céline—and we—shuttle back and forth among them, reaching now into one, now into the other. There are no watertight compartments. There is not even the certainty of having arrived beyond the pale. Like some restless Theseus, Céline's reader is driven in and out of the labyrinth, propelled

forward and pulled back, a puppet at the end of a length of
string. No calm or fixity must be achieved. The work subjects us
to a series of almost continual flashbacks from one world to
the other. This is probably among the main factors which make
Céline's writing so powerful, or even overpowering. The reader
is unsettled, repeatedly traumatized by this forced switch from
hard reality to pliable fantasy, from furious railing to glacial
silence, from the banality of the present scene to the vast
panorama of cosmic scope.

    Yet, this is also the great strength of Céline's visions. It
is the basis of his ability to give literature a singular scale of
sounds and to create "that new tone . . . which unites the
harshest realism and the most profound poetry, and from which
springs . . . the *myth*." [11] The double function of the writer,
his aptitude for straddling two worlds at once, for looking
forwards and backwards, out and in, with the harsh glance of
the realist and the veiled gaze of the seer, makes him as powerful
and enigmatic as Janus, god of the gates. Is it surprising that
he appeared, to those who saw him at the end of his life, as
having the dual visage of "an inspired *clochard* . . . a visionary
beggar."? [12]

"L'EXTRA-VOYANT LUCIDE"

    The role of the seer—whether in myth or in literature—
has always been reserved for those who could pierce the veil of
appearances to reveal what lies beneath and beyond. From
Tiresias to Rimbaud and on, the gift of second sight has been
the province of those who could penetrate into the universe
that lies on the other side of the mirror. The visions, which
are the result of such a vantage point, are both magnificent
and terrifying. They range from the image of the snake-crowned
Medusa to that of the winged Pegasus, from rending jackals
to the smiling Isis, from the thundering beasts of the Apocalypse
to the mystic rose.

    "L'extra-voyant lucide" (the "lucid super-seer"), as one
of his characters calls Céline (*C.*, 76), has often been classed
with those authors whose visions are concentrated at the
terrifying, the hideous end of the spectrum. "Céline has the
eye which sees things from the bottom and the back, the kind

of second sight which discerns the Gorgon's head through the mask of outer appearances," [13] one critic insists. While it is perfectly true that Céline is principally allied with the night world and is a familiar spirit among the dark powers of primeval anger, destruction, and chaos, he has also—on occasion—traveled in the land of Pegasus, of Isis, of the rose.

Céline, the creator of legends, the mythmaker, the poet, the bard, is less well understood than his implacably realistic double. Yet one is as vital as the other to the understanding of the author's complex personality. Just as "le docteur Destouches" cannot be separated from Louis-Ferdinand Céline, the realistic cannot be extricated from the poetic side of his character. Together, they form the several voices with which Céline is able to speak at one and the same time, the synthesis of worlds he knows how to effect. The author himself states: "As a Breton I'm mystical, messianic." [14] This and a number of other statements indicate that he considers himself among the dealers in legends, visions, myths. The mission of those who are familiars of this domain is, first, to *see* beyond reality. Céline seems amply fitted for this task. Le Vigan, the chief character involved in one of the hallucinatory visions of *D'un château l'autre*, recognizes this and tells the author-narrator of the work: "you're made to see us . . . especially." (85) As in legends or myths, the specialist or the seer is the only one able to perceive visions, and has been chosen to do so. Once he has seen beyond reality, he must synthesize his vision, and render it in the form of words for those who wait. The synthesis and interpretation of visionary or mythical experiences, which is the second stage in the process of making them known to the populace, is entrusted to the oracle, the bard, the poet.

While some of those who knew him well tend to see Céline as a mystic in the medieval tradition—although stripped of religious involvements—an illuminated, ascetic visionary, or a thundering preacher of nonreligious sermons, it seems much closer to the truth to include him among the members of another time-honored cult: "the ancient tradition of the poet who raves and prophesizes." [15] What is central, is the role of the poet, a role which Céline reserves for himself in no uncertain terms. Equally important is the term "to rave." As we have already pointed out in reference to other aspects of Céline's work, delirium—whether evoked by fever dreams, trances, madness, or artistic fervor—is one of the central themes as well as one of the predominant techniques in his writing. In discussing some of his past work, Céline states, for example: "I had to raise everything to the level of delirium. Then, things began to fit together naturally. . . ." In the same breath he mentions, however: "I am lucid; that's my redeeming quality." [16] These two seemingly contradictory statements illuminate the paradoxical epithet of "extra-voyant lucide" which Céline has given himself in *D'un château l'autre*. At the same time, it explains the curious nature of Céline's poetic vision: one in which delirium and lucidity [17] alternate, where the other side of the world joins with this, or poetry and reality merge to create the myth.

Perhaps Céline would best be placed in the bardic tradition: that of the *aède*, or the illuminated tramps of Celtic origins, the Breton jugglers, or those old men of North Africa and the Balkan countries who still practice the art of the oral epic—all the tellers of tales, the creators and perpetuators of legends and of myths. The figure of the bard has many affinities with that of Céline (one might suggest that Céline, indulging in a characteristic play on words when naming a character, chose his hero's name "Bardamu" for its connection with "bard"). Thus, the oral quality of his work is striking; the epic elements can easily be discerned; the emphasis on the poetic aspect is undeniable. The author himself gives us a clear picture of such a role, full of characteristic humor and directness, while suggesting more serious overtones: "I'm first of all a Celt-*day-dreamer, bard*, I can turn out legends like taking a leak . . . . legends are my music." [18]

The author's preoccupation with legend or myth is fairly pronounced. Many examples of it can be found in his writings. *Voyage au bout de la nuit* already gives evidence of such a tendency in its very epigraph. Added to this, we have the presence of Bardamu's mysterious double, Robinson, who flits phantomlike in and out of the novel. Bardamu himself embarks on a voyage which can be compared to that of the traditional hero journey to the other world and back. There are also many accounts of almost legendary adventures which include Bardamu's travels through the African jungle, his journey on a galley, etc. Céline's own opinion can be glimpsed through the fact that he is reported to have been extremely pleased with a comparison made by a French critic who likened *Voyage au bout de la nuit* to those gigantic stone blocks—or heads— found on Easter Island,[19] whose origins and meaning are unknown, but which undoubtedly have legendary or mythical significance. In *Mort à crédit*, the emphasis on legend increases. Among the most important passages concerning this facet of Céline's writing are those dealing with "the legend of King Krogold" (512-14, 519, 635).[20] The story of Krogold, almost childlike at the outset, or symbolic of childhood, seems close to the realm of the fairy tale or that of pure escape literature, with the help of which one can flee from the miseries of existence. However, it evolves and erupts at various points in the novel to indicate major crises in the clash of the two opposite poles of existence: that of the dream and that of brutal reality. Variously referred to as "an epic romance" or "a Celtic legend,"[21] it first appears in a chapter characterized by its down-to-earth level and provides a sharp contrast through its elevated, poetic tone (512).

The most important statement contained in the Krogold legend is found in the dialogue between Death and Gwendor, "the magnificent," who is the hero of the tale. The former insists: "There is no kindness in this world, Gwendor! nothing but a legend! All kingdoms end in a dream!" Death's severe judgment of existence is borne out. The bestial, monstrous forces of Krogold win out over Gwendor, the melancholy dreamer. The barbarous triumphs. The monster fails to be slain by the hero. The tale ends in his defeat. And the fate of the legend itself is almost as sad as that of its protagonist. The forces of harsh reality assail it in a way which turns it into a danger for its creator, Ferdinand. Accused of having debauched a fellow employee by this subversive exercise of the imagination, he is chastised for having dared to bring some glimpse of poetry into a world of brutal misery. Yet, he finds it impossible to totally renounce the realm of dream, legend, myth. Even as an adult, Ferdinand has not been cured of this penchant: he affirms his right to tell tales, even though it might be at the risk of his life (502); he is willing, if necessary, to make degrading bargains in order to preserve this right, to trade stories with Mireille, the local whore. Thus, he proposes: "You tell me some filthy stories . . . and I in turn will let you hear a beautiful legend." (502) The dichotomy between "filth" and "legends" marks the entire novel with the former characteristically outweighing the latter.

The legend of King Krogold, while it provides a key to some of the important basic themes of *Mort à crédit*, also interests us because certain of its elements appear in Céline's late novels. Krogold's castle, which only appears in silhouette form in *Mort à crédit*, will emerge more fully in the monstrous habitations of the last works: the nightmare castle of *D'un château l'autre*, the Schertz estate of *Nord*. Krogold himself, who massacred the population of an entire village with the help of his mace and a pack of Great Danes (635) could easily be the ancestor of Aïcha and her hounds, as well as of the various other tormentors who figure in the late novels of Céline. The descendants of Gwendor, on the other hand, can be found among the graceful, harmonious creatures who inhabit the author's "coins de tendresse": Lili, Mme Bonnard, the old couple of musicians, Bessy, and others.

Legend or myth appears to be a fragile thing. It can easily be soiled, damaged, destroyed. In *Mort à crédit* we had already been told "it's as fragile as a butterfly. At the drop of a hat it falls apart, sullies you" (513). In *Féerie pour une autre fois* it becomes "lace so finely . . . spun, so delicate, that if you but touch it, you tear it all! . . . irreparably!" (144) The beings associated with this realm are equally perishable and have, like Mme Bonnard, "that delicate, fragile invalid . . . that finesse, like a lacework of waves" (*C.*, 218). While both the legends and the people connected with them are easily harmed or lost, while they disappear or perish at the hands of more brutal forces, they are a necessary if painful affirmation of a realm which Céline claims for his own: that of poetry.

It must of course be added that Céline's own poetry is much more robust than the legends created by his characters. This is mainly due to its constant cross-fertilization with brutal realism, and to its forceful delivery. Neither limited to the description of delicate domains which depend on a lacework of subtlety, nor based on a style which has the fragility of a butterfly's wings, the poetic vision of Céline can withstand the onslaught of many more attacks than that of Ferdinand or Gwendor. His myth-making activities are much more powerful than any of theirs, for the former are protected by a barrage of verbal arrows and defended by a flow of invectives as lethal as boiling pitch.

Besides, the myths themselves are couched in terms which are a demand, almost an attack on our feeling and senses. Legends are attained by means of one of Céline's major stylistic devices, colorfully named "le métro émotif" ("the subway of the emotions") and aptly described in these terms:

> I take everybody along! . . . willingly or by force! . . . along with me . . . the subway of emotions, mine! . . . direct! into emotion! . . . from one end to the other! . . . let the travelers be in a dream . . . let them not realize what's happening . . . enchantment, magic . . . violence too! . . . I admit it . . . all the travelers crammed in, locked up, double-locked. . . .[22]

The poet then coerces the reader to submit to his visions. He locks him in the moving vehicle which takes hold of his feelings by force or violence, in order to project him into the world of dream, legend, alchemy, magic. The writer's craft is both weapon and vehicle. It is that style considered as terrorism by which the author attempts to "force the dream into reality." [23] The work involved is difficult, demanding to the utmost. It combines the arts of the composer, the oracle, the surgeon, and the witch doctor. The following statement affirms this:

> This kind of versified prose which is my genre . . . is work as fastidious as crossword puzzles or composing music. It's lace-makers' work, devised with emotion and violence, but without showing its threads.
>
> It's like making tables turn. That trance state wears me out. Only few mediums are enthusiastic ones. . . .[24]

While the task is exhausting, the tables must continue to turn, the medium cannot refuse the trance, "l'extra-voyant lucide" must go on seeing and proclaiming his visions.

The knitting together of two worlds, of dream and reality, of verse and prose, of delicacy and violence, is done in elaborate lacemaker's fashion and forms a pattern so tight that no one thread can be pulled out or even distinguished from the other. In this fascinating network of opposites, mere dichotomy would seem elementary. Céline's work does more than simply partaking of two worlds. It *is* true that the author "drinks only water, yet is capable of Dionysian laughter." [25] However, the water and the wine, sober realism and violent exaltation are so intermingled as to be inseparable. By the same token, it is not sufficient to point out Céline's "antibiotic prose which, like the dragons in fairy-tales, defends the entrance to the realm of poetry." [26] For the prose often brusquely switches to poetry, the dragons move in and out of the gates, breathe their fiery fumes in the pure ether, carrying terrified and bewitched riders on their backs.

What Céline seems to find when he probes beneath the superficial layer of opposites—a layer in which raw emotion and poetic utterance, formal perfection and wild delirium, meticulous discipline and utter freedom are considered diametrically opposed—is that there is a basic unity which can be grasped and rendered visible, palpable, through the skill of the writer. He is willing to reveal the formula by which such alchemy is achieved:

> I follow emotion close behind the words . . . take hold of it raw—in its poetic state—for in spite of everything, the deepest layer in man is poetry.[27]

THE DANCING GOD

"The meaning of tragedy," Nietzsche said, "can be interpreted only as a concrete manifestation of Dionysiac conditions, music made visible, an ecstatic dream-world." [28] "In tragedy," he continues, "the tragic myth is reborn from the matrix of music." [29] Céline, who is reported to have read Nietzsche avidly in his youth, seems to reflect a number of the philosopher's concepts in his last novels. We note Céline's own Dionysiac tendencies as manifested in his writings: the dithyrambic quality of much of his language; the trancelike penetration into the realm of man's destructive, primal drives;

the dizzy stare into the abyss; the triumph of the irrational forces of existence; the involvement with myth. In the last works, and especially in *Nord*, we witness the performance of age-old tragedy in modern dress. It is as if Céline were giving the answer to Nietzsche's demand for that tragic myth which is to be reborn from the matrix of music. For both writers, if tragedy is to have meaning and power, it must be founded in music. Céline is as clear on this as Nietzsche. The former affirms: "I have to transpose everything. If a thing doesn't sing, the soul doesn't know it exists. To hell with reality! I want to die in music, not in reason or in prose." [30] He enlarges on this statement, this time speaking in a more virulent vein: "Anything that doesn't sing is a pile of crap. 'A man who doesn't dance confesses some disgraceful weakness,' says an old French proverb. I put dancing into everything." [31] Céline then goes on to reaffirm one of Nietzsche's central ideas—expressed in *Thus Spake Zarathustra*—when he states: "We don't dance anymore —everything's in *Dancing*. Nietzsche (so overblown usually) wasn't wrong when he wrote 'I'll believe in a God only if he dances!' " [32]

It is under the aegis of this dancing god—or goddess— that much of Céline's writing takes place. Dance from the simplest to the most complex manifestation, from the most literal to the most symbolic, plays a significant role in the work of the author. We need not here dwell on his lifelong predilection for dancers, nor on his technical and almost medical interest in the dance form,[33] or even the literary genre which he termed "ballet" and used for his more lighthearted creations. What is much more significant is the author's passionate involvement with movement of all kinds and his equal hatred of fixity: that of words, thoughts, feelings, states of being. Dance, which is the essence of movement, free from random gestures and contingent acts, is then diametrically opposed to fixity, lethargy, death. It can be considered the movement of life, synthesized, formalized, transfigured into art. The dancer who performs the acts necessary to this art becomes then a kind of priest, just as does the poet or musician. Céline tends to see himself in all these roles, for he assures us: "Legends are my music . . . I *hate* prose . . . . I'm a poet and would-be musician. What interests me is a direct message to the nervous system." [34] (The nervous system, in Céline's thinking, seems akin to the center of man's feelings, his inner core or "soul" without, however, attributing any religious connotations to the last term.)

It becomes clear that Céline feels that his art, like that of the dance or of music, goes beyond the prosaic manifestations of movement, sound, or language. It penetrates to a level of experience which belongs to the realm of poetry, illumination, myth. It is an expression of the harmony—actually the only harmony which Céline allows in his great dissonant creations—between the human being and the cosmos. The dance itself would then become a mystical rite by which the world of appearances is shorn away or transgressed. More than that, it becomes an act of creation. A world is born or reborn by the action of a dancing god—not unlike Siva of the Hindu religion, but more like the recent incarnation provided by Nietzsche—and the dance then takes the shape of final affirmation. It is a savage affirmation, for the rebirth of a world takes place in true Dionysian fashion: it must first be rent to pieces in order to be resurrected in a transfigured state.

We can most clearly observe this act of destruction and creation if we study a phenomenon in the works of Céline which, on the surface, seems paradoxical but which, when considered with the enactment of Dionysian ritual in mind, becomes deeply revealing: it is the ascendancy of the maimed hero paralleled by that of his opposite, the dancer, which we have already alluded to early in this study. A progression may be noted by comparing *Voyage au bout de la nuit*, which contains only some indirect references to the dance and in which the disablement of the principal characters is of a passing nature (Robinson's temporary blindness, Bardamu's war injuries), to the last works, in which the narrator is "75 per cent mutilated" and in which one of the central figures is a double amputee, but the figure of Arlette, Lili, Lucette—the dancer—grows more and more prominent. As the world is progressively torn to pieces, dismembered or devoured by bloodthirsty maenads or more mechanical destroyers, the urgency of the dance becomes even greater. The figure of the dancer—the dancing goddess—emerges clearer and stronger from the bloody rubble and the destruction. Hers is the sole remaining matrix, through her the only rebirth possible.

In simplest terms, the dancer incarnates form, firmness, unity in a universe that is amorphous, chaotic, devoid of meaning. She can be considered "a small island of grace and nobility, lost in the sordid disintegration of being." [35] Indeed, she appears in this guise in the last works of Céline. But she is also a symbol of much larger dimensions, a link with the most ancient rituals of destruction and creation, death and resurrection. Seen in this light, woman or the dancer, the author or interpreter of a creative force, becomes either a priestess or the goddess herself. Her functions achieve a mystical meaning, and union with her becomes a way of attaining the infinite.

The goddess can take on a variety of forms: that of an old woman who opens a world of subtle and profound relationships, of wave lengths seldom captured which reveal "une sorte de musique de fond" (a kind of subterranean music) (*C.*, 218); that of a charming, laughing, tantalizing nymphette (*P.L.*); or of a forlorn young woman living in the English countryside whose song enchants the listener, and whose very presence is "an enchantment, a mirage . . . when she passed from one room into another, it created a void in one's soul" (*M.C.*, 729). In similar fashion, Virginia has "a sweet majesty . . . in her slightest gesture," a bearing that makes her appear "a creature between earth and heaven." (*P.L.*, 86) Woman's dreamlike, legendary, or mystical aspect is also—and perhaps most clearly —incarnated in Molly of *Voyage* who, when seen in this light, appears to be akin to the sacred rather than the profane whore. She then takes on the role and the functions of the healer and becomes the matrix from which man may be reborn, emerge anew, after having been rent by existence. In this guise, her gift to Bardamu (the record "No More Worries") resembles that of her lesser sisters, those "splendid, gracious hostesses," who offer Bardamu "the erotic promiscuities . . . needed to rebuild [his] soul." (*V.*, 227)

Sexual union, which Céline sometimes considers only to be a momentary delirium that brings man into contact with nature, at other times resembles the doctrines of Shaktism, in

which coitus is considered a means of attaining Nirvana.[36] In
the first instance, Céline suggests that sexual gratification is
really "a bonus which nature gives to coitus and reproduction:
it allows a guy a few seconds' delirium which permits him to
communicate with her." [37] In the second case, we are confronted with an experience which Céline describes as "that
profound adventure . . . mystically anatomical" (V., 55).
There, woman becomes a divinity, a vessel embarked on a
mythical voyage (V., 463), a door to the infinite. Her awakening from sleep, that moment of blinding beauty "when matter
becomes life," reveals all her powers of resurrection and creation. In the act of possessing her, "one rises to that infinite
plain which opens up before man." (V., 464) Rather than the
quest for Nirvana or oblivion, sexual union appears a voyage
toward discovery, transfiguration, and renewal. It is a mystical
experience, leading to a confrontation with the central vision of
existence. Not in vain does Vera (the dancer) say to the hero
of *L'Eglise*: "Ah, Ferdinand . . . as long as you live you will
always search for the secret of the universe in the loins of
women!" (E., 232) For both Ferdinand and his author are con-
firmed adherents of the cult of "érotico-mysticisme."

The cult, thus entitled by Céline, is based on a triple doctrine: the worship of perfect forms (described earlier in this
study); the movement of these forms as expressed in dance or
sexual union; finally, the mystical experience of all rituals observed. The secret of the universe, which woman holds within
her, is not that of repose or fixity but that of motion, purified,
refined, or of dross, or of contingency, of the rhythmic pulsa-
tions of a dance performed "de l'autre côté de la vie."

As the vessel of motion, she also becomes the vehicle
which carries man to the realms of the beyond. Her image
is linked to that of the barge, the ship, the ark. She is then addressed as: "the three-masted schooner of tender joy, en route
to the Infinite!" (V., 463) While boats of all kinds are quite
clearly associated with the world of dreams, delirium, and death,
the works of Céline also establish similar roles for woman. She
is included among the moving, graceful, tender, magical vessels
which appear here and there in his novels (V., 343, 531–32;
M.C., 516, 601, 707, 711, 714, 785, 792, *et al.*). Their task, and

hers, is to carry the voyager through the locks of existence, across
rapids and shallows, into the realms of freedom and vast motion: the infinite sea. The glimpse, even though it lasts only
for an instant, justifies the voyage. Men, although limited to
the narrow confines of their disintegrating bodies, are no longer
implacably damned to being "cuckolds of the infinite" (V.,
333). Or at least, only after having embraced the infinite in the
shape of woman.

The goddess, however, has a double face. The female incarnation of the dancing god Siva also reveals the dread visage
of Kali, the destroyer. Her rite demands victims, the dance can
also become the annihilator of life. Both mother-goddess and
terrible divinity, her kingdom is no reassuring haven, but the
primordial cradle of death and birth alike. Céline shares this
vision, as the many hideous and bloodthirsty female figures in
his works can testify. This is not surprising, for in the realm of
delirium, whether poetic or religious, mutilation and annihilation are as imminent as renewal and rebirth.

This dualism can be related to two important categories
in Céline's vision of existence: "the hard pole" as opposed to
"the soft" one, a dichotomy also reflected in his stylistic pen-
chants. The disintegration of the individual, the falling apart, the
process of dissolving, putrefying, and liquefying, can all be
classed in the category of "softening" as can the fragmented
nature of the language. It is a loss of form, unity, and direction,
and can be connected with disease, maiming, and destruction.
At the opposite pole, we find the "hardening," which relates to
formal movement, unity, direction, creativity. While it is true
that the author despises fixity and advocates motion in everything he does, we see that this motion is in itself of a twofold
nature and that it can lead in diametrically opposed directions:
disintegration or construction. In similar fashion, the deformed,
crippled movements of creatures as maimed as Emile in *D'un
château l'autre* and Schertz in *Nord*, can be contrasted with the
effortless grace of the women dancers whose every motion is
an affirmation of form in a progressively formless universe. The
soft, rotting corpse of the world is sharply juxtaposed with the
hard, brilliant silhouette of the dancer.

The role of the artist, the creator, giving form to chaos is

thus similar to that of the god who dances. The dance of the
writer occurs in his style, in the construction and elaboration
that is the end product of his craft. The very architecture of a
work of art provides that firm framework which opposes it to
the amorphous, liquefying nature of existence which Céline
emphasizes. The domain of language remains the realm from
which the literary craftsman must draw his raw materials. The
manner in which he hammers, forges, tempers them, determines
the shape of his creation. The apprenticeship is long, the work
conditions hard, the risks great. The creative process, when it
has as vital a function as it does for Céline, involves all the anguish of labor, all the triumph of birth. In the task of conceiv-
ing, nurturing, and giving life to the work of art, the artist plays
all three roles: progenitor, parturient, and midwife. All join
in the final act of expelling the newly created entity, all labor
"to force the dream into reality." [38]

The conditions necessary for this process can be related to
the cult of "érotico-mysticisme" of which we have already
spoken. Thus, during the preparatory stages of creation, artistic
foreplay demands an ambiance of dream, mirage, trance, delirium—all terms which we have seen applied to erotic experiences, but which hold as true for the poetic act as for the carnal
one. Poetic delirium is thus defined as "that free-flowing quality,
like an open tap . . . [which] to do it right, has to come from a
man's core . . . not from his head." [39] We note the emphasis
on the nonrational and even antirational approach to creation
in Céline. The cerebral realm seems both sterile and lowly to
him: "There's nothing more vulgar, more common, more disgusting than ideas! . . . All the impotent are overflowing with
ideas!" (Y., 19) Does not the statement suggest that emphasis
on the rational is injurious to both artistic and physical potency?
Mirage, trance, drunkenness, the unleashing of the various
Dionysiac forces is then considered to be paramount, if any
act of procreation is to begin.

The role of the progenitor is variously described. At times
he is termed a medium, an alchemist, or a seer: a being who
can reveal or transfigure the world about him. "I know how to
make tables turn," Céline insists in one of his last interviews.[40]
At other times, he describes the process of "transmutation from

mirage to paper . . . [as] Alchemy!" [41] Emphasizing both the
difficulty of the task and the artist's powers, he states further: "I
know the music at the bottom of things. . . . If needed, I
could make alligators dance to Pan's flute. But then again, it
takes time to make the flute and strength to blow: and often
my flute feels so light, it seems to slip out of my fingers." [42] In
other moods, Céline tends to assign the role of *accoucheur* to
the artist, in which he is only instrumental in bringing an already completed creation into being: "Everything's there; I
don't really create a thing. I clean off a forgotten medallion, a
statue sunk in the clay." [43] We might be led to read a Neo-
platonic notion into this remark, were we not immediately re-
called to Céline's universe by the sentence which follows. There
he describes the process of creation as taking place in this order:
"mirage, digging, then cleaning house," and thus ascribes a
simple workman's role to the artist.

However, whether the artist is portrayed as a medium, a
seer, an alchemist, or a midwife, whether as a master of metamorphoses he is as great as Orpheus or Pan, his role remains
fundamentally a dynamic one. It is this dynamism which, for
Céline, is at the center of the creative act and gives impetus to
the dance. This does not mean to imply of course that this dynamism is necessarily a joyful or lighthearted one. The frolick-
ing figure of Pan can at a moment's notice reveal its other
aspect, which is that of profound terror. The Orphic spell not
only enchants rocks and beasts, but can also result in the dis-
memberment of him who casts it. The dancing god has several
incarnations. His creative powers encompass those opposites
which make for the deepest unity of experience: dread and joy,
brutality and tenderness, negation and affirmation, destruction
and rebirth.

Style, which is the visible form given to the dance, the
vehicle which transports the mirage onto paper, the shape
given to the flute so that it may emit the necessary sound, the
formula which makes the alchemist's craft become manifest,
must then encompass all the elements it wishes to convey. In
order to produce the dread which is central to Céline's vision,
he uses an approach by which "style [becomes] like a terrorism." [44] We must pause here, to re-emphasize the tonic powers

of terror which liberate and activate the emotions. Its cathartic
and bloodletting virtues are as potent today as they were in
ancient tragedy. The reader is both cleansed of previous or
superficial notions, and reduced to a state of momentary weakness or paralysis, during which he is at the mercy of the writer.
In such a condition, he can be willingly or against his will confronted with the vision of the artist. Céline is well aware of the
power such a situation gives him. Brutally, yet with extreme
care, he thrusts his work in the reader's path, allowing him no
escape. As we have already seen, the author then takes the
reader—by force if necessary—on a voyage made possible by
the stylistic vehicle he has described as "the subway-all-nerves-
magic-rails-across-those-three-dots" (Y., 116). The destination
of this "métro émotif" is the dream, spontaneous poetry which
the author considers one of man's earliest and most meaningful forms of expression, emotion in its most direct state. The
entire aim of Céline's style—and in a sense the aim of his whole
work, since he considers himself first and foremost a stylist—is
then to render emotion raw, as it is experienced, fresh, una-
dorned, unadulterated. Such a concept carries out the fundamental purpose of the work of art, as far as Céline is concerned,
which is the stripping away of all that is contingent, superficial,
glossy, facile, nonessential.

The technique used to achieve this might be described by
the term stream-of-emotion, different from the stream-of-con-
sciousness we know so well yet not totally unrelated to it. Basically, its aims are similar to those of interior monologue since
the major preoccupation is with recording, as directly as possible, the workings of the mind or the experience of feeling states.
However, since Céline is basically antirational and anti-intel-
lectual, his major emphasis is on the recording of emotions, not
thoughts. The author himself is quite conscious in the use of
his technique. While he at times dismisses it as a mere trick [45]
(un truc), he also emphasizes its revolutionary stylistic innovations: "[It is] a little find, but [one] which nevertheless shakes
the novel up so hard that it will never recover from it! the
Novel doesn't exist any longer!" (Y., 86)

The invention which the author lords over his contemporaries—the authors of "the Novel" who were working in the traditional prose form when Céline embarked on his literary career and emphasized the distinction between the *written* and the *spoken* language—is an intriguing one. The author seems to have arrived at it by a path which proceeds along the following lines: spontaneous poetry, which is one of man's deepest forms of expression, has its roots in emotion; it is this which must then be captured and set down. However, "emotion is fussy, flighty, slippery . . . by its very essence: evanescent." (35) The author concludes—and this is his "little find"—that "emotion can only be captured and transcribed through spoken language . . . the memory of spoken language!" (28) We see that Céline is a conscious enough artist to realize that what he is transcribing is the *memory* of such language, that his use of spoken language in written narrative is an artifice. He makes no attempt to record what he hears, as some writers do who set down, almost phonetically, various forms of speech that are either dialects or colloquialisms. He quite clearly asserts that his aim is to "artificially remake, in writing, an *ideal* spoken language." [46] His method for doing so is compared by the author to that of the Impressionists: they did not invent " 'the out-of-doors' as one claims! . . . they weren't as dumb as that! . . . but the 'impression' of the 'outdoors' " (36). In other words, what counts is not to record spoken language (or the outdoors, in the case of the Impressionists) but to create the *impression* of spoken language. Céline's means for achieving this are extremely intriguing: they involve distortion, refraction. When describing the process, the author returns to the image of "le métro émotif," whose rails lead straight into emotion. However, they only *seem* to be straight and in actuality are not. "It's really quite simple . . . the rails which give the 'impression' of emotion, appear absolutely straight, but aren't so at all" (111). The trick for achieving seeming directness resembles "the whole secret of Impressionism . . . that of refraction!" He continues to explain: "your stick will seem straight . . . if you break it first . . . before plunging it into water!" (123) What Céline describes is a method which reverses the usual phenomenon of plunging a straight stick into

water and, with the aid of refraction, making it appear bent or
broken. In other words, the stick—or sentence—is broken first,
so that, as a result of refraction, it will appear to be straight.

Much of Céline's stylistic individuality is clarified by an
understanding of this principle. The breaking up of traditional
sentence structure, the famous use of the three dots, the often
fragmentary appearance of the narrative, the ellipsis of phrases,
the jagged rhythms are all related to the fundamental idea of
obtaining seeming directness by means of what the author
terms "the impressionistic trick." It is true that quite a few
critics interpret his technique mainly as reflection of his vision
of existence,[47] whence such extreme statements as that of J.-P.
Richard, who insists that "the very movement of the dialogue
imitates the gestures of flowing or falling apart: the language
responds to the scandalous diarrhea of the human being with
its banter, its own logorrhea." [48] It seems evident, however,
from Céline's own statements concerning his literary techniques,
that he is aiming to do something quite different. It is not that
his sentences have been allowed to fall apart, to spill unimpeded
unto the page, in an effort to echo or imitate the state of human
existence as he sees it. Instead, the author seems to have taken
the traditional sentence—so venerated in French prose—and
subjected it to rigorous treatment of the "impressionist" sort
in order to obtain the desired illusion. It is a *controlled* effort,
purposely designed and carefully aimed to do violence to "the
lovely seventeenth century sentence . . . taking the wind out
of it, dismantling it, disarticulating it, reducing it to its prime
elements and reconstructing it according to his own rhythm.
. . . His journey to the end of language has led him to the
lands of a new language." [49]

In order to attain the realm of this new language, that
"*ideal* spoken language" which can depict and activate the
stream-of-emotion, it is then necessary to utterly destroy syntax
and literary language of the traditional variety. The first of these
transgressions is certainly not novel and has been brilliantly
achieved by such poets as Rimbaud and others; the destruction
of literary language, or of the boundary between written and
spoken language, is much more original. It is in this area of
stylistic exploration where Céline appears as an innovator of

major proportions. Paradoxically, it is the very success of his stylistic innovation which prevents us from appreciating it in all its magnitude: the use of spoken language has become so much a part of contemporary literature that we find it hard to imagine what a truly revolutionary stylistic contribution it was at the time of its first appearance.[50]

While the foregoing statements emphasize the side of Céline that is the destroyer—in terms of style, just as we had already noted a similar role in terms of vision—we must also affirm that he was a conscious, conscientious, and even meticulous creator. At first glance, the last of these affirmations seems untrue or at least unfounded: for one of the most striking features of Céline's style is its apparent nonchalance, carelessness, or *débraillage* (negligence), to use one of the author's own terms. The words, the phrases appear to be thrown unto the page, artlessly and without effort. This however, is further proof of Céline's powers of *trucage*, of mystification. For in actuality, Céline filed and chiseled his phrases as carefully as any Parnassian; as obsessively perfectionistic as Flaubert, he wrote and rewrote, corrected, retouched, built up, enriched, elaborated. The thousands of pages of rough drafts which led to a finished work of several hundred, the endless trials and corrections which can be found in the manuscripts, the exhaustive bouts of revisions to which his secretaries attest—all are proof of this. Céline himself is explicit on this phase of creation: "I start every sentence over again, 10 or 20 times . . . and those poor idiots who think that I improvise! . . . It's all measured to the millimeter, man!" [51] This meticulous labor, reminiscent of the lacemaker's art, necessary in the devotee of virtuosity of any kind, is the effort Céline demands of his craft. With the deep involvement and the almost ritualistic perfection necessary in the pursuit of any art—whether music, dance, or literature—Céline erects the only edifice which he will allow to remain standing, with all the care and precision of a master builder.

Céline the destroyer builds no temples to art. We have seen him take a sledgehammer to existing structures. Thus, the only edifice he will admit to is not a motionless monument. It consists rather of the structure of the rite itself: the act of writ-

ing, a ritual as moving and full of movement as a dance, as
formal and yet continually being formed as a gesture in space,
as timeless and timely as the human voice, as dreadful and
brutal as destruction, as exhilarating as creation. It is an age-
old rite of affirmation, the recognition of primal forces, the
joining of opposites, a profound and difficult unity of vision.
And this act must be performed in accord with the fundamental
dynamism of life and the ruthless perfection of art: The dancer
must move with flawless grace, the musician play the tune which
drowns out all lesser melodies, the poet forge his language into
a harsh and joyous mold, if out of the blackness, the work of
art is to emerge and the night of wrath be made fruitful.

Notes

1 See for example: Trotsky, Brodin, Orlando, Brasillach, Epting,
Nadeau, Suarès. Glicksberg, in his *Nihilism in Contemporary Literature*
suggests, however, "the tragic sense of life may prove enormously heartening
aesthetically, even when it ends in absolute nihilism as in the case of
Journey" (218).

2 Letters to Milton Hindus, *Texas Quarterly*, V, No. 4 (1962),
32.

3 Letter to E. Pollet, August 1933, *L'Herne*, No. 3, 100.

4 Pol Vandromme, *Céline* (Paris: Editions Universitaires, 1963), p. 46.

5 Michel Beaujour, "La Quête du Délire," *L'Herne*, No. 3, 282.

6 *Ibid.*, p. 280.

7 Marc Hanrez, *Céline* (Paris: Gallimard, 1961), p. 75.

8 As he himself says: "I'm a bit of an alchemist, as you've probably
already noticed. . . ." Manuscript of an early variation of *D'un château
l'autre*. Unpublished. In the special manuscript collection of New York
University Libraries.

9 Nicole Debrie-Panel, *Céline* (Lyon: E. Vitte, 1961), p. 131.

10 Robert Stromberg, "La Source qui ne rafraîchit pas," *L'Herne*, No.
3, 269.

11 Henri Thomas, "A propos 'd'Un château l'autre,'" *L'Herne*, No. 3,
296.

12 Marcel Audinet, "Dernières rencontres avec Céline," *Les Nouvelles
Littéraires* (July 6, 1961), p. 4.

13 Karl Epting, *Frankreich im Widerspruch* (Hamburg: Hanseatische
Verlagsanstalt, 1946), p. 53.

14 Letters to Hindus, *op. cit.*, 4, 34.

15 Robert Poulet, *Entretiens familiers avec Louis-Ferdinand Céline*
(Paris: Plon, 1958), p. 10.

16 Letter to Eugène Dabit, *L'Herne*, No. 3, 88.

17 Céline's "lucidity" is of a special brand. Not in the line of rational
thought, it comes closer to describing the unflinching confrontation of the
misery and absurdity of existence.

18 Letter to Hindus, *op. cit.*, p. 27. For the French version, see *L'Herne*, No. 5, pp. 67–111.

19 Reported by Jeanne Carayon, Céline's first secretary, during a personal interview in the fall of 1962.

20 See also my article on this subject, "Céline et le thème du roi Krogold," *L'Herne*, No. 5, 201–206.

21 Manuscript version of *D'un château l'autre*, in the private collection of Mme Lucette Destouches.

22 *Entretiens avec le Professeur Y*, p. 102. Note also the remarks by the author concerning his use of argot: "[It's] a language of hatred which knocks the reader out, annihilates him! . . . puts him at your mercy!" (*Ibid.*, pp. 71–72.) In reference to this, see also Céline's "L'argot est né de la haine. Il n'existe plus," *L'Herne*, No. 5, 31.

23 Letters to Hindus, *op. cit.*, p. 37.

24 Letter to R. Poulet, "Lettres de l'exil," *Ecrits de Paris*, XCIII (October 1961), 109–110.

25 Hanrez, *Céline*, p. 155

26 Philippe Sollers, "Interférences," *L'Herne*, No. 3, 207.

27 Letters to Hindus, *op. cit.*, p. 25.

28 *The Birth of Tragedy* (New York: Doubleday Anchor, 1956), p. 89.

29 *Ibid.*, p. 144.

30 Letters to Hindus, *op. cit.*, pp. 32–33.

31 *Ibid.*, p. 30.

32 *Ibid.*, p. 31.

33 Céline's widow stated, in my latest interview with her, that the author was planning to write a booklength study on the dance, with her as co-author, when death overtook him.

34 Letters to Hindus, *op. cit.*, pp. 27–28.

35 J.-P. Richard, "La Nausée chez Céline," *La Nouvelle Revue Française*, X, No. 116, 242.

36 Hanrez, *Céline*, p. 83.

37 Hanrez, "Céline au magnétophone," *Le Nouveau Candide* (November 23, 1961), 14.

38 Letters to Hindus, *op. cit.*, p. 37.

39 *Ibid.*, p. 31.

40 André Parinaud, "L.-F. Céline" (interview), *Arts*, LCCCXXX (July 1961), 3.

41 Letters to Hindus, *op. cit.*, p. 32.

42 *Ibid.*, p. 25.

43 *Ibid.*, p. 37.

44 J.-L. Bory, "Du Braoum dans la Littérature," *L'Herne*, No. 3, 225.

45 Letters to Hindus, *op. cit.*, p. 26.

46 *Ibid.*, p. 36.

47 Richard, *op. cit.*; Drieu La Rochelle, *Le Français d'Europe* (Paris: Editions Balzac, 1944), p. 43.

48 "La Nausée chez Céline," *La Nouvelle Revue Française*, CXVI, 239. It should be noted that Céline himself makes joking references to his "logorrhée" ("Brouillons," unpublished, in the collection of M. Bolloré, pp. 7, 38).

49 Maurice Nadeau, *Littérature présente* (Paris: Corréa, 1952), p. 162.

50 A critic like R. Poulet feels that Céline's first work had such an enormous impact that it could be considered "an event comparable in

importance to the creation of Stravinsky's *Rite of Spring*." (Statement made during a personal interview with the writer of this study in September 1962.)

51 Poulet, *Entretiens* . . . , p. 5. The author of this study can testify to the truth of this statement, having consulted and studied the thousands of pages of revisions which go into each of Céline's novels.

I. WORKS OF LOUIS-FERDINAND CÉLINE

In French

A l'agité du bocal. Pamphlet. Paris: P. Lanouve de Tartas, 1948. Also republished in L'Herne, No. 5 (1964), 22–27.

Bagatelles pour un massacre. New edition with 20 photographs. Paris: Denoël, 1943.

Ballets, sans musique, sans personne, sans rien, 2nd ed. Paris: Gallimard, 1959.

"Carnet du cuirassier Destouches." L'Herne, No. 5, 9–11.

Casse-pipe. 4th ed. Paris: Gallimard, 1952.

"Casse-pipe" (fragment). Manuscript in the possession of the author of this study. Also published in L'Herne, No. 3, 167–69.

D'un Château l'autre. 20th ed. Paris: Gallimard, 1957.

"D'un Château l'autre." Manuscript version in the hand of the author. In the private collection of Michel Bolloré, Paris.

Entretiens avec le Professeur Y. Paris: Gallimard, 1955.

Féerie pour une autre fois, I. 12th ed. Paris: Gallimard, 1952.

Féerie pour une autre fois, Normance II. Paris: Gallimard, 1952.

Foudres et flèches, ballet mythologique. Actes des Apôtres. Paris: C. de Jonquières, 1948.

Guignol's Band. I. Paris: Gallimard, 1952.

L'Ecole des cadavres. Paris: Denoël, 1938.

L'Eglise, comédie en cinq actes. 4th ed. Paris: Gallimard, 1952.

Les beaux draps. Paris: Nouvelles Editions Françaises, 1941

Le Pont de Londres (Guignol's Band II). Paris: Gallimard, 1964.

Mea Culpa suivi de La Vie et l'oeuvre de Semmelweiss. Paris: Denoël et Steele, 1936.

Mort à crédit. Revised edition. Paris: Gallimard, 1950.

Nord. Paris: Gallimard, 1960.

Nord. Definitive edition. Paris: Gallimard, 1964.

Semmelweiss. 10th ed. Paris: Gallimard, 1952.

Voyage au bout de la nuit. Paris: Denoël et Steele, 1932.

Voyage au bout de la nuit suivi de Mort à crédit. Bibliothèque de la Pléïade. Paris: Gallimard, 1962.

In English Translations

Death on the Installment Plan. Tr. H. P. Marks. New York: New Directions, 1938 and 1966; London, England, The Bodley Head, 1966.

Guignol's Band. Tr. B. Frechtman and J. T. Nile. New York: New Directions, 1954.

Guignol's Band. Tr. B. Frechtman and J. T. Nile. London: Vision, 1954.

Journey to the End of Night. Tr. H. P. Marks. New York: Little, McClelland, 1934. New York: Grosset, 1936. New York: New Directions, 1934 and 1961. London: Vision, 1950. New York: New Directions (paperback), 1959, 1960.

Mea Culpa and The Life and Work of Semmelweiss. Tr. and with an introduction by Robert Allerton Parker. New York: Little, 1937. London: G. Allen, 1937.

Articles, Pamphlets, Talks, Prefaces, Lyrics, Correspondence of Louis-Ferdinand Céline

"Chansons," *L'Herne*, No. 5, 25–27.

"Correspondance de Céline" (letters to such persons as Léon Daudet, Eugène Dabit, Lucien Descaves, Eveline Pollet, le Docteur Camus, Albert Paraz, etc.), *L'Herne*, No. 3, 85–160.

"Correspondance de Céline" (letters to such persons as Erika Landry, Elie Faure, Lucien Combelle, Milton Hindus, Perrot, Galtier-Boissière, Georges Altman, etc.), *L'Herne*, No. 5, 35–137.

"Des pays où personne ne va jamais. . . ." (taped interview with Céline by Jean Guénot and Jacques Darribehaude), *L'Herne*, No. 3, 185–90.

Hommage à Emile Zola. Talk by Céline, in *Apologie de "Mort à crédit"* by Robert Denoël. Paris: Denoël et Steele, 1936.

"L'argot est né de la haine. Il n'existe plus," *L'Herne*, No. 5, 31.

"La médecine chez Ford," *L'Herne*, No. 3, 173–80.

"Les assurances sociales et une politique de la Santé Publique," *L'Herne*, No. 5, 12–18.

Letters of Céline in *Le Gala des vaches* by Albert Paraz. Paris: Editions de l'Elan, 1948.

Letters of Céline in *Le Menuet du haricot* by Albert Paraz. Geneva, 1958.

"Lettre de prison." *L'Herne*, No. 5, 310.

"Lettres de l'exil" (Introduction by Robert Poulet). *Ecrits de Paris*, XCIII (October 1961), 103–10.

"Le 'Voyage' au cinéma" (recorded conversation between Céline and Jacques Darribehaude about a cinematographic adaptation of V*oyage au bout de la nuit*). *L'Herne*, No. 3, 191–94.

"Louis-Ferdinand Céline: Excerpts from his Letters to Milton Hindus" (Introduction by Milton Hindus). *Texas Quarterly*, V, No. 4 (1962), 22–38. See also the French originals of these letters and the introduction by Milton Hindus in *L'Herne*, No. 5, 67–111.

Preface to *Bezons à travers les âges* by Albert Serouille. Paris: Denoël, 1944.

"Préface inédite de Semmelweiss." *L'Herne*, No. 3, 163–64.

"Rabelais, il a raté son coup." *L'Herne*, No. 5, 19–21.

"Réponse aux accusations." *L'Herne*, No. 5, 319–25 (Céline's defense against accusations of collaboration, written during his exile in Denmark).

Unpublished Material

Letters from Céline to Lucien Descaves. In the private collection of Jean-Claude Descaves, Paris.

Manuscript copies of "D'un château l'autre," "Féerie pour une autre fois," "Guignol's Band." In the hand of the author.

In the private collection of Mme Lucette Destouches (Céline's widow).

Manuscript, in the author's hand, of what the writer of this study considers an early version of parts of "D'un château l'autre." Originally in the private collection of Jean-Claude Descaves, Paris, now property of New York University Libraries.

Rough drafts ("Brouillons") of various portions of "D'un château l'autre." In the private collection of Michel Bolloré, Paris.

Typist's copies with corrections in the hand of the author of portions of "Guignol's Band," "Normance," "Féerie pour une autre fois. [I]" In the private collection of Céline's secretary, Marie Canavaggia.

II. CRITICAL WORKS DEVOTED TO CÉLINE; COMMENTARIES ON HIS LIFE AND WORKS (Major studies or those of unusual interest will be indicated by *.)

Anissimov, Ivan. "Préface à la traduction russe de 'Voyage au bout de la nuit.'" L'Herne, No. 5, 165–72.

Accamo, Giano. "Céline, prophète de la Décadence orientale," L'Herne, No. 3, 218–22.

Antonini, Giacomo. "Fortune e sfortune di Ferdinand Céline," Corriere Mercantile-Genova (May 13, 1965):

———. "Misericordia per Céline," Il Gazzetino-Venezia (May 4, 1965), p. 3.

Audinet, Marcel. "Dernières rencontres avec Céline," Les Nouvelles Littéraires (July 6, 1961), pp. 1, 4.

Audouard, Yvan. "Que dites-vous de Céline," Le Nouveau Candide (July 7–13, 1961), p. 16.

Aymé, Marcel. "Sur une légende," L'Herne, No. 3, 213–18.

*Beaujour, Michel. "La Quête du délire," L'Herne, No. 3, 279–89.

———. "Temps et substances dan 'Voyage au bout de la nuit,'" L'Herne, No. 5, 173–82.

Benn, Gottfried. "Letter to M. Oelze," L'Herne, No. 5, 141.

Bernanos, Georges. "Céline," Le Nouveau Candide (July 6, 1961), p. 16. Reprint of Bernanos' article on Céline written for Le Figaro in 1932.

*Boisdeffre, Pierre de. "Sur la postérité de Céline," *L'Herne*, No. 5, 213–22.

Bory, Jean-Louis. "Du Braoum dans la littérature," *L'Herne*, No. 3, 223–26.

———. "Que faire avec. . . . ?" *Le Nouvel Observateur* (February 25, 1965).

Bory, Jean-Louis, Maurice Clavel, and Dr. Quentin-Ritzen. "Trois écrivains parlent de Céline, Rabelais de l'ère atomique," *Arts*, LCCCXXVII (July 1961), pp. 3, 5.

Brasillach, Robert. "Céline prophète," in *Les quatre jeudis. Images d'avant guerre*. Paris: Editions Balzac, 1944, pp. 23–59.

Brissaud, André. "Voyage au bout de la tendresse," *L'Herne*, No. 3, 226–32.

Brochard, Marcel. "Céline à Rennes," *L'Herne*, No. 3, 13–18.

C. (Canavaggia), Marie. "Mademoiselle Marie, ma secrétaire," *L'Herne*, No. 3, 30–33.

C. (Carayon), Jeanne. "Le docteur écrit un roman," *L'Herne*, No. 3, 20–25.

*Cardiarelli, Dinamo. "Il dottor Louis-Ferdinand Destouches: Céline," *Il Secolo d'Italia* (March 23, 1965), p. 4.

Cartier, J.-L. "Bardamu le paria," *Tant qu'il fait jour* (April 1965), p. 11.

Cattabiani, Alfredo. "Il 'maledetto' rivalutato," *Corriere Lombardo-Milano* (April 30, 1965).

Chamfleury, Robert. "Céline ne nous a pas trahis," *L'Herne*, No. 3, 60–67.

*Debrie-Panel, Nicole. *Louis-Ferdinand Céline*. Lyon-Paris: Editions E. Vitte, 1961.

Dedet, Christian. "La condition médicale de L.-F. Céline," *L'Herne*, No. 3, 312–14.

Delteil, Joseph. "Céline l'oral," *L'Herne*, No. 3, 41–42.

Denoël, Robert. *Apologie de "Mort à crédit."* Paris: Denoël et Steele, 1936.

Déon, Michel. "Les beaux draps," *L'Herne*, No. 3, 238–40.

Docteur Guy Morin. "Destouches médecin," *L'Herne*, No. 3, 18–20.

Docteur R. B. "Le médecin de Meudon," *L'Herne*, No. 3, 81–82.

*Donley, Michaël, "L'identification cosmique," *L'Herne*, No. 5, 189–200.

Dorian, Max. "Céline rue Amélie," *L'Herne*, No. 3, 25–28.

Dubuffet, Jean. "Céline Pilote," *L'Herne*, No. 5, 223–27.

Duckworth, Colin. Review of *L'Herne*, No. 3, in: *French Studies*, XIX, No. 2, 202–203. London.

Epting, Karl. "Il ne nous aimait pas," *L'Herne*, No. 3, 56–60.

Faure, Elie. "D'un 'Voyage au bout de la nuit,' " *L'Herne*, No. 5, 228–33.

Faurisson, Robert. "La leçon de Bardamu," *L'Herne*, No. 3, 306–11.

Frohock, W. M. "Céline's Quest for Love," *Accent*, II, No. 2, 79–84.

Gide, André. "Les Juifs, Céline et Maritain," *La Nouvelle Revue Française*, CCXCV (April 1938), 630–34. Reprinted in *L'Herne*, No. 5, 335–38.

Geoffroy, Georges. "Céline en Angleterre," *L'Herne*, No. 3, 11–12.

Grover, E.-J. "Céline et Drieu La Rochelle," *L'Herne*, No. 3, 302–305.

*Guénot, Jean. "Voyage au bout de la parole," *L'Herne*, No. 5, 246–67.

Guicciardi, Elena. "Gli inediti di Céline," *Il Giorno* (April 14, 1965).

Halperine-Kaminski, E. *Céline en chemise brune ou le Mal du présent*. Paris: Les Nouvelles Editions Excelsior, 1938.

*Hanrez, Marc. *Céline*. La Bibliothèque Idéale. Paris: Gallimard, 1961.

———. "Céline au magnétophone" (Interview), *Le Nouveau Candide* (November 23, 1961), p. 14.

———. "Le Prince des hommes libres," *L'Herne*, No. 3, 240–43.

Hardy, Alain. "Rigodon," *L'Herne*, No. 5, 268–77.

Hindus, Milton. "Dire, redire et se contredire," *L'Herne*, No. 3, 244–48.

*———. *The Crippled Giant*. New York: Boar's Head Books, 1950.

———. Introduction to a new edition of *Death on the Installment Plan*, New York: New Directions, 1947.

Howe, Irving. "Céline: The Sod Beneath the Skin," *The New Republic* (July 20–27, 1963), pp. 19–21.

Ikor, Roger. "Au feu de l'enfer," *L'Herne*, No. 3, 249–51.

Josslin, J.-F. "Céline, l'admirable monstre," *Nouvelles Littéraires* (April 22, 1965), p. 6.

Laurent, Jacques. "Céline," *Le Nouveau Candide* (July 6–13, 1961), p. 16.

Legris, Michel. "L'Antisémite," *Le Monde* (June 5, 1961), p. 16.

Lioret, André. "Une doctrine biologique?" *L'Herne*, No. 5, 210–12.

Magrini, César. "Céline et Lautréamont," *L'Herne*, No. 3, 298–301.

Mandel, Arnold. "L'âme irresponsable ou Céline et le Dibbouk," *L'Herne*, No. 5, 207–209.

———. "D'un Céline Juif," *L'Herne*, No. 3, 252–56.

Matzneff, Gabriel. "Pour l'amour de Céline," *Combat* (March 4, 1965).

Mazeline, Guy. "Cher Bardamu, mon concurrent," *L'Herne*, No. 3, 28–29.

Mondor, Henri. "Céline," *L'Express* (June 6, 1961), p. 30.

———. "Avant-propos," Pléïade edition of Céline, Paris: Gallimard, 1962.

Monnier, Pierre. "Résidence surveillée," *L'Herne*, No. 3, 72–80.

Morand, Paul. "Céline et Bernanos," *L'Herne*, No. 3, 257–58.

Nadeau, Maurice. "Céline," *L'Express* (June 6, 1961), pp. 31, 32.

———. "Une nouvelle littérature," *Mercure de France*, CCCVIII, No. 1039, 499–503.

Nimier, Roger. "Céline au catéchisme," *La Nouvelle NRF*, V, No. 54, 1032–37.

———. "Donnez à Céline le Prix Nobel," *Les Nouvelles Littéraires* (October 18, 1958), pp. 1, 8.

———. *Le Nouveau Céline: 'D'un château l'autre.'* Pamphlet. Paris: Gallimard, 1957.

Nizan, Paul. "Voyage au bout de la nuit," *L'Herne*, No. 5, 145. Reprinted from *L'Humanité* (September 12, 1932).

Orlando, Walter. "Grandeurs et misères de Bardamu," *La Table Ronde*, No. 57 (1952), 171–74.

Ostrovsky, Erika. "Céline et le thème du roi Krogold," *L'Herne*, No. 5, 201–206.

Parinaud, André. "L.-F. Céline" (interview), *Arts*, LCCCXXX (July 1961), 3.

Pia, Pascal, "Céline au bout de la nuit," *Carrefour* (February 13, 1963), p. 18.

Piatier, Jacqueline. "Louis-Ferdinand Céline," *Le Monde* (May 5, 1961), p. 16.

Pommery, Jean. "Bestiaire de Céline," *L'Herne*, No. 5, 300–306.

Poulet, Robert. "Céline et son château," *La Table Ronde*, No. 121 (1958), 76–88.

*———. *Entretiens familiers avec Louis-Ferdinand Céline.* Paris: Plon, 1958.

———. "Métamorphoses de Bardamu," *L'Herne*, No. 3, 259–61.

———. "Où l'on retrouve Bardamu," *La Meuse* (September 28, 1933).

Rabi. "Un ennemi de l'homme," *L'Herne*, No. 3, 262–67.

Rebatet, Lucien. "D'un Céline l'autre," *L'Herne*, No. 3, 42–55.

———. "Nouvelles découvertes sur Céline," *Rivarol* (June 17, 1965), 11.

*Richard, Jean-Pierre. "La Nausée de Céline," *La Nouvelle Revue Française*, X, No. 115, 33–47; continued in X, No. 116, 235–52.

Rolin, Dominique. "Ni avant, ni après, ni ailleurs," *L'Herne*, No. 3, 289–91.

Romani, Bruno. "Che farne di questo Céline?" *Il Messagero* (March 5, 1965).

Rousseaux, André. "Chevaux de retour," *Le Figaro Littéraire* (June 6, 1957), 2.

———. "Justice pour Céline écrivain," *Le Figaro Littéraire* (June 8, 1961), 1, 2.

Simon, Pierre-Henri. "L'aurore est au bout de la nuit," *L'Herne*, No. 3, 292–94.

———. "Céline le forcéné," *Le Monde* (June 6, 1961), p. 1.

Sinclair, Andrew. "Prophet of the Apocalypse," *Spectator* (April 19, 1965), p. 508.

Sperber, Manès. "Louis-Ferdinand Céline," *Preuves*, CXXVII (1961), 18–22.

Spitzer, Leo. "Une habitude de style, le rappel chez Céline," *L'Herne*, No. 5, 153–64.

Stromberg, Robert. "A Talk with Louis-Ferdinand Céline," *Evergreen Review*, V, No. 19, 102–107.

———. "La source qui ne rafraîchit pas," *L'Herne*, No. 3, 268–71.

Suarès, André. "A propos de Céline," *La Nouvelle Revue Française*, IX, No. 104, 326–29.

Thomas, Henri. "A propos 'd'Un château l'autre,'" *L'Herne*, No. 3, 295–97.

Trotsky, Leon. "Céline et Poincaré," *L'Herne*, No. 5, 146–47. Reprinted from Trotsky's *Littérature et Révolution*, Collection des Lettres Nouvelles, Paris: Julliard. N.d.

*———. "Céline—novelist and politician," *Atlantic Monthly*, CLVI, No. 4, 413–20.

*Vandromme, Pol. *Céline*. Paris: Editions Universitaires, 1963.

———. "L'esprit des pamphlets," *L'Herne*, No. 3, 272–76.

Vanino, Maurice. *L'Affaire Céline. La Résistance ouvre ses dossiers*. Paris: Editions Créator, 1952. Reprinted in part in *L'Herne*, No. 5, 326–32.

Villefosse, R.-H. de. "Prophéties et litanies de Céline," *L'Herne*, No. 3, 33–35.

Vinding, Ole. "Vu par son ami Danois," *L'Herne*, No. 3, 69–71.

Waller, William. "Journey into Nihilism," *The South Atlantic Quarterly*, XVIII, No. 3, 288–91.

III. CRITICAL WORKS CONTAINING STUDIES OR COMMENTS ON CÉLINE

Arland, Marcel. *Essais et nouveaux essais critiques*. Paris: Gallimard, 1952.

Baldensperger, Fernand. *La littérature française entre les deux guerres*. Los Angeles: Lymanhouse, 1943.

Barjavel, René. *Journal d'un homme simple*. Paris: Frédéric Chambriand, 1951.

Barthes, Roland. *Le degré zéro de la littérature*. Paris: Editions du Seuil, 1953.

Bernanos, Georges. *Le crépuscule des vieux*. Paris: Gallimard, 1956.

Boisdeffre, Pierre de. *Histoire vivante de la littérature d'aujourd'hui*. Paris: Le Livre Contemporain, 1959.

Brée, Germaine. *Twentieth Century French Literature*. New York: Macmillan, 1962.

Brée, Germaine and Guiton, Margaret. *An Age of Fiction*. New Brunswick, N.J.: Rutgers University Press, 1957.

Brodin, Pierre, *Présences contemporaines*, III. Paris: Debresse, 1957.

Clouard, Henri. *Histoire de la littérature française du symbolisme à nos jours, 1915–1960*, II. Paris: Albin Michel, 1962.

Epting, Karl. *Frankreich im Widerspruch*. Hamburg: Hanseatische Verlagsanstalt, 1943.

Etiemble, P. *La hygiène des lettres*, II. *Littérature dégagée*. 1942–1953. Paris: Gallimard, 1955.

Glicksberg, Charles I. "Nihilism in Contemporary Literature," *The Nineteenth Century and After*, CXIV, 214–22.

Jamet, Claude. *Images de la littérature*. Paris: F. Sorlot, 1943.

Lalou, René. *Histoire de la littérature française contemporaine. De 1870 à nos jours*, II. Paris: Presses Universitaires, 1953.

La Rochelle, Drieu. *Le Français d'Europe*. Paris: Editions Balzac, 1944.

———. *Notes pour comprendre le siècle*. Paris: Gallimard, 1941.

Miller, Henry. *Sunday After the War*. Norfolk, Conn.: New Directions, 1944.

Nadeau, Maurice. *Littérature présente*. Paris: Corréa, 1952.

Paraz, Albert. *Le Gala des vaches*. Paris: Editions de l'Elan, 1948.

———. *Le Menuet du haricot*. Geneva, 1958.

Peyre, Henri. *The Contemporary French Novel*. New York: Oxford University Press, 1955.

Picon, Gaëtan. *Panorama de la nouvelle littérature française*. Paris: Gallimard, 1951.

Poulet, Robert. *La Lanterne magique.* Paris: Nouvelles Editions Debresse, 1956.

Radine, Serge. *Lumières dans la nuit.* Paris: Editions du Vieux Colombier, 1956.

Sartre, Jean-Paul. "Portrait de l'Antisémite," *Les Temps Modernes*, I, No. 3, 442–70.

———. *Réflexions sur la question juive.* Paris: Paul Morihieu, 1947.

Sérant, Paul. *Le romantisme fasciste ou l'oeuvre politique de quelques écrivains français.* Paris: Fasquelle, 1959.

Slochower, Harry. *No Voice Is Wholly Lost. Writers and Thinkers in War and Peace.* London: D. Dobson, 1946.

Steel, Eric M. "The French Writer Looks at America," *Antioch Review*, LV, No. 3, 414–31.

Vial, Fernand. "French Intellectuals and the Collapse of Communism," *Thought*, XV, No. 58, 429–44.

Weidle, Wladimir. *Les Abeilles d'Aristée. Essai sur le destin des lettres et des arts.* Paris: Gallimard, 1954.

IV. OTHER CÉLINIANA

Lecture on Louis-Ferdinand Céline, delivered by Michel Beaujour at the Institut Français of New York, March 19, 1963.

Lecture delivered by Serge Doubrowsky, "Louis-Ferdinand Céline, un mort inquiétant," March 26, 1962, at the Alliance Française, New York.

Personal interviews with Marcel Aymé, Arletty, Marie Canavaggia, Jeanne Carayon, J. Delannoy, Bernard de Fallois, Roger Nimier, Robert Poulet, Dominique de Roux. (See Preface of this study for further details.)

Personal interviews and conversations with the author's widow, Lucette Destouches. Visits to the author's home in Meudon.

Recording of an interview with Louis-Ferdinand Céline. Collection "Leur Oeuvre et leur Voix," Festival Records, Paris. FLD 149 M.

Recording of Two Songs by Louis-Ferdinand Céline (sung by the author). Pacific Records, Paris. L.D.P.-F 199.

Various documents concerning Céline's trial and final acquittal. *L'Herne*, No. 5, 309–25.

Note:

For the most complete bibliography on Céline to date, consult Dominique de Roux, "Essai de bibliographie," *L'Herne*, No. 3, 317–39; "Complément bibliographique," *L'Herne*, No. 5, 345–47.

Aïcha (in *D'un château l'autre*), 105, 149, 172, 192
Aimée (in *Voyage*), 46, 103, 119
Alcide (in *Voyage*), 115, 118
Alliance Française of New York, 107
Anarchism, 31–32
André (in *Mort à crédit*), 46
Animals, feeling for, 120–22
Annihilation, 174–75, 199
Apocalypse, the, 157–80
Apollinaire, Guillaume, 19
Aragon, Louis, 7
Aristophanes, 17
Arlette (in *D'un château l'autre*), 124, 196
Armandine, Mme (in *D'un château l'autre*), 96, 99
Art, realm of, 184–85
Artaud, Antonin, 24
Aymé, Marcel, 20

Bagatelles pour un massacre (Céline), 8, 164
Ballets sans musique, sans personne, sans rien (Céline), 12, 85
Bardamu (in *Voyage*), 34, 40–41, 42, 43, 49, 50, 52, 53, 55, 59, 61, 62, 63, 69, 70, 71, 78, 89, 93–94, 95, 99, 103, 104, 107, 108, 109–11, 112, 113, 116, 117, 118, 120, 121, 122, 123, 133, 135, 136, 140, 143, 145, 146, 157, 159,

Bardamu (*Cont.*): 163, 165, 168, 184, 187, 190–91, 196, 197
Baryton, Dr. (in *Voyage*), 103, 105
Baudelaire, Charles Pierre, 19, 32, 165, 184
Beaujour, Michel, 34, 35
Beaux draps, Les (Céline), 8, 164
Bébert (in *Mort à crédit*), 43, 46
Bébert (in *Voyage*), 99, 115, 119, 120, 121, 134, 143
Bébert the cat, 9, 121
Beckett, Samuel, 17, 24, 25
Berenge, Mme (in *Mort à crédit*), 100, 121
Berlin, Germany, 8–9
Bernanos, Georges, 20
Bestombes, Professor (in *Voyage*), 104
Blackness within, the, 65–79
Bonnard, Mme (in *D'un château l'autre*), 115, 117, 134, 192
Bosch, Hieronymus, 170, 174
Brueghel, 169
Burroughs, William, 20, 21, 22–23

Canavaggia, Marie, 7
Carayon, Jeanne, 4, 5
Casse-pipe (Céline), 2
Céline (Destouches), Louis-Ferdinand: animals, feeling for, 120–22; birth of, 2; childhood of, 2; collaboration charges against, 10–

Céline (*Cont.*):
  11, 13; death, concernment with,
  130–52; death of, 11, 12; educa-
  tion of, 2, 3; eroticism of, 53–55,
  75, 115, 123; exile in Denmark,
  9–11, 12; feminine beauty, cult
  of, 122–25, 198; hatred of, 35–
  37, 66, 174; heroes of, unheroic,
  106–14; horseman of the apocalypse, 157–80; impact of, 20–25;
  internment during Second World
  War, 9; inverted humanism of,
  85–125; legend or myth, preoccupation with, 190–96; literary
  career of, 4–8, 10–13; literary
  estate, settlement of, 12–13;
  lucid super-seer, the, 188–94; mar-
  riages of, 3, 9; medical career of,
  3–4, 8, 9, 60, 88, 97–106; metamorphoses, 183–88; military service of, 2–3; night muses of,
  29–37; passing of things, on, 133–
  37; passivity, hatred of, 99; pity
  of, merciless, 91–97; poetry of,
  192–94, 203; position in French
  literature of, 14–25; progenitor,
  role of, 200–201; psychiatry, interest in, 102–106; scapegoat, the,
  162–68; seer, role of, 188–94;
  self-depreciation, 56–65; self-
  image, 63–65; style of, 19–20,
  201–206; technique of, 202–203;
  tenderness of, 114–22; travels
  abroad, 3–4, 7, 88; visceral revolt
  of, 65–79; war, reaction to, 48–
  49; works of, 209–12
Cervantes, Miguel de, 17
Champfleury, R., 9
Chekhov, Anton, 97
Childhood and children, 42–47, 65,
  71, 119–21, 141
Children's Games (Brueghel), 169
Clotilde (in *D'un château l'autre*),
  115, 118
Comedy of death, 149–50
Contradictory pattern, 60–63
Copenhagen National Hospital, 10
Cornière, Édouard Joachim, 19
Corso, Gregory, 22
Courbevoie (Seine), France, 2
Cowardice, 50–51
Craig, Elizabeth, 4, 124

Dance of death, 130–52
Dancing god (or goddess), the,
  194–206
Death, muse of, 130–33
Death on the Installment Plan (Cé-
  line), see *Mort à crédit*
Debrie-Panel, Nicole, 87
Degradation of man, 40–56
Delaunay (in *D'un château l'autre*),
  105, 141
Delirium, 175–76, 185, 190, 197–
  98, 199, 200
Denmark, 8, 9, 10, 12, 64
Denoël & Steele (publishers), 4–5,
  6, 7, 8, 50
Des Pereires, Courtial (in *Mort à
  crédit*), 76–77, 78, 89, 101, 105,
  119, 136, 147–48, 149, 177, 183,
  184, 186
Des Pereires, Mme (in *Mort à
  crédit*), 139, 148–49
Destouches, Colette (Céline's daugh-
  ter), 3
Destouches, Edith Follet (Céline's
  wife), 3
Destouches, Louis-Ferdinand, see
  Céline, Louis-Ferdinand
Destouches, Louise-Céline Guillou
  (author's mother), 2, 9, 167
Destouches, Lucette Almansor (Cé-
  line's second wife, 8, 9, 10, 11
Dickinson, Emily, 22
Dissolution, decomposition, and dis-
  integration, 177–80
Dos Passos, John, 19
Dostoevsky, Fëdor M., 17
Doubrowsky, Serge, 107
Dread and laughter, 170–74
Du Bouchet, André, 24
D'un château l'autre (Céline), 9,
  12, 39, 40, 41, 42, 44, 48, 54, 55,
  61, 62, 89, 98, 99, 101, 105, 115,
  119, 120, 132, 136, 137, 143,
  149, 150, 169, 171–72, 176, 178,
  180, 186, 189, 190, 192, 199

Ecole des cadavres, L' (Céline), 8,
  50, 164
Edouard (in *Mort à crédit*), 114,
  115, 118

Eglise, L' (Céline), 6, 49, 124, 165, 168, 198
Eliot, T. S., 158
Emile (in *D'un château l'autre*), 178, 199
Entretiens avec le Professeur Y (Céline), 11–12, 57
Epting, Karl, 160
Eroticism, 53–55, 75, 115, 123
Erotico-mysticisme, cult of, 198, 200
Existentialism, 17, 19

Fantasy, realm of, 184–85
Faulkner, William, 19
Fear, 50–52, 101, 173
Féerie pour une autre fois, I (Céline), 11, 115, 139, 177, 192
Féerie pour une autre fois, II (Céline), 11, 139, 160, 177
Feminine beauty, cult of, 122–25, 198
Ferdinand (in *D'un château l'autre*), 89
Ferdinand (in *Mort à crédit*), 34, 38–39, 43, 44–46, 47, 50, 52, 62, 71, 72, 73, 74, 78, 89, 94, 101, 105, 112, 116, 117, 118, 119, 135–36, 157, 163–64, 168, 184, 186, 191
Ferdine (in *Nord*), 121, 140, 142, 143, 150, 163
Ferlinghetti, Lawrence, 22
Flaubert, Gustave, 17, 24, 184, 205
Freud, Sigmund, 165
Frucht, Frau (in *D'un château l'autre*), 54, 149

Gaige, Elizabeth (in *L'Eglise*), 124
Gallimard (publisher), 4, 5, 8, 9, 11, 12
Genet, E., 24
Geneviève (in *Mort à crédit*), 117
Gide, André, 19, 24
Ginsberg, Allen, 20, 21–22
Girard de Charbonnière, G. de, 10
Goya, Francisco José de, 169–70
Grappa, Lieutenant (in *Voyage*), 95, 143

Guignol's Band (Céline), 3, 9, 13, 117
Gustin (in *Mort à crédit*), 98, 100, 108

Hate, 35–37, 66, 174
Herne, L', 13
Hegel, Georg Wilhelm Friedrich, 165
Hemingway, Ernest, 19
Henrouille, M. (in *Voyage*), 141–42
Henrouille, Mme (in *Voyage*), 148
Heroes, unheroic, 106–14
Hilda (in *D'un château l'autre*), 54
Hommage à Zola (Céline), 6
Humanism, inverted, 85–125

"Ignu" (Ginsberg), 21
Impressionism, 203, 204
Incantational delirium, 185
Insanity, 102–106, 176
Ionesco, Eugene, 24

Jarry, Alfred, 24
Jonkind (in *Mort à crédit*), 46, 105, 119
Journey to the End of Night (Céline), see *Voyage au bout de la nuit*
Joyce, James, 14, 25

Kafka, Franz, 14, 25, 32
Kerouac, Jack, 20, 21, 22
Kierkegaard, Sören Aabye, 17
Klarskovgard, Denmark, 10
Körsor, Denmark, 10
Kratzmühl, Frau (in *Nord*), 150, 167, 176
Kressling, Germany, 9
Krogold legend (in *Mort à crédit*), 191–92

Laforgue, Jules, 19
Laughter and dread, 170–74
Lautréamont, Comte de, 24
La Vigue (in *Nord*), 105, 115, 121, 141
La Vitruve (in *Mort à crédit*), 71
League of Nations, 6, 165
Legend, preoccupation with, 190–96
Le Vigan (in *D'un château l'autre*), 9, 143, 144, 176, 189
Libel suits, 13
Lili (in *D'un château l'autre*), 54, 115, 117, 121, 124, 144, 192, 196
Lola (in *Voyage*), 52, 96, 122, 123
Lucid super-seer, the, 188–94

Madelon (in *Voyage*), 75, 76, 123, 147
Madmen's Feast (Brueghel), 169
Maimed, the, 139–41
Mallarmé, Stéphane, 19
Maquis, 9
Matchke (in *Nord*), 149, 150
Mea culpa (Céline), 7
Metamorphoses, 183–88
Meudon, France, 11, 12, 64
Michaux, André, 24, 25
Michelangelo, 39
Miller, Henry, 20, 21, 23–24
Molly (in *Voyage*), 93, 94, 115, 116–17, 118, 119, 122–23, 134, 197
Mondor, Henri, 33
Mort à crédit (*Death on the Installment Plan*) (Céline), 2, 6, 7, 15, 37, 38–39, 40, 42, 43, 44–46, 47, 50, 52, 54, 55, 60, 61, 62, 65, 70, 71, 72–74, 75, 76, 79, 85, 89, 94, 98, 100, 101, 114, 115, 117, 118, 119, 121, 123, 132, 135, 139, 141, 142, 147, 157, 163, 164, 168, 169, 171, 177, 183, 184, 185, 186, 191–92
Myth, preoccupation with, 190–96

Naked Lunch (Burroughs), 21, 22
Nerval, Gérard de, 32

Niçoise, Mme (in *D'un château l'autre*), 99
Nietzsche, Friedrich Wilhelm, 17, 32, 194, 195, 196
Night muses, 29–37
Nora (in *Mort à crédit*), 52, 105, 115, 116, 117, 123, 124
Nord (Céline), 9, 12, 13, 15, 29, 39, 40, 41, 48, 61, 63, 76, 89, 104, 105, 109, 115, 118, 119, 120, 121, 132, 138, 139, 140, 141, 149, 150, 158, 160, 161, 163, 167, 169, 175, 176, 178, 180, 192, 195, 199
Normance (Céline), 11

Odor of death, 72, 77, 138
On the Road (Kerouac), 22
Orphize (in *D'un château l'autre*), 172

Papillon (in *D'un château l'autre*), 115, 118
Parapine (in *Voyage*), 103
Pascal, Blaise, 17, 24, 112
Passing of things, the, 133–37
Passivity, hatred of, 99
Paul et Virginie (Saint-Pierre), 12
Paulo (in *Voyage*), 46
Perfect forms, cult of, 122–25, 198
Picasso, Pablo, 39
Pirandello, Luigi, 64
Pity, merciless, 91–97
Poe, Edgar Allan, 22, 134
Poetry, 192–94, 203
Pont de Londres, Le (Céline), 3, 12, 115, 116, 117, 119, 123, 132, 149, 186
Poulet, Robert, 13, 14, 33
Pound, Ezra, 22
Prix Théophraste Renaudot, 4
Progenitor, role of, 200–201
Protiste, Abbé (in *Voyage*), 67, 70
Proust, Marcel, 14, 19, 25
Psychiatry, 102

Queneau, Raymond, 20

Rabelais, François, 17, 97
Raumnitz, von (in *D'un château l'autre*), 149
Resistance movement, 8, 9
Richard, J.-P., 67, 77, 104, 204
"Rigodon" (Céline), 12, 13
Rimbaud, Arthur, 19, 188, 204
Rittmeister (in *Nord*), 141, 149, 150, 176
Robbe-Grillet, A., 24
Robinson (in *Voyage*), 34, 43, 49, 52, 59, 61, 62, 70, 71, 75, 76, 78, 89, 90, 94, 95, 99–100, 103, 111, 113–14, 120, 134, 140, 142, 146–47, 148, 186, 190, 196
Rockefeller Foundation, 3, 4
Rodolphe (in *Mort à crédit*), 134
"Rottenness" of man, the, 38, 53–56
Rousseau, Jean Jacques, 17

Saint-Pierre, Bernardin de, 12
San Francisco Renaissance, 21
Sartre, Jean-Paul, 17, 19, 24, 25, 40, 58
"Scandale aux abysses" (Céline), 12
Scapegoat, the, 162–68
Schertz (in *Nord*), 76, 139, 141, 149, 150, 175, 176, 178, 199
Schertz, Isis (in *Nord*), 149, 150
Second sight, gift of, 188
Second World War, 8–10
Seer, role of, 188–94
Self-depreciation, 56–65
Self-image, 63–65
Semmelring (in *Nord*), 150
Semmelweiss (Céline), see *Vie et l'oeuvre de Philippe Ignace Semmelweiss, La*
Semmelweiss, Philippe Ignace, 3, 62, 85–87, 88, 89, 90, 92, 94, 100, 107, 163, 168, 184
Sexual union, 197–98
Siegmaringen, Germany, 9
Sophie (in *Voyage*), 123, 124–25
Sullied mirror, the, 38–39
Swift, Jonathan, 17

Tenderness, 114–22
Thoreau, Henry David, 22
Thus Spake Zarathustra (Nietzsche), 195
Tiresias, 188
Tragedy, 151–52, 194
Triolet, Elsa, 7

Vanoš, Géjra, 20
Vera (in *L'Eglise*), 198
Vie et l'oeuvre de Philippe Ignace Semmelweiss, La (Céline), 3, 29, 61–62, 87, 88–91, 99, 102, 104, 107, 108, 118, 132, 146, 158, 166
Villon, François, 17
Violette (in *Mort à crédit*), 115, 117
Virginia (in *Pont de Londres*), 115, 116, 123, 124, 197
Visceral revolt, 65–79
Voltaire, 17
Voyage au bout de la nuit (*Journey to the End of Night*) (Céline), 2–3, 4, 5–6, 7, 15, 21, 22, 35, 36–37, 38, 39, 41, 42–44, 47, 48, 50, 53, 54, 55, 62, 67, 68, 69, 70, 71, 75, 77, 88, 89, 90, 95, 97, 98, 99, 103, 104, 107, 109, 115, 116, 119, 120, 121, 124, 132, 133, 134, 137, 141–42, 143, 144, 146, 147, 148, 162, 164, 165, 168, 169, 171, 173, 175, 177, 183, 184, 185, 186, 190, 196, 197
"Voyou Paul. Brave Virginie" (Céline), 12

War, reaction to, 48–49

Zola, Emile, 6